D0125443

Shakespeare in London

*Hannah Crawforth,
Sarah Dustagheer
and Jennifer Young*

Bloomsbury Arden Shakespeare
An Imprint of Bloomsbury Publishing Plc

B L O O M S B U R Y
LONDON • NEW DELHI • NEW YORK • SYDNEY

Bloomsbury Arden Shakespeare

An imprint of Bloomsbury Publishing Plc

50 Bedford Square	1385 Broadway
London	New York
WC1B 3DP	NY 10018
UK	USA

www.bloomsbury.com

BLOOMSBURY, THE ARDEN SHAKESPEARE and the Diana logo are trademarks of Bloomsbury Publishing Plc

British Library Cataloguing-in-Publication Data
A catalogue record for this book is available from the British Library.

ISBN: HB: 978-1-4725-7372-8
PB: 978-1-4081-4596-8
ePDF: 978-1-4081-5179-2
ePub: 978-1-4081-5180-8

Library of Congress Cataloging-in-Publication Data
A catalog record for this book is available from the Library of Congress

Typeset by RefineCatch Limited, Bungay, Suffolk
Printed and bound in India

CONTENTS

List of Illustrations   vii

Acknowledgements   viii

Note on the Text   x

A Chronology of Shakespeare's Life and Early Modern London   xi

Introduction: Shakespeare's London   1

1 Violence in Shakespeare's London:
   Titus Andronicus (1594) and Tyburn   21

2 Politics in Shakespeare's London:
   Richard II (1595) and Whitehall   47

3 Class in Shakespeare's London:
   Romeo and Juliet (1595–6) and The Strand   73

4 Law in Shakespeare's London:
   The Merchant of Venice (1596–8) and the
   Inns of Court   99

5 Religion in Shakespeare's London:
   Hamlet (1600–1) and St Paul's   121

6 Medicine in Shakespeare's London:
   King Lear (1605–6) and Bedlam   147

7   Economics in Shakespeare's London:
    Timon of Athens (1607) and the King's
    Bench Prison, Southwark   171

8   Experimentation in Shakespeare's London: *The
    Tempest* (1610–11) and Lime Street   195

    Epilogue: *Henry VIII* (1613) and the Tower of
    London   221

Works Cited   237
Suggested Further Reading   245
Index   253

LIST OF ILLUSTRATIONS

1   Braun and Hogenberg's map of London (1572)   4
2   From Richard Verstegan, [*Theatre of Cruelty*]
    Theatrum Crudelitatum (1587)   32
3   From John Norden, *Speculum Britanniae* (1593)   50
4   Jonathan Slinger as Richard II, RSC Histories
    Cycle (2008)   71
5   Shakespeare's testimony in the Mountjoy case
    (11 May, 1612)   100
6   William Shakespeare, *Hamlet* (1601), with Ling's
    commonplace markers (C2r)   141
7   From Thomas Harman's *A Caveat for Cursitors,
    &c.* (1567)   167
8   The Sam Wanamaker Playhouse (2014)   214

ACKNOWLEDGEMENTS

Our first thanks must go to the students at King's College London who have taken our course, 'Shakespeare in London', from which this book originated. Our aim in writing it has been to further explore and illuminate the question of the playwright's relationship to his city that students taking this course first helped us to explore; they have in many ways been our ideal imagined readers as we write.

Several colleagues have taught 'Shakespeare in London' with us, and thus have had a role in shaping this book; special thanks to Sarah Lewis, Lucy Munro and Chloe Porter in this regard. A particular feature of the course is the weeks our students spend studying at Shakespeare's Globe Theatre, whose education department are much-valued research collaborators. Farah Karim-Cooper, Gwilym Jones, Simon Smith and the Globe practitioners who work with our students there deserve particular mention, as does Madeline Knights.

In writing this project we have been supported by the London Shakespeare Centre: Gordon McMullan, Ann Thompson, Sonia Massai, John Lavagnino and Elizabeth Scott-Baumann (as well as those already named above). The English Department at King's College London has provided us all with a home at different points in our careers, and we are thankful to Jo McDonagh, who has generously served as Head of Department during this period.

Other colleagues who have been particularly influential in our work for this book include Eugene Giddens, Andy Kesson, Farah Mendlesohn, Harry Newman, Catherine Richardson, Renee Weis and Clare Wright. We would also like to thank participants in an SAA seminar on Shakespeare in Place (2012), organized by Julie Sanders, who commented on an early draft of Chapter 4.

Margaret Bartley has been an absolute delight to work with on this project. Her enthusiasm, boundless positivity, flexibility and considerable patience have been very much appreciated as we have written *Shakespeare in London*. Everyone we have dealt with at Bloomsbury has been kind and superbly efficient; thanks especially to Emily Hockley, our cover designer and the anonymous readers at the press who helped us refine both our proposal and manuscript.

Our families have supported and sustained us as we wrote this book. In grateful recognition of their love and assistance we would like to thank them here: Sue, Graham and Eleanor Crawforth, Hadrian, Lucian and Rufus Green, Ibrahim, Angela and Adam Dustagheer, Tom Chivers, Marc Viera, and James and Nancy Young.

NOTE ON THE TEXT

As this book is intended for a general readership we have
silently modernized all spellings from texts other than those by
Shakespeare (although we have preserved early modern book
titles so that they can be more easily traced). All quotations
from his plays are taken from the Arden third series editions,
unless otherwise stated. In the interests of readability we have
kept referencing to a minimum. Page numbers and brief
references are included in the text; please consult the list of
Works Cited for fuller attribution of quotations.

A CHRONOLOGY OF SHAKESPEARE'S LIFE AND EARLY MODERN LONDON

Our chronology positions important dates from Shakespeare's life alongside key events that happened in, or were significant to, London, including important dates we mention in the book. We have also consulted the following texts, which offer their own useful chronologies: Jane Armstrong, *The Arden Shakespeare Miscellany* (Bloomsbury Arden Shakespeare, 2011); David Crystal and Ben Crystal, *The Shakespeare Miscellany* (Penguin, 2005); and Tarnya Cooper, with Jane Eade, *Elizabeth I and her People* (London, 2013).

Year	Shakespeare	London
1558		Death of Mary Tudor; Ascension of Elizabeth I on 17 November
1559		Elizabeth's Coronation at Westminster Abbey on 15 January
1561		Spire of St Paul's destroyed by lightning
1563		John Foxe's *Book of Martyrs* first edition

Year	Shakespeare	London
1564	William Shakespeare born in Stratford-upon-Avon, third child of John and Mary Shakespeare, on 23 April	
1566		James, later James I, born to Mary Queen of Scots (in Scotland) on 19 June
1568		Completion of Gresham's Exchange
1570		Middle Temple Hall built
1571	Shakespeare eligible to attend King Edward VI Grammar School in Stratford	Elizabeth visits Gresham's Exchange and in her honour it is renamed 'the Royal Exchange' Tyburn Tree – execution site – constructed
1572		Birth of John Donne and Ben Jonson Braun and Hogenberg map of London produced
1576	John Shakespeare applies for a coat of arms but is denied	The Theatre opens in Shoreditch
1577		The Curtain opens in Shoreditch Francis Drake sets sail to circumnavigate the world (returns 1580)
1582	Shakespeare marries Anne Hathaway some time in November	

Year	Shakespeare	London
1583	Daughter Susanna born, baptized 26 May	
1585	Twins Hamnet and Judith are born, baptized 2 February The beginning of the 'lost years'	
1587	Shakespeare leaves Stratford (?)	The Rose opens on the Southbank First performances of Thomas Kyd's *The Spanish Tragedy* Mary, Queen of Scots, executed
1588		Defeat of the Spanish Armada – mass of Thanksgiving held at St Paul's
1589	*1, 2, 3 Henry VI* (1589–91)	
1590	*Taming of the Shrew* (1590–5?) *The Two Gentlemen of Verona* (1590–4) *King John* (1590–1)	
1591	*Richard III* (*c.*1591–3)	
1592	Shakespeare is described as an 'up-start crow' in *Greene's Groats-worth of Wit*, suggesting he is in London by this time *Titus Andronicus* (*c.*1592–4) *Edward III* (*c.*1592–4)	Plague in London Rose closed by order of Privy Council after riots in Southwark

Year	Shakespeare	London
1593	*Venus and Adonis* published with a dedication to the Earl of Southampton	Christopher Marlowe dies Plague – all theatres closed from January John Norden, *Speculum Britanniae* published, includes map of Westminster
1594	*The Rape of Lucrece* published *Titus Andronicus* published – first Shakespeare play to appear in print *The Comedy of Errors* (*c.*1594 or earlier) *Love's Labour's Lost* (*c.*1594–5) *A Midsummer Night's Dream* (c. 1594–6)	Four year famine begins Roderigo Lopez, Elizabeth I's former doctor, hanged *Titus Andronicus* first performed on 24 January, according to Henslowe's Diary *The Comedy of Errors* performed at Gray's Inn on 28 December Theatre company formed under Lord Chamberlain, Henry Cary, Baron Hunsdon
1595	First recorded as a member of the Chamberlain's Men *Richard II* (*c.*1595) *Romeo and Juliet* (*c.*1595–6)	Possible performance of *Richard II* at Sir Edward Hoby's house, Westminster on 7 December Apprentices riot in Southwark and at the Tower over the price of fish and butter in June; five hanged for treason
1596	Death of Hamnet Granted coat of arms *Merchant of Venice* (*c.*1596–8) *1 Henry IV* (1596–7)	Burbage builds the Blackfriars Playhouse

Year	Shakespeare	London
1597	Purchases New Place in Stratford-upon-Avon *2 Henry IV* (1597–8) *The Merry Wives of Windsor* (1597)	
1598	Described as 'best for comedy and tragedy . . . among the English' in Francis Meres' *Palladia Tamia* *Much Ado About Nothing* (1598–9)	John Stow, *Survey of London* published
1599	*Henry V* (1599) *Julius Caesar* (1599) *As You Like It* (*c.*1599–1600)	The Globe opens on Bankside
1600	*Hamlet* (1600–1)	
1601	Death of John Shakespeare *Twelfth Night* (1601) *Troilus and Cressida* (1601–2)	Essex Rebellion – Essex's supporters request performance of *Richard II* Earl of Essex executed Earl of Southampton imprisoned in the Tower of London
1602	Shakespeare buys additional property in Stratford including a garden and a cottage opposite New Place *All's Well That Ends Well* (*c.*1602–5)	*Twelfth Night* performed at the Middle Temple in February

Year	Shakespeare	London
1603	*Othello* (1603–4) *Sir Thomas More* (1603–4)	Death of Elizabeth I at Richmond Palace on 24 March Ascension of James I Chamberlain's Men win patronage of James, become the King's Men Virulent plague kills one in five Londoners
1604	Living on Silver Street *Measure For Measure* (*c*.1604) *King Lear* (1604–6)	
1605		Gunpowder Plot
1606	*Macbeth* (*c*.1606) *Antony and Cleopatra* (*c*.1606)	
1607	Daughter Susanna marries the physician John Hall Death of Shakespeare's brother Edmund, an actor with the King's Men *Timon of Athens* (*c*.1607) *Pericles* (1607–8)	River Thames freezes over – first Frost Fair held English colonists found Jamestown in Virginia, America
1608	*Coriolanus* (*c*.1608)	*King Lear* performed at Whitehall on 26 December
1609	*Sonnets* published	The King's Men begin performing at the Blackfriars Playhouse in the winter

Year	Shakespeare	London
1610	*Cymbeline* (*c.*1610) *The Winter's Tale* (1610–11) *The Tempest* (1610–11)	
1612	*Cardenio*, lost play (1612–13) Shakespeare appears as witness at Court of Requests on 11 May	James' son Prince Henry dies on 6 November
1613	Buys property in the Blackfriars precinct *Henry VIII* (1613) *Two Noble Kinsmen* (*c.*1613–14)	James' daughter Princess Elizabeth marries Frederick, elector palatine and future king of Bohemia on 14 February Globe theatre burns down during performance of *Henry VIII* on 29 June
1614		Rebuilt Globe opens
1616	Burial of 'William Shakespeare gent' recorded in parish register, Stratford-upon-Avon Daughter Judith marries Thomas Quiney Baptism of Judith's son, Shakespeare Quiney	
1623	Anne Shakespeare dies *Mr. William Shakespeare's Comedies, Histories and Tragedies* (also known as The First Folio) published	

Introduction:
Shakespeare's London

Shakespeare in London

We do not know the day, month or even the year in which the young William Shakespeare first came to London, the city in which he would establish himself as a playwright and where he would spend the most active years of his professional life. Indeed, much of Shakespeare's life is unknown to us in the 1580s, the decade he would first encounter the city. What we do know of this period makes the fact he came to London at all rather surprising. In November 1582 he was in Stratford-upon Avon, where he married Anne Hathaway, daughter of a farmer from a neighbouring village. In May the following year their daughter Susanna was baptized, followed by twins Hamnet and Judith in February 1585. The young family lived with Shakespeare's parents in a two-level house on Henley Street, in the bustling centre of Stratford. At the end of the 1580s Shakespeare does not look like a man who is about to uproot his life and move to the most rapidly growing city in early modern Europe. But then he does not look like the man who will write what are near-universally acclaimed as our greatest plays, either. This book will explore these great plays – amongst them *Romeo and Juliet*, *The Merchant of Venice*, *Hamlet*, *King Lear* and *The Tempest* – in relation to Shakespeare's life in London.

By 1592 Shakespeare was living and working in London, where he would reside for the next twenty years of his life, an existence punctuated by regular trips back to Stratford to visit his wife and family, who would remain there throughout these years. London would be the city in which Shakespeare made his name, in which he produced his greatest work, and embarked upon his most fruitful collaborations with fellow actors and writers. It would be the place where he earned his money, where he nurtured his connections to the highest reaches of society, and where he achieved mastery of the emerging world of the commercial playhouses. Shakespeare did not just live and thrive in London, however. Rather the city became a part of him and his writing. This book will suggest that London holds a central place in the Shakespearean imagination, underwriting the plays that he created there, even while they are set elsewhere. It is a notorious fact that Shakespeare rarely writes about London directly, and yet his life was enmeshed with that of his adopted city – through the ownership of property there, his investment in its theatrical world, and his roles at the heart of some of its most prominent acting companies. For all of the plays set in Venice, Padua, or Verona, in ancient Britain, Rome, or Greece, not one of Shakespeare's works is set in the London of his own day. And yet, as we shall discover, the size, diversity, noise, smell, chaos, anarchy and sheer excitement of London can be felt in all that Shakespeare writes. Understanding the important presence of this exhilarating city within his work can thus help us to read the plays anew, to capture something of the freshness of the moment – and the place – in which they were written.

Let us imagine for a moment that we are with Shakespeare on the day he first sets foot in London. Assuming he had been travelling there from Stratford Shakespeare would have already been on the road for several days. Journeying on foot, by horse or by carriage, and putting up for the night in the coaching inns that dotted the roads through the English countryside, Shakespeare would have been weary by the time he reached the metropolis. It was not an easy journey. But something drove him to endure the dangers and discomforts of the road. The 37 plays and the poems that followed suggest that what drew him to London was his desire to be a writer. Shakespeare's early life is largely lost to us. One popular theory based on gossip reported by early modern biographer John Aubrey suggests that he spent a period as a schoolmaster in the country (possibly in Lancashire), another posits that he joined the touring company the Lord Strange's Men to hone his acting (and writing) skills. But once he arrives in London Shakespeare becomes somewhat more visible to us. By 1592 he was in the city and his first forays into its literary world had attracted the attention of local writers. *Greenes Groats-Worth of Wit*, a pamphlet published that year, famously derides Shakespeare as 'an upstart crow, beautified with our feathers' (F1ᵛ), suggesting that by this point he had made his presence sufficiently felt amongst London dramatists as to have ruffled some of this plumage.

If the pamphlet provides us with our first glimpse of Shakespeare in London, then what would the young Shakespeare's own first perspective upon that city have been? The famous Braun and Hogenberg map, produced by two German cartographers in 1572, gives us our best clue (Figure 1). What immediately strikes the modern eye on looking at this map is the sheer amount of green space it includes; south of the river is largely agricultural land with little by way of building upon it, and to the north one rapidly leaves the labyrinth of narrow streets for fields once past Holborn. The West End, now a densely packed area of urban development to the north of Charing Cross and the centre of today's theatreland, simply does not exist. 'Spyttel fields' (Spitalfields) are still fields and 'Convent Garden' (Covent Garden) is actually a garden at this time. The vast outlying suburbs that now characterize London are nowhere to be seen; Westminster remains a village cut off from the rest of the city by intervening farmland, joined only by a single street. But London was changing quickly, more than doubling in size over the course of Shakespeare's lifetime. Jeremy Boulton estimates that its population rose rapidly from 70,000 in 1550 to reach 400,000 by 1650 (Boulton [1987], 3).

FIGURE 1 *Braun and Hogenberg's map of London (1572)*
(© Museum of London)

Entering the city from the west, a traveller arriving from Stratford would first encounter the home of 'The Corte' (court), the village of Westminster where parliament sat – then as now. A major royal palace here provided a London home for the monarch in days long before the iconic Buckingham Palace with which we are now familiar (adopted by the royal family as their official residence in 1837). Walking north up the main thoroughfare from Westminster brings our early modern visitor to 'Chayncros' (Charing Cross), before turning east onto the Strand, fashionable home of some of the most aristocratic and wealthy members of London society, such as the Lord Suffolk and Earl of Arundel, whose enormous mansions stretched right down to the river. The Duke of Somerset's home is also conspicuous on Braun and Hogenberg's map, as it would have been to young Shakespeare, the only one of these grand dwellings to survive in modern form in its more recent, neoclassical, incarnation as Somerset House. Another familiar landmark, the Savoy, was in his time not the luxury hotel it is today, but rather a hospital for 'the relieving of a hundred poor people', described by John Stow, whose famous *Survey of London* (1598) will be an invaluable companion to us as we make our journey with Shakespeare through London (372).

Walking eastward through London Shakespeare and his contemporaries would next have gone through the medieval walls that mark off the limits of the City of London itself, passable via a series of gates. Moorgate, Aldgate and Bishopsgate, where there are now railway stations, are all well-known to any modern tube traveller, but in Shakespeare's London these were the gated entryways into the City, an area stretching to the Tower of London in the east that fell under the legal jurisdiction of the city fathers and Lord Mayor. Within the walls behaviour was also moderated and commerce tightly controlled by a series of guilds belonging to the major trades. Immediately within their confines lies the large and imposing structure identified by Braun and Hogenberg as 'S.Paule' (St Paul's) cathedral. But this massive landmark, so familiar to Shakespeare, is unrecognizable to modern viewers.

The building that served as the focal point for the Elizabethan Church in London was subject to a series of fires throughout the early modern period, losing its spire in one of the worst of these, which started when it was struck by a lightning bolt in June 1561 (its appearance on the 1572 map is perhaps best explained by a fit of nostalgia on the parts of Braun and Hogenberg). Christopher Wren would eventually rebuild the whole thing following the destruction wrought by the Great Fire of London in 1666; it would take him until 1708 to complete the famous domed structure of St Paul's today.

The last thing we might notice is the river Thames, snaking its way through the heart of London, crossed only by a single bridge. Providing the sole thoroughfare for coach and foot traffic across the Thames in Shakespeare's day, London Bridge is covered in houses, 'so that it seemeth rather a continual street than a bridge,' Stow writes (45). This is especially apparent in our cover image, based upon John Norden's sixteenth-century depiction of the bridge. Braun and Hogenberg also depict the many small boats and skiffs that transported people across the river. But why would they want to cross? As we have noted, there is remarkably little south of the river in Shakespeare's day. What is there, however, would draw a crowd. For there, just west of Southwark, we see two circular amphitheatres, marked 'The Bowll bayting' (bull-baiting) and 'The Beare bayting' (bear-baiting). These insalubrious venues were not only the location for the barbaric but hugely popular blood sports that entertained early modern Londoners. They were also sites for putting on plays, and by the turn of the century would have a new neighbour, a purpose-built theatre called the Globe.

'So many little worlds in her': London's multitudes

It was not the Globe that brought Shakespeare to London in the later 1580s, however (it would not be constructed until

1599), but instead the earlier theatres with which he would first be associated. These included the inns and taverns where travelling theatre companies performed, and which must surely have produced the most memorable impression upon the young man who first came to London, hungry for a theatrical and literary career. Bankside's first commercial playhouse was the Rose, built in 1587 amidst the bull and bear baiting, brothels and gaming houses, and near to the site that would house the Globe. The Rose saw the first performances of Christopher Marlowe's *Doctor Faustus, Jew of Malta* and *Tamburlaine the Great*, Thomas Kyd's *Spanish Tragedy* and Shakespeare's own early plays, *Henry VI part I* and *Titus Andronicus*. But most important for Shakespeare initially was The Theatre in Shoreditch, the neighbourhood to which he moved upon first arriving in the city. Shakespeare's new local theatre had been constructed in 1576 as the first permanent home for the Lord Chamberlain's Men, a group of itinerant players with whom the young Shakespeare may have occasionally acted and who performed some of his first plays. From 1594 onwards he would write exclusively for the company, who would later still become the King's Men on the accession of James I in 1603.

On arriving in the city Shakespeare took lodgings in Shoreditch, a mixed neighbourhood lying well beyond London's walls and thus outside of the jurisdiction of the City Fathers. It also lies beyond the outer reaches of Braun and Hogenberg's map, although if an early modern Londoner walked north up Bishopsgate Street he or she would come to Shoreditch in under half a mile. (Shakespeare would himself retrace the steps of this journey when he moved to live within the City walls, in the wealthier neighbourhood of Bishopsgate, later in his life.) All of London life might be found in early modern Shoreditch, a bustling and hugely diverse area in which a wide variety of people crowded through its narrow streets. In this regard the area was a highly representative part of London for a newcomer to the city like Shakespeare to choose, packed with immigrants, a range of trades, people of differing ages, and differing degrees of affluence, from the rich to the very poor indeed.

Shakespeare would later evoke this diversity for his audience at the Globe in his history play of 1599, *Henry V*, possibly one of the first works to be staged at the theatre upon the playhouse's completion. The play's final act begins with a prologue spoken by a Chorus, which gives an extraordinary introduction to the play's hero and events, addressed to those who 'have not read the story' (5.0.1). Shakespeare stages the imaginary journey of his returning King Henry, travelling across 'the deep-mouth'd sea' (5.0.11) from Calais, France to Dover, and then up through Blackheath, to the south-east of London. As he proceeds into the capital Henry begins to conjure the city itself, out of nothing but his own words and the imaginative capabilities of the play's audience:

> But now behold,
> In the quick forge and working-house of thought,
> How London doth pour out her citizens.
> The Mayor and all his brethren in best sort,
> Like to the senators of th'antique Rome
> With the plebeians swarming at their heels,
> Go forth and fetch their conquering Caesar in

(5.0.22–28)

Shakespeare does two remarkable things here. First, he compares 'The Mayor and all his brethren' – the London aldermen and City Fathers – to 'the senators of th'antique Rome', affording them the status and prestige of these officials from the classical past, in preparation for the (perhaps ominous) metaphor figuring Henry as 'Caesar' in the final lines of this passage. Second, he surrounds these nobles by 'plebeians swarming at their heels' in uncontrollable proliferation, like bees – or rats. Shakespeare resolutely refuses to ignore the realities of his own city in imagining both the medieval London of his history play and also the 'antique Rome' that stands in for it here; these cities are not just the preserve of the elite, but also of the masses, the poor, the dispossessed. Shakespeare's London is a city of teeming activity, inhabited by 'citizens', 'senators', 'plebeians' and 'conquering Caesar' alike, its bustle as insistent as the noise of swarming insects.

This is precisely the metaphor that another visitor to the city, Donald Lupton, would employ in his 1632 account, *London and the Country Carbonadoed*. London, he writes, 'is the great beehive of Christendom, I am sure of England' (1). It is not just the density of London's population or the frenzied activity of the city that merits its comparison to a beehive for Lupton, but also its diversity; just as worker, drone and queen bee all have their distinct roles to fulfil in the carefully modulated hierarchy of the hive, so 'She swarms four times in a year, with people of all ages, natures, sexes, callings' (1). For London contains multitudes, Lupton makes clear: 'She seems to be a glutton, for she desires always to be full,' he writes, 'She may be said to be always with child, for she grows greater every day than other' (2, 3). There is something almost cannibalistic in the juxtaposition of these two images: London's voracious appetite threatens to swallow up everything before her; she will grow ever fatter on a diet of her inhabitants. In fact, Lupton says, London 'is grown so great that I am almost afraid to meddle with her', a note of awe – if not terror – creeping into his voice at the sheer omnivorousness of this city (1).

'All the world's a stage': The Globe as microcosm

In fact, London is by nature all consuming, Lupton suggests. 'She's certainly a great world, there are so many little worlds in her,' he writes, evoking the popular early modern idea of the microcosm (1). A microcosm is a world in miniature that can represent or stand in for a bigger one. Early modern Londoners were fascinated by this concept. In 1603 the poet and prolific writer John Davies would publish a whole book devoted to the subject, called *Microcosmos: The Discovery of the Little World*; Peter Heylyn's *Microcosmus, or A little description of the great world* would follow in 1621. London itself served as a microcosm in this way, embodying all that stood beyond the city limits – to the extent that the travel writer Thomas Platter, visiting the city in 1599, remarked that 'London is the capital of England and so superior to other English towns that London is not said to be in England, but rather England to be in London' (Platter, 364–65). London's diversity is representative of the whole country for which the city serves as capital. We know that Shakespeare himself was intrigued by the idea of conjuring small worlds, 'little kingdoms' that could evoke greater ones; this is exactly what he set about doing in the theatre, as we will see. At times it must have seemed that it was impossible to capture all that London encompassed. Angela Stock and Anne-Julia Zwierlein have observed that even the names used to refer to the city struggled to do justice to the worlds it contained: 'it was Troynovant, the New Jerusalem, the epitome or breviary of all Britain; it was a virgin, a mother, a fickle mistress, a monster;' they write, 'it was a beehive or Babylon, a jewel, a sea, a wood, a sprawling palace, and again and again a stage, a theatre' (4). This last image is particularly telling. If all of life was on display in early modern London, the theatre offers one of the most compelling metaphors for capturing this multitudinous aspect of the city.

This is of course one of Shakespeare's most distinctive insights. Indeed, the popular analogy between theatre and city might go some of the way to explaining the attractions of London for Shakespeare, beyond the access it offered him to the world of the stage. The particular energy of the metropolis in turn allowed his stage to become a world, to serve as a microcosm in just the way London itself encapsulated the broader diversity of England as a whole. It is not insignificant that one of Shakespeare's most famous lines of verse is Jacques' comment that 'All the world's a stage' in *As You Like It*, another play written in 1599, the year of both *Henry V* and Platter's extraordinary account (2.7.140). Nor should we forget that the Globe would adopt as its motto the Latin tag, *totus mundus agit historionem*, 'because all the world plays the actor'. But perhaps the most potent expression of this idea in all of Shakespeare's writing is the opening prologue with which *Henry V* begins. This play, which we have already touched upon, represents a key moment in the history of early modern theatre. It commences with a Chorus who startlingly acknowledges onstage the artificiality of what is about to occur (and which other dramatists more commonly try to ignore) by drawing attention to the boards on which he stands and the walls of the theatre that surround him. The particular nature of the Globe – the circular structure its name plays upon and the timbers out of which it is built – are alluded to in the opening of *Henry V*, when the Chorus asks his audience to behold the 'wooden O' in which they stand:

> But pardon, gentles all,
> The flat unraised spirits that hath dared
> On this unworthy scaffold to bring forth
> So great an object. Can this cockpit hold
> The vasty fields of France? Or may we cram
> Within this wooden O the very casques
> That did affright the air at Agincourt?
> O pardon, since a crooked figure may
> Attest in little place a million,
> And let us, ciphers to this great account,
> On your imaginary forces work.
> Suppose within the girdle of these walls
> Are now confined two mighty monarchies,
> Whose high upreared and abutting fronts
> The perilous narrow ocean parts asunder.
> Piece out our imperfections with your thoughts.
> Into a thousand parts divide one man
> And make imaginary puissance.

Think, when we talk of horses, that you see them
Printing their proud hoofs i'th' receiving earth.
For 'tis your thoughts that now must deck our kings,
Carry them here and there, jumping o'er times,
Turning th'accomplishment of many years
Into an hour-glass: for the which supply,
Admit me Chorus to this history,
Who prologue-like your humble patience pray,
Gently to hear, kindly to judge, our play.

(1.0.8–34)

Shakespeare's entire speech embodies the idea of the microcosm that his own experience of London would have rendered so vividly to him. A 'crooked figure may | Attest in little place a million,' the Chorus reminds his audience; there may only be one man on the stage, or a dozen actors, but they are a microcosm for the 'million' who (in Shakespeare's imagining at least) fought in the battle of Agincourt. By alluding to the actors' mysterious ability to replicate themselves on the stage Shakespeare may also nod to early modern practices of doubling roles in the theatre, to reduce the number needed to perform a given play. Just as a single actor can evoke multitudes, so this 'little place' can likewise become 'The vasty fields of France'. The theatre, in short, could contain the world. Of course this speech is also a carefully calibrated piece of flattery designed to please the nobles amongst Shakespeare's audience, 'gentles all', as well as those with noble pretensions. For without them, this extraordinary transformation of Globe into the globe cannot take place. 'Piece out our imperfections,' the Chorus asks, imploring his audience to use their 'imaginary forces' in the service of the creative magic Shakespeare and his actors will attempt to perform. The audience must supply for themselves the sound effect of horses charging across a battlefield; Shakespeare will provide them with their cue – the alliterative phrase 'Printing their proud hoofs,' – but they must do the rest. While the world of the play is dominated by the actions of a King and his nobles, here power is put into the hands of Shakespeare's London audience, who are asked 'Gently to hear' and 'kindly to judge' his play. In this way he makes them part of its world.

It is likely that Shakespeare wrote this speech with the Globe theatre specifically in mind. In 1599, the year of *Henry V*'s first performance, a major dispute had arisen as to who owned the land that its predecessor the Shoreditch Theatre stood upon. According to the legal testimony of Giles Alleyn, landlord of the Theatre, the company of players decided to seize what indisputably did belong to them: the building itself. In the middle of a cold and wintry night they supposedly dismantled the wooden structure and carried it piece by piece across the bridge to Bankside, where it would be reconstructed in the new form of the Globe. Whether we choose to believe this rather romanticized story or not (and the likelihood of achieving such a feat in the space of a single evening), the Globe certainly was constructed out of timbers that had been reclaimed from the Theatre. And as we have seen from the Prologue to *Henry V*, the key element of this story – the aura that attaches to the construction of the Globe as an almost magical space – is evident both in the fact this myth took hold, and in the plays Shakespeare wrote to be performed there.

Mapping our journey through Shakespeare's London

In these opening pages we have plunged into the heart of the city in which Shakespeare arrived in the late 1580s, offering a short biographical narrative of how and why the young dramatist came to London. We have also given a brief historical account of the emerging urban centre from the point of view of Shakespeare himself, who saw in the city a microcosm for all the world had to offer and believed his theatre could in turn contain all this variety within its 'wooden O'. And we have begun to trace certain important metaphorical connections between Shakespeare's London and the world of his plays, as we will do throughout this study. In the case of *Henry V* we have seen the way that the idea of the microcosm, so fundamental to popular conceptions of London at this time, comes to characterize how Shakespeare thinks about the power of the theatre. The metaphor of the microcosm thus draws together text and context, play and place. This way of approaching Shakespeare's work will be characteristic of each of the chapters that follow, in which we will show how the experience of life in early modern London underwrites some of his major plays by identifying the symbolic power that certain locations within the city hold for him.

This book continues the journey into the heart of the city in which Shakespeare would live and work that we have undertaken in this introduction, moving through London from west to east, in imitation of a traveller approaching from Stratford. We will also move chronologically from the beginning to the end of Shakespeare's dramatic career, taking in a variety of different plays in different genres, and drawing upon the latest scholarship from an extensive range of disciplines encompassing geography, politics, economics, the law, and the history of medicine, for instance, to reanimate our understanding of the plays. As we go we will offer new readings of some of Shakespeare's most important works, informed by close attention to the language of his drama. Each chapter will focus on one play and one key location, drawing out the thematic connections between that place and the drama it informs.

We begin at Tyburn, site of early modern executions, particularly the gruesome disembowelling of Catholic priests who defied the practices of the Protestant English church following the Reformation. Proximity to such violence was one of the defining features of life in Shakespeare's London. From bear and dog fighting to these gruesome hangings, early modern Londoners were exposed to an astonishing amount of bloodshed while going about their day-to-day business. In our first chapter we relate what many critics (particularly the Victorians) consider the excessive brutality and gore of Shakespeare's early tragedy *Titus Andronicus* (1594) to the violent city in which the play was written. We suggest that any attempts to give meaning to otherwise senseless violence in *Titus Andronicus* reflect early modern narratives that sought to turn those who suffered at Tyburn into religious martyrs. While this tradition can help us to contextualize the brutal events of Shakespeare's play, the drama itself consistently refuses to interpret – and thus recuperate or redeem – violence, ultimately insisting that it remains meaningless.

In our second chapter we explore the ways in which history play *Richard II* (1595) stages the political life of early modern London as much as that of the medieval city in which it is set. An unflinching portrayal of the institution of kingship and the nature of power itself, the play scrutinizes the ambitions of both Richard and his would-be successor, Bolingbroke, who plots to seize the crown. We explore the shifting allegiances of the English nobles who – like Shakespeare's audience perhaps – gradually transfer their loyalty from one king to the next, situating such fickleness within the context of the vicissitudes of Elizabethan court life. In a reflection of the architecture of Westminster, which constructed a series of concentric circles of increasingly sacrosanct authority around the monarch, the play embodies the mechanisms of inclusion and exclusion by which royal favour was granted or revoked. Shakespeare makes clear that Richard and Bolingbroke's political fates are interconnected, the rise of one character contingent upon the fall of the other. This insight is mirrored in both the structure and language of the play, and derives from the playwright's familiarity with the workings of power in his city.

In Chapter 3 we explore representations of class in *Romeo and Juliet* (1595) using one of the city's most vibrant thoroughfares at the time, the Strand, as our geographic focus. Home to an eclectic mix of elite and working classes, the public and private spaces of the Strand offer a compelling social context for considering the interactions of Shakespeare's Capulet and Montague families. We will explore ways in which the geographic layout of the Strand offers a blueprint for envisioning multiple places in the play and their class-based connotations. We will then consider the range of social and professional classes who intermingled on the Strand. Reading the well-known 'Queen Mab' speech as a commentary upon the frictions between upper and lower classes, we suggest ways in which Shakespeare's representation of masters and servants in *Romeo and Juliet* speaks to similar social concerns in 1590s London. With the power of names to express identity a major concern of this play, early modern London and indeed Shakespeare's personal history, we will conclude by considering how the act of naming (or denying names) challenges traditional social boundaries, positioning *Romeo and Juliet* as a space of dynamic social engagement, much like the Strand itself.

The focus of our fourth chapter is *The Merchant of Venice* (1596–7), a play that reflects the legal life of Shakespeare's London and particularly his personal dealings with the law. We chart the ways in which his own experience of entering into a legal bond informs one of the key features of the play's plot, the bond between Bassanio and the Jewish moneylender Shylock for which Antonio has agreed to act as guarantor and now stands to forfeit. The Inns of Court, where early modern law students were educated, were very familiar to Shakespeare, and we explore them in order to better understand the legal language of the play and especially the famous trial scene with which it reaches a dramatic climax. Finally we offer a new reading of the play by arguing that the tensions between public justice and private mercy evident in this work reflect not a clash between Old and New Testament ideals, as it has so often been interpreted, but instead mirrors the difference in values between the contrasting forms of law being practised in the city at the time in which Shakespeare was writing the play, pitting the relative inflexibility of precedent-based common law against the equitable approach of the Chancery courts.

If our version of *The Merchant* is more secular than that of many other critics, Chapter 5 considers the sacred spaces of Shakespeare's city, addressing religion in relation to *Hamlet* (1600–1), by focusing upon the play's relationship to the Cathedral and churchyard of St Paul's. This part of early modern London was not just the nation's religious focus and the major site for preachers to gather in the city, where they delivered their theological arguments to large crowds, but was also the centre of the early modern printing industry, which disseminated religious texts and doctrinal polemic as well as playbooks, political pamphlets, salacious ballads, recipe books and volumes of jokes. The clash of sacred and secular in the bustling environs of the Cathedral cloisters gives one of Shakespeare's greatest tragedies its particular energy, we will show, and an awareness of the unstable religious landscape of early modern London can therefore help us to better understand Hamlet's central dilemma.

Continuing our journey from the west to the east of early modern London, our sixth chapter visits the Bethlehem Hospital near Bishopsgate, better known as Bedlam, which makes up an important part of the imaginative universe of *King Lear* (1605–6). This former priory became London's most infamous institution for the mentally ill, attracting spectators who themselves displayed an unappealing fascination with its deeply disturbed inmates. It is this aspect of Bedlam that lies beneath both Edgar's performed madness as Tom'o'Bedlam and Lear's own descent into a world that loses all meaning, we argue. This chapter situates one of Shakespeare's greatest tragedies in the context of London's medical practices, and shows how the play is underpinned by the commonly held fear that what is intended to cure might in fact harm. We chart the physical and mental ordeals undergone by its central characters, seeking to cast new light on the precise nature of the King's affliction by examining his symptoms alongside early modern accounts of mental illness.

Our seventh chapter visits the area of London most explicitly associated with Shakespeare: Southwark, the home of the

Globe. We seek to re-evaluate received ideas about Southwark as a subversive area outside the City walls. In particular, this chapter examines punitive powers exercised in this area of London, the prisons that stood near to the Globe and the culture of credit and debt that saw many members of Southwark's theatre community imprisoned. It is this culture that informs Shakespeare and Middleton's collaborative play *Timon of Athens* (1607). The play explores the implications of early modern London's new economic systems, and the resulting anxieties produced by the looming threat of debtors' prison. When Timon finds himself destitute outside the walls of his city, the fictional setting of the play and the real-life location of the Globe align. Through this alignment of imaginary Athens and real Southwark, Middleton and Shakespeare raise significant questions about London's emerging economy.

Our final chapter considers the various kinds of experiment that coalesced around early modern Lime Street. This single thoroughfare served as a centre for scientific investigations that attracted national and international attention. We suggest that the extraordinary scientific practices of the inhabitants of Lime Street provide a key context for Prospero's magic in *The Tempest* (1610–11). This chapter also considers theatrical experimentation, exploring the consequences of the fact that *The Tempest* is thought by many to have been written specifically for the King's Men's new playhouse: the Blackfriars. By examining the location of the Blackfriars, and the specific performance conditions of an indoor theatre, we outline the ways in which the thematic, acoustic and visual qualities of *The Tempest* demonstrate Shakespeare's engagement with his company's new theatrical venture.

A brief epilogue summarizes the journey we have taken through Shakespeare's London and reflects upon the intimate relationship between his plays and the city that our study uncovers. We conclude the book with an examination of one of his last, collaborative works (co-written with John Fletcher), *Henry VIII* (1613). Here we address the play from the viewpoint of the Tower of London, where medieval and early modern monarchs spent the night before their coronations, and where two of the play's characters – Buckingham and, later, Anne Boleyn – reach the end of their own journeys. Our epilogue considers briefly the relationship between the play and history, at the moment that Shakespeare looks back upon his own personal history in the city that has inspired him.

1

Violence in Shakespeare's London:

Titus Andronicus (1594) and Tyburn

Introduction

We begin our journey through Shakespeare's London at the western edge of the early modern city, in an area whose significance derives partly from its location at the furthest limits of the metropolis. Approaching early modern London from the west, as a traveller from Stratford would, some of the first sights, sounds and smells to greet the visitor would have been those of Tyburn, the city's site for public executions from 1176 to 1783. Originally a small village on the outskirts of London, by Shakespeare's day Tyburn had become part of the early modern city's urban sprawl as built-up areas quickly encompassed the surrounding fields. The gruesome scene was dominated by the infamous 'Tyburn tree', a three-sided gibbet that had been constructed in 1571 from which up to nine people could be hung at once (as its name suggests, in its early beginnings trees were used as makeshift scaffolds). It is thought that between 40,000 and 60,000 people died at Tyburn during its years of use. It was here that many martyrs were made,

Protestant and then later Catholic priests who were tortured and executed for their faith. A further notable feature of the execution ground was the seating set up by enterprising local residents. Their attempts to cash in on the violent spectacle by such means (including selling refreshments) has been taken to suggest that early modern Londoners saw executions at Tyburn as quasi-theatrical events.

Shakespeare inhabited this mental space of extreme violence as public spectacle when he composed the first play we will study in detail here, the early tragedy *Titus Andronicus* (1594). The sense of excess, of a proliferation of bloodshed and suffering that Shakespeare would have encountered at Tyburn provides the play's keynote, culminating in a bloodbath considered extreme even by the standards of Elizabethan dramatists. In an orgy of violence Titus feeds his enemy Tamora her own sons baked in a pie, before killing her, his daughter Lavinia, and finally himself being killed by Saturninus – who is in turn killed in revenge by Titus' son Lucius. Martyrdom, of the kind achieved at Tyburn by extremists of both faiths, further underpins the play's action as its central character Titus attempts to impose some kind of meaning upon the suffering that he and his family experience, much as death and bloodshed conferred a particular significance upon those who suffered for their faith in Shakespeare's London. Like accounts of the torture of priests at Tyburn that we will explore here, Titus tries – but fails – to fully assimilate the sheer scale and multitude of torments he is faced with; the play's violence simply cannot be contained by any efforts to make it meaningful, resisting all suggestions that it might be symbolic of some greater purpose.

Let us begin with an example of very direct contact between *Titus Andronicus* and the executions at Tyburn, as we explore how and where this location in Shakespeare's city connects to his play. On 31 March 1593 two puritans were taken to the scaffold at Tyburn to face their fates, believing they were about to be executed. At the very last possible minute, however, they received a reprieve, were taken down, and returned to prison.

One can only imagine that their relief must have been considerable, although perhaps tinged with a sense of disappointment that they were not to achieve the martyrdom they had sought. Such feelings were short-lived. Seven days later, with little warning, they were taken back to Tyburn and hanged.

There is reason to think that Shakespeare, who was living in London at this time, may have witnessed one or other of these billed executions. *Titus Andronicus* contains a scene that suggests the ways in which the everyday reality of such incidents in early modern London might have affected Shakespeare's writing of his plays. It features an exchange between Titus and a rather morbid Clown. Titus' daughter Lavinia has been brutally attacked by the sons of his arch-enemy Tamora, the Queen of the Goths; in the play's pivotal dramatic action, Lavinia has been raped and mutilated by Chiron and Demetrius, her hands cut off and her tongue cut out. In act four, scene three the increasingly desperate Titus – who has resorted to firing arrows into the sky as an attempt to convey a message to the gods imploring them to help him – thinks that the Clown and his pigeons bring a message from heaven. It is a moment of both black comedy and deep-rooted pathos as Titus is forced to seek understanding from a figure who talks only incomprehensible gibberish and even gets the names of the gods wrong:

Enter the Clown *with a basket and two pigeons in it.*

TITUS   News, news from heaven! Marcus, the post is come.
        Sirrah, what tidings? Have you any letters?
        Shall I have justice? What says Jupiter?

CLOWN   Ho, the gibbet-maker? He says that he hath taken
        them down again, for the man must not be hanged
        till the next week.

TITUS   But what says Jupiter, I ask thee?

CLOWN   Alas, sir, I know not Jupiter, I never drank
        with him in all my life.

TITUS   Why, villain, art not thou the carrier?

CLOWN   Ay, of my pigeons, sir – nothing else.
TITUS   Why, didst thou not come from heaven?

(4.3.77–88)

In his commentary on the play its Arden editor Jonathan Bate detects an echo of what had just happened to those puritans in London at the time Shakespeare was composing the play in this scene's allusion to a 'gibbet-maker' having 'taken them down again' from the scaffold, 'for the man must not be hanged till the next week'. In this bleakly comic dialogue, the figure trapped in an endless cycle of being strung up to die and cut down again represents a moment of extremely dark humour, a kind of grisly joke that the play's first audience of early modern Londoners would have been attuned to. Shakespeare's imagination has seized upon a detail of life in his own time, and his own city, and used it in the most unexpected of ways, discerning comedy in a tragedy, and the tragic within the comic.

As such, his treatment of early modern London life both serves to connect his play to its first audience, drawing upon events with which they may have been familiar, and also to transcend his own time and place, reaching beyond the specifics of this moment into a more universal realm of human experience. We can see the same impulse at work in another evocation of the early modern executions carried out at Tyburn later in the play. Aaron, Tamora's co-conspirator and the father of her illegitimate baby son, is captured by Titus' son Lucius (who is declared Emperor at the play's conclusion and is one of the very few characters to survive its gruesome events). Lucius threatens to hang the child, urging: 'Get me a ladder' (5.1.53). In Elizabethan executions at Tyburn ladders were used to ascend the scaffold, and the detail may have provoked a moment of recognition among the play's first audiences. As such it represents a momentary incursion of Shakespeare's London into the classical world of the play, serving to bring the action – for a brief instant – into the time and place of its composition. At the same time Shakespeare goes beyond the realities of the world and city in which he lives; the idea that a baby might be subjected to such brutalities would have seemed excessive even to early modern Londoners. He at once places his drama within a context familiar to the theatregoers of his city and, at the same time, takes the documented violence of London to an otherworldly extreme.

Shakespeare's tendency to simultaneously evoke and transcend the realities of life in early modern London is replicated throughout the play, and in fact typifies the dramatist's work as a whole, as this book will show. In *Titus Andronicus* it is manifested at both the most general and the most local levels. We begin this chapter by considering the broadest ways in which the play reflects the extraordinarily violent city in which it was written, a place of political unrest, plague and religious upheaval. We will then consider some more particular points of contact between the proliferation of violence in Shakespeare's city and what many have considered the excessive bloodshed of the play itself, addressing gruesomely theatrical early modern blood sports, the popular Elizabethan genre of revenge tragedy and the spectacle of public executions. In the final part of this chapter we uncover more specific connections between the execution of certain notorious religious martyrs at Tyburn in the late sixteenth century and the language of *Titus Andronicus* itself. At every level we will see how Shakespeare's London suffuses the words of his text, how he writes for – and out of – the time and place in which he lives, and how doing so simultaneously brings *Titus Andronicus* closer to that world and also allows Shakespeare to go far beyond it.

The settings of *Titus Andronicus*

Like almost all of Shakespeare's other drama *Titus Andronicus* is not set in London. Instead the events of the play take place in a non-specific Roman locale. While it used to be thought that the time of the play was much later than Shakespeare's other Roman tragedies (such as *Julius Caesar* and *Antony and Cleopatra*) in fact the text itself makes no concrete references to the historical moment in which its actions occur. In addition, while its main subject is the war of attrition between the Roman general Titus and the conquered Queen of the Goths, Tamora (who seeks revenge because Titus has killed her sons), the play is unusual amongst Shakespeare's work in not having a source in classical literature or history. The plot is a composite, borrowing elements from Ovid's Latin *Metamorphoses* (familiar reading to every schoolboy in Elizabethan England), but also drawn out of contemporary drama fashionable in Shakespeare's London, as well as the life of that city itself. In keeping with the other kinds of multiplicity and excess we will encounter in the play, this proliferation of differing sources and settings shows how – even at this very early stage in his career – Shakespeare's writing cannot or will not be restrained by any single frame of reference, but rather draws upon a great diversity of contexts in order to best reach his audience of early modern Londoners.

The amalgamation of ancient, classical and early modern sources for *Titus Andronicus* is reflected in a rare sketch of a scene from the play made by Henry Peacham, a writer of conduct books and a manual of literary style born around 1576. We have no evidence Peacham actually saw the tragedy staged, but his illustration usefully indicates how one of Shakespeare's contemporaries visualized the play. His famous pen and ink drawing, reproduced in the introduction to the Arden edition of the play (39), shows the actors in stylistically mixed costumes reflecting its ambiguous setting; Titus wears a toga, but the soldiers are Elizabethan in their dress, while Tamora wears medieval attire. Peacham imagines *Titus Andronicus* peopled by a cast of characters combining figures who might very well inhabit Shakespeare's London with others from various historical and literary pasts.

The political climate of Shakespeare's London at the time he was writing the drama may partly explain its composite setting. *Titus Andronicus* is a play profoundly interested by what it means to rule and how power should be passed on from heads of state to their heirs. This thematic concern connects the play to the particular moment and location in which it was produced;

the issue of the Elizabethan succession dominated political discourse in early modern London and is a recurring preoccupation for Shakespeare, as we will see. With Queen Elizabeth I still unmarried and now unlikely – at the age of sixty – to produce any biological offspring, political tensions ran high as to who would inherit her kingdom, and with it the control of a rapidly expanding empire and an extremely unstable Reformed church. One of the few early modern productions of *Titus Andronicus* for which records survive took place on 1 January 1596, in the household of Sir John Harington in Rutland (where the play was presumably performed by Shakespeare's company, the Lord Chamberlain's Men). Harington was part of a circle particularly concerned with the political crisis surrounding the succession. Amongst its members was the Earl of Essex, whose dissatisfaction with the situation would eventually inspire him to march upon the City of London itself, leading a party of armed nobles in an uprising against the Queen for which he would himself be executed in 1601. The preoccupation with dynastic succession evident in *Titus Andronicus* – the question of who will outlive the terrible events of the tragedy in order to claim the crown at the end – is thus as much a feature of Shakespeare's London as the gruesome violence the play depicts.

Violence in Shakespeare's London

The turbulent world presented in *Titus Andronicus* reflects life in early modern London in other ways, too. The play made its debut on the city's stage at a time of deep instability for the city's inhabitants, in which mass death was a recurrent phenomenon and suffering proliferated everywhere Shakespeare and his contemporaries looked. The Rose Theatre, where *Titus* received its premiere, had been closed in 1592 by order of the Privy Council after a violent riot in Southwark. The theatre had barely reopened again when it was once more shut down, this time owing to an outbreak of the plague in January 1593. It was common practice to close theatres during plague epidemics in early modern London, in an attempt to halt the spread of the disease, of which the residents and governors of the city were morbidly (and justifiably) afraid. In 1603 a particularly virulent plague outbreak would kill one out of five Londoners in the space of just a few months, prompting pamphleteer and playwright Thomas Dekker to ask in his pamphlet, *The Dead Terme*: 'Shall our fair bodies never recover of this Disease, which so often and often has run all over them, and does now again begin to be as a plague unto us?' (G1^r). Amidst such loss and bleak despair the notoriously high body count of Shakespeare's *Titus* starts to appear less outlandish and more a sorry reflection of the state of his city. The play seems to have been introduced into the repertoire during a brief reopening of the Rose between plague outbreaks, from 27 December 1593 to 6 February 1594. According to theatre producer and impresario Philip Henslowe's diaries (one of the most important records of early modern theatre that have survived to us today), the play was first performed on Thursday 24 January 1594. It took three pounds and eight shillings in receipts – among the best returns of the season – suggesting that something about the tragedy immediately struck a chord with the early modern Londoners who were losing their loved ones to a seemingly incurable and insatiable disease. Titus' desperate efforts to understand the pain the gods have inflicted upon his family take on a new resonance in the light of such loss, felt on an incomprehensible scale and owing to an illness that nobody understood.

In addition to Henslowe's account of its takings, further evidence for the play's relevance to early modern Londoners comes from the unusual speed with which it was rushed into print. This may have been prompted in part by yet another closure of the theatres owing to the plague. On 6 February, with the Rose once more silent, the printer and publisher John Danter recorded the play in the Stationers' Register (the early modern equivalent of registering its copyright, although no such authorial privilege existed in Shakespeare's day). Stating his intention to publish *Titus Andronicus*, Danter prepared the way for his edition, which would appear in 1594 when it could be readily purchased in St Paul's churchyard (the centre of the early modern book-trade, and a key context for *Hamlet*, we will see in Chapter 5). Issued as a small, inexpensive quarto volume (a little smaller than a modern paperback), the title page to *Titus Andronicus* announces that it could be purchased from Edward White and Thomas Millington at the sign of the Gun, by the door of St Paul's in the heart of London.

Such rapid publication seems to have been motivated by a desire to capitalize on the popularity of Shakespeare's play, particularly within the city in which it was written. But its success would not endure. While the evidence we have just examined suggests that it was initially extremely well received, the play fell out of favour in the eighteenth and nineteenth centuries, when it was rarely performed and frequently denounced; it only returned to the repertoire in the twentieth century. The reason for its fluctuating fortunes seems to be the extreme violence for which the play became infamous, and which was out of keeping with notions of taste held in the intervening years. But how would this crucial aspect of the play have appeared to Shakespeare's original London audience? How would the play's undoubted brutality have seemed to them? Audience members at the Rose in the winter of 1594 would have chosen their afternoon's entertainment from a range of activities on offer to them that included going to watch bull or bear-baiting at the nearby arenas, some of which also staged plays on days when the animals were unavailable. While it would be reductive to compare the suffering seen onstage in Shakespeare's *Titus* to the violence encountered during such blood sports, the popularity of the play should nonetheless be understood in this context; early modern Londoners chose to spend their leisure time – and hard-earned money – watching activities that would today be considered extremely gruesome.

This predilection for bloodshed and gore as a form of entertainment is reflected in the popularity of the genre now known as 'Revenge Tragedy', which originated in the late 1580s and early 1590s. Particularly successful examples of this extremely bloody drama would include Thomas Middleton's *The Revenger's Tragedy* (1607), John Webster's *Duchess of*

Malfi (1613–14) – which today remains the most frequently performed non-Shakespearean play of the early modern period – and *The Changeling* (1622), by Thomas Middleton and William Rowley. These tragedies feature gruesome tales of brutalities inflicted upon one's enemies, and a kind of excessive violence that was designed to be not just effective but, most of all, spectacular – including severed limbs and fingers and elaborate murders. Much like *Titus* they often end in bloodbaths in which almost no characters survive the events of the play. By far the most notorious of these dramas in the period that Shakespeare composed *Titus Andronicus* was Thomas Kyd's *Spanish Tragedy* (*c*.1587), a play that in modern terms would be considered a box-office sensation. It features a particularly stomach-churning scene in which the play's troubled hero, Hieronimo, and his wife, Isabella, find the body of their son, who has been hanged and stabbed. The rest of the action is driven by Hieronimo's desire to exact revenge upon those who have tortured and killed his child, much as Titus' need to avenge Lavinia's rape and mutilation becomes the central preoccupation of Shakespeare's own play. In fact Shakespeare directly alludes to *The Spanish Tragedy* as a precursor to *Titus*, drawing attention to the tradition of theatrical violence of which his own very bloody play is a part. Watching Lavinia weep after the brutal attack upon her, Titus asks her if he should weep too:

> And in the fountain shall we gaze so long
> Till the fresh taste be taken from that clearness
> And made a brine pit with our bitter tears?
> Or shall we cut away our hands like thine?
> Or shall we bite our tongues and in dumb shows
> Pass the remainder of our hateful days?

> (3.1.128–33)

Titus imagines putting on 'dumb shows', miming suffering akin to his daughter's. This is exactly what Hieronimo does at the end of *The Spanish Tragedy*; the play concludes with a dumb show, under the cover of which he finally kills the enemies who have murdered his son. In another moment that resonates with the actions of *Titus*, Hieronimo bites out his own tongue in the play's final scene, in order to ensure that he cannot give away what he has done should he be captured and tortured. When Shakespeare's Lavinia has her own tongue cut out so she cannot identify her rapists the dramatist places the play and the tradition of violent revenge tragedy to which it belongs firmly in the context of the city in which it was performed, where bloody spectacle of a not dissimilar kind was on view to the public regularly at Tyburn. It is this location to which we wish to turn in more detail now.

Titus Andronicus and the violent language of martyrdom

Shakespeare was living and writing in London at a time when the torture and execution of religious non-conformists in the metropolis was at its height, and in which the martyrdom of Catholic priests at Tyburn was a familiar public event. The two instances of the removal of characters' tongues onstage that we have just encountered mirror the treatment of those Elizabethans who continued to adhere to the outlawed Catholic faith at the execution site, who were often tortured and mutilated in public displays intended to warn others against such religious non-compliance. The removal of nails, fingers, genitals, limbs and even internal organs from the still-living bodies of those accused of secretly maintaining Catholic practices was a common occurrence at Tyburn.

We get a sense of the extent of this violence from a popular book published by the Catholic spy Richard Verstegan in 1587. His *Theatre of Cruelty* was a catalogue of brutality, documenting in agonizing and highly detailed images the treatment of Catholic priests who had been captured by the Protestant government. In Figure 2, an illustration typical of Verstegan's book, a tormenter is shown casting grain into the

Horribilia ſcelera ab Huguenotis
in Gallijs perpetrata.

Thracia Biſtonij ſtabulo portenta tyranni
Non vidit tam multa truci, quot noſtra tulerunt
Sæcula, quum magnis animam cruciatibus orbi
Non ſatis eripuiſſe fuit, ſæuitur in ipſum
Funus, & exanguem faciunt præſepia truncum,
Turpe miniſterium, & plusquam monſtroſa tyrannis.

FIGURE 2 *From Richard Verstegan,* [Theatre of Cruelty] *Theatrum Crudelitatum (1587) (by kind permission of Bibliothekarische Auskunft)*

disembowelled torso of a naked man; a donkey is eating the feed directly out of the man's stomach, along with any remaining insides he may possess (53). A death's head and a well-dressed, well-fed Elizabethan gentleman look on. In the background another group of men are dragging other figures (captured priests, we presume) to a well, where they are being dunked upside down under the water. What is perhaps most striking of all, however, is the relative normality of the rest of Verstegan's picture; these terrible events are taking place against the most prosaic of backdrops. We see a river, down which a man is rowing a small boat, seemingly unconcerned by what is happening on its banks; a bridge, over which several small groups are walking purposefully towards the gruesome spectacle; and, in the background, an extremely ordinary-looking urban street, featuring what appears to be a church, a fortified tower and a set of residential dwellings. The scene looks not unlike early modern London. And in fact, this is what it represents; Verstegan's images juxtapose the most cruel and unusual forms of punishment imaginable with the everyday realities of life in Shakespeare's city. In what follows we will take three key instances of notable public executions at Tyburn (and elsewhere) and examine their significance as important contexts that help us to interpret three corresponding moments in *Titus Andronicus*. These are the deaths of Edmund Campion, Anne Askew and Thomas Cranmer, each of which has something important to contribute to our understanding of Shakespeare's treatment of the death of Bassanius, Lavinia's mutilation and Titus' severing of his own hand, respectively.

Meaningful death: Edmund Campion and Bassanius

Let us begin with the example of Campion, one of the most infamous Jesuit priests of Shakespeare's lifetime, martyred in 1581. While Campion's execution occurred some time before the dramatist's arrival in London, its impact continued to be felt through the proliferation of the written word. Print and manuscript accounts of his final days were widely circulated in the city in the years after his death by both Protestants and Catholics, who each wanted to make an example of him in their very different ways. Campion had been working as a secret Catholic missionary after returning to England on 24 June 1580 from continental Europe, where he had been inducted into the novitiate at the Jesuit College in Rome. Campion's task was to preach to – and foster the growth of – the underground community of English Catholics known as recusants. They were, in the words of Anne Sweeney, 'a congregation denied a church', owing to the incompatibility of their religious beliefs with the doctrines espoused in England following the Reformation, a movement that we will analyse in much more detail in Chapter 5. We might think of Campion's role as that of creating a virtual church in which this community might worship, preaching secret masses and tending to the spiritual concerns of his fragmented congregation.

While Campion and his fellow recusant missionaries travelled throughout England in the service of these aims, he also spent a significant amount of time in London, where the population density ensured a significant proportion of closet Catholics (other strongholds of the Roman faith included the north of England, particularly Lancashire, where Shakespeare is rumoured to have spent some of his so-called 'lost years' prior to coming to the city). It was to London that Campion himself repaired upon his return to England in the summer of 1580 (disguised as an Irish jewel salesman). He was to find shelter in the house of the wealthy young Catholic convert George Gilbert, a friend of his companion Robert Persons, another leading Jesuit of his day. Campion even preached at Smithfield a few days after arriving back in the country, despite the vast risk of doing so. It would be outside London (at Lyford Grange, the Berkshire house of the Catholic Edward Yates) that Campion would finally be arrested, however. His presence there was made known to authorities and he was imprisoned on 17 July 1581, after just over a year at large as a recusant preacher. What happened next can help us to understand how early modern Londoners might have perceived some of the more extreme moments of brutality staged in *Titus Andronicus*. Campion was taken to the Tower of London by horse, with his hands and feet tied under the animal's belly. Upon arrival there he was placed in a room known as the 'Little Ease', in which he could neither stand up nor lie down. Campion was then repeatedly interrogated over the next three months. After refusing to answer any questions he was put to the rack and tortured by having metal spikes driven between the flesh and nails of his fingers and the nails pulled out. So severe were his torments that when he was indicted for treason before the

grand jury in Westminster Hall on 12 November he was unable
even to lift his hands to plead 'not guilty' without assistance.
Campion's plea was futile. On 1 December he was dragged to
Tyburn through the streets on a wicker hurdle, where he would
be hung, drawn and quartered. The end of Campion's life
represented the beginning of his career as a martyr; Persons
took a piece of the rope used to hang his colleague and fellow
Jesuit, and carried it with him as a relic for the remainder of
his life.

Titus Andronicus is a play that is born out of this world of
martyr making, and shares the preoccupation of early modern
Londoners with the after-effects of such gruesome deaths. For,
as critic Daryl Palmer has argued in relation to the play,
martyrdoms are a very particular kind of death, not only in
their extreme violence but – more importantly – in the fact
that they have symbolic value. They are deaths that give
meaning to the life that preceded them, according to their
particular rhetoric of sacrifice, and therefore might, in Palmer's
view, be said to signify. We see this kind of attribution of
sacrificial meaning to a bloody death early on in Titus, as
Shakespeare begins to establish the theme of martyrdom that
will run throughout the play. The Emperor's son Bassanius has
been murdered by Chiron and Demetrius (who will go on to
attack Lavinia). Martius comes across his battered corpse,
dumped in a pit in the forest, and he describes his brother's
death in the language of sacrifice:

> Lord Bassanius lies berayed in blood
> All on a heap, like to a slaughtered lamb,
> In this detested, dark, blood-drinking pit.

> (2.2.222–4)

The simile of the 'slaughtered lamb' here is a Christ-like
image, familiar from much poetry of the early modern period,
where it is frequently used to evoke the idea of martyrdom, or
meaningful death. Robert Southwell, another Jesuit who

would himself be martyred at Tyburn in 1595 (hung, drawn and quartered, like Campion) presents a vision of an imagined execution in which he uses a metaphor strikingly similar to that Shakespeare employs here, for instance. Writing in the persona of the Catholic Earl of Arundel, who was at that time imprisoned and believed his own violent death to be imminent, Southwell's speaker entreats his interlocutor to find in his heart the same sympathy for the recusant's plight that he would feel for a 'Relinquished Lamb in solitary wood' who 'With dying bleat doth move the toughest mind' ('I Die without Desert', ll.7–8). Such images recur repeatedly throughout the literature of martyrdom, suggesting that each of these deaths symbolically evokes the original signifying violent death of Christ. It is this kind of poetry, and this kind of bloody logic, that the image of Bassanius as a 'slaughtered lamb' arises out of, and speaks to.

Martyring Lavinia: The silence of Anne Askew

Shakespeare's comparison of Bassanius 'like to a slaughtered lamb' thus establishes a language of martyrdom that evoked the familiar brutalities of Tyburn for the play's original London audience. It is, however, the treatment of Titus' daughter Lavinia in the play that most overtly situates it within the context of the early modern execution of religious martyrs. Lavinia's suffering at the hands of Chiron and Demetrius, who rape her, cut off her hands and remove her tongue, has seemed gratuitous or excessive to many audiences, and goes a long way to explaining the play's fall from favour between the years of its first performance and more recent times. 'Speak, gentle niece, what stern ungentle hands | Hath lopped and hewed and made thy body bare | Of her two branches,' urges Marcus when he first encounters her after their brutal attack (2.3.16–18). He continues:

> Why dost not speak to me?
> Alas, a crimson river of warm blood,
> Like to a bubbling fountain stirred with wind,
> Doth rise and fall between thy rosed lips,
> Coming and going with thy honey breath.
> But sure some Tereus hath deflowered thee
> And, lest thou shouldst detect him, cut thy tongue.
> Ah, now thou turn'st away thy face for shame,
> And notwithstanding all this loss of blood,
> As from a conduit with three issuing spouts,
> Yet do thy cheeks look red as Titan's face,
> Blushing to be encountered with a cloud.

(2.3.21–32)

Marcus' response is notable for its distinctly literary qualities; his first instinct is to turn what he sees into metaphor (the 'crimson river') and simile ('Like to a bubbling fountain'). He reaches for familiar allusions as he struggles to grasp what he sees, referring to the Ovidian story of Tereus who raped and mutilated his wife's sister Philomela, for example. The incongruity of this highly poetic register is highlighted by the rather practical, prosaic image that follows, of the 'conduit with three issuing spouts', a sight familiar to Shakespeare's contemporaries from many an early modern street corner. Adrian Prockter and Robert Taylor, editors of *The A to Z of Elizabethan London*, an invaluable resource for anyone interested in Shakespeare's city, mark thirty conduits and wells in the city, although they believe many more existed (57). It is as if Marcus is fighting to render what he sees in literary terms while the reality of Lavinia's disfigured and bleeding body threatens to overwhelm his efforts in the form of this most quotidian image.

This struggle to give literary significance to Lavinia's suffering is typical of a recurrent desire throughout the play to portray all that happens to her as having symbolic value, in just the way that the torture and execution of priests was made to signify in

the discourse of martyrdom. Lavinia is herself explicitly
described in such terms by Titus, who says he will read her
'martyred signs', for instance (3.2.35). He goes on to promise:

> Thou shalt not sigh, nor hold thy stumps to heaven,
> Nor wink, nor nod, nor kneel, nor make a sign,
> But I of these will wrest an alphabet
> And by still practice learn to know thy meaning.

> (3.2.42–5)

Unable to speak, only 'sigh', or to write, only 'hold thy stumps
to heaven', Titus nonetheless makes clear to his daughter that
one thing that her torturers have not taken away from her is an
ability to communicate, to make meaning. He will 'learn' the
symbolic significance of every 'wink', 'nod' or gesture. Even in
her torment she can yet 'make a sign', in the same way that the
brutalities undergone by Catholic priests at Tyburn would
become symbolic for those wishing to make martyrs of them.

This attempt to make meaning out of Lavinia's suffering is
lent particular emphasis by the fact that when she is finally
able to communicate to her family the full horror of what has
happened she does so in a gesture that could be considered the
most overtly literary moment of the play. Unable to speak, or
indeed to write, Lavinia turns instead to a selection of books,
frantically turning them over with the stumps that are all that
is left of her hands, in search of one particular volume that she
wishes to show her father and which contains an episode she
feels can explain her own fate to him:

> [*Lavinia turns over the books*]

> TITUS   How now, Lavinia? Marcus, what means this?
>   Some book there is that she desires to see.
>   Which is it, girl, of these? Open them, boy.

>   [*to Lavinia*]
>   But thou art deeper read and better skilled:
>   Come and take choice of all my library,
>   And so beguile thy sorrow till the heavens

Reveal the damned contriver of this deed.
Why lifts she up her arms in sequence thus?

MARCUS   I think she means that there were more than one
Confederate in the fact. Ay, more there was –
Or else to heaven she heaves them for revenge.

TITUS   Lucius, what book is that she tosseth so?

BOY   Grandsire, 'tis Ovid's *Metamorphosis*;
My mother gave it me.

MARCUS   For love of her that's gone,
Perhaps she culled it from among the rest.

TITUS   Soft, so busily she turns the leaves!
What would she find? Lavinia, shall I read?
This is the tragic tale of Philomel,
And treats of Tereus' treason and his rape –
And rape, I fear, was root of thy annoy.

MARCUS   See, brother, see: note how she quotes the leaves.

(4.1.30–50)

Turning to the page of Ovid's *Metamorphoses* that tells the story of the rape of Philomela at the hands of Tereus, already alluded to by Marcus above, Lavinia not only seeks to communicate the basic facts of what has happened to her (that there was 'more than one' attacker, for instance, and that they raped her), but also attempts to make her suffering mean something, to make it signify. Marcus' unusual – and ironic – usage of the verb 'quote' in the last line reproduced here (to mean something closer to 'touches') is especially poignant; quoting – writing or speaking the words of another – is something Lavinia now cannot do. Yet by turning to a literary precedent in order to explain her ordeal to her father she is also in some sense interpreting her experience, trying to understand its significance by casting it in the words of another, her Ovidian precursor Philomela.

A more immediate precedent for Lavinia's martyrdom can, however, be found in Shakespeare's own city. At the time he wrote the play the execution of one of the most famous female martyrs of early modern London might have been in

Shakespeare's mind. The Protestant Anne Askew was burned at the stake in Smithfield in 1546, under the rule of the Catholic Queen Mary. Her violent death is recounted in one of the most frequently reprinted and widely read books of the Elizabethan period, John Foxe's *Book of Martyrs*, as it was popularly known (its official title was *Acts and Monuments*, the first edition of which appeared in 1563, the second – considerably revised and augmented – in 1570). Foxe's book contains a series of accounts of those martyred in the service of their faith that collectively make up a history of the English church. The episode describing the death of Anne Askew is one of the most commonly cited moments in Foxe's vast work (the book stretched to over 1,800 pages, and filled two large folio volumes in the second edition). It reports Askew's extraordinary silence while enduring enormous physical pain, documenting a (possibly apocryphal) story that tells how she did not begin to scream until the flames reached her chest, while the men executed alongside her began to shout the moment they first felt the heat of the fire. This model, with all the hyperbole such an account carries with it, provides an important context for Shakespeare's Lavinia, who is likewise silent in her suffering and whose stoicism is also interpreted as highly symbolic of her innocence and moral strength by those around her. Lavinia's composite character draws not just upon the Ovidian Philomela but also, perhaps more directly, upon London's female martyrs, such as the celebrated Askew, accounts of whose death proliferated in Shakespeare's imaginative universe.

'Lend me thy hand': Titus and the death of Thomas Cranmer

The point of Foxe's book, which reproduces a seemingly endless number of similarly violent tales of martyrdom, is of course to inspire comparable actions amongst his readers, hoping to instil in them similar courage in confronting suffering in their own lives. This is the third aspect of the language of martyrdom associated with Tyburn that Shakespeare plays upon in his early tragedy, in which Titus' decision to cut off his own hand echoes what has happened to Lavinia, like those who sought to emulate the acts of martyrs. In a futile attempt to save the lives of his sons Martius and Quintus, which he has been led to believe can be achieved by sending a severed hand in substitution for their deaths, Titus quickly offers his own, asking: 'Good Aaron, wilt thou help to chop it off?' (3.1.162). In a morbid pun he then goes on, 'Lend me thy hand and I will give thee mine' (3.1.188). He asks,

> Good Aaron, give his majesty my hand.
> Tell him it was a hand that warded him
> From thousand dangers, bid him bury it:
> More hath it merited; that let it have.
> As for my sons, say I account of them
> As jewels purchased at an easy price,
> And yet dear too, because I bought mine own.

> (3.1.194–200)

Titus' speech plays upon the differing senses of 'hand', as both a physical body part and a metaphor for helpfulness (Shakespeare uses the literary device of synecdoche, by which a part can stand in for a whole, with 'hand' here representing the efforts of an entire body). Titus mistakenly thinks that he can make his own suffering signify like that of a martyr, and that its symbolic value will be considered equal to the life of his sons, 'an easy price', in his estimation. In fact, in the tragic world he finds himself, there is no such mechanism for translating pain into meaning or rewarding suffering; his severed hand turns out to be far too 'dear', sent back to him along with the heads of his sons.

This episode recalls the circumstances of another famous martyr, whose death is also told of in Foxe's book. Thomas Cranmer was executed in Oxford by being burned at the stake in March 1556 for having denounced the authority of the Pope. The archbishop supposedly held his hand up to the fire to be burned first, because it had written (under duress) a statement recanting his beliefs. But where accounts of Cranmer's death emphasize this symbolism, Titus' own gesture is shown by Shakespeare to be ultimately meaningless. In one of the embodiments of excess for which the tragedy is infamous, his action is repaid not just in kind but with a kind of surplus, the gratuitous beheading of two of his children. As in each of the other key moments of *Titus Andronicus* illuminated by the accounts of martyrdom proliferating in early modern London examined in this chapter, Shakespeare's own version of violent death resists any attempts at understanding. Where Campion's dismemberment made him a revered martyr amongst his fellow Catholics, Bassanius' martyrdom is senseless. Askew's stoicism provides an example of graceful suffering to her co-religionists, whereas Lavinia's silence bespeaks only of more suffering, the literary terms in which she expresses what has happened to her brutally and irredeemably at odds with the attack she has been subjected to. And while Cranmer's tendering of his hand to the fire has been interpreted as a highly symbolic restatement of the beliefs he had denied under torture, Titus' comparable gesture leads only to pointless bloodshed. In each of these three case studies reading moments from *Titus Andronicus* alongside the episodes in the history of martyrdom studied here reveals Shakespeare's insistence that any effort to impose meaning or signification upon suffering results only in further violence and loss.

'No funeral rite': Death and the Reformation in Shakespeare's London

We catch a final glimpse of the gruesome world of Elizabethan London's executions and the language of martyrdom in last scene of the play. Here Titus' victorious heir Lucius declares that the malignant Aaron, who has conspired with Tamora to bring about the Romans' downfall, will be punished not by death, but rather will be buried alive:

> Set him breast-deep in earth and famish him;
> There let him stand and rave and cry for food.
> If anyone relieves or pities him,
> For the offence he dies.
>
> (5.3.178–81)

This cruel and unusual punishment would not have been out of place at Tyburn, where the expression of sympathy for priests suffering such a fate was similarly forbidden. In effect Aaron will be interred without any proper ritual. As such his end echoes that of Tamora, to whom he has remained loyal throughout his life and who will not be afforded the rites of a burial. Like those executed at Tyburn, Lucius commands that she receive

> No funeral rite, nor man in mourning weed,
> No mournful bell shall ring her burial,
> But throw her forth to beasts and birds to prey:
> Her life was beastly and devoid of pity,
> And being dead, let birds on her take pity.
>
> (5.3.195–99)

The question of how one should properly be buried was one of the key issues underlying the English Reformation; Lucius' reference to the 'mournful bell' recalls the defunct Catholic ritual of tolling a bell for the dead, a point of doctrinal contention that we will explore further in our study of *Hamlet* in Chapter 5. There we will see Ophelia denied a proper burial, of which she is considered undeserving having committed suicide. At a time when huge importance was attached to the correct way of mourning for the dead, early modern Londoners could imagine no worse fate than receiving 'No funeral rite' at all.

This brings us to the reason why the language of martyrdom that we have traced throughout Shakespeare's *Titus Andronicus* is so important to the play and its context. Not only does it reflect life in early modern London, where events such as the execution of Campion were regular occurrences; it also reveals the play's deeper concern with what must have been for many the traumatic after-effects of the English Reformation. The violence undergone by Lavinia, Bassianus, Titus himself, and even Tamora and Aaron, reflects the violent upheaval experienced by English society in the wake of the cataclysmic series of events that led England's separation from the Roman Church. The Reformation is a fundamental sub-text of the play as a whole, in which the corruption of Rome is a recurring motif and where Aaron, the personification of evil in the drama, is accused of 'popish tricks' (5.1.75). One of the play's goriest moments (responsible for a particularly large number of faintings during a recent Globe staging) is when Titus ritually lets the blood of Chiron and Demetrius in preparation for making the gruesome pie that Tamora will be forced to eat. He tells them:

> And now, prepare your throats. Lavinia, come,
> Receive the blood, and when that they are dead
> Let me go grind their bones to powder small,
> And with this hateful liquor temper it,
> And in that paste let their vile heads be baked.

> (5.2.196–200)

'Receive the blood' here echoes the words of the communion service in the Book of Common Prayer. As such, this moment alludes to one of the key questions underpinning the religious upheavals of Shakespeare's time: the debate about what actually happens during the Eucharist. One of the central points of reformed doctrine was an insistence that the bread and wine do not actually become the body and blood of Christ during the process of communion (as Catholics believe) but that the transformation was purely symbolic. Shakespeare's first great tragedy shows us – as it showed his first London audience – the problematic nature of any attempt to make the language of death and violence operate in a symbolic way. In this way it exactly mirrors the debate being staged in doctrinal disputes as he wrote. The play's constant emphasis on the idea of proliferation, of taking everything to its utmost extreme or excess, is Shakespeare's way of taking the gruesome realities of life in early modern London and turning them into something yet more profound. By drawing upon the experiences of plague, violent spectacle and public execution that were part of the daily lives of his contemporary Londoners, Shakespeare is able to imbue *Titus Andronicus* with his own much deeper insight about the ultimate meaninglessness of violence.

2

Politics in Shakespeare's London:

Richard II (1595) and Whitehall

Introduction

Richard II is one of the very few Shakespeare plays to contain scenes that are specifically set in London, albeit the historical city inhabited by the medieval king whose downfall it charts, rather than that of the dramatist himself. The play explores the behaviour that causes Richard II to lose the support of his nobles and the country at large, his subsequent deposition and the ascent to the throne of Bolingbroke, future King Henry IV. It contains episodes set at the Duke of Lancaster's London residence, Ely House, to which we will turn in a moment, and a pivotal scene between Queen Isabel and her recently deposed husband that takes place amongst the bustle of a London street. The Queen is forced to wait amongst the crowds there in the hope of interrupting the procession in which Richard is being taken 'To Julius Caesar's ill-erected tower, | To whose flint bosom my condemned lord | Is doomed a prisoner by proud Bolingbroke' (5.1.2–4). Shakespeare even refers to the seedier side of London in the closing moments of *Richard II*,

when the newly crowned Henry IV wonders where his son
might be:

> Can no man tell me of my unthrifty son?
> 'Tis full three months since I did see him last.
> If any plague hang over us, 'tis he.
> I would to God, my lords, he might be found.
> Enquire at London, 'mongst the taverns there,
> For there, they say, he daily doth frequent,
> With unrestrained loose companions.

(5.3.1–7)

This passage is not only specifically placed in London, it also
speaks the language of everyday life in the metropolis, with its
concerns about money ('my unthrifty son'), fear of the 'plague'
that hangs over its inhabitants and talk of the 'taverns' full of
'loose companions'. As such it shares the city's preoccupations
with credit and debt, sickness and health, and tensions between
social classes that we examine in our chapters on *Timon of
Athens*, *King Lear* and *Romeo and Juliet*, respectively. The
young man lost for more than 'three months' amongst the
lowlife of the capital is of course the dissolute Prince Hal,
whose exploits form much of the plot of the two *Henry IV*
plays and who eventually becomes the warrior king seen in
Henry V. Hal's mettle is tested in an odyssey through the
teeming streets of London's dark underbelly; it is the city itself
that takes the measure of the man who will one day wear the
crown. The prince who is heir to the throne of England through
his blood ties to the house of Lancaster is equally connected to
the 'unrestrained' inhabitants of the drinking holes he 'daily
doth frequent' in London. Hal is as much at home on Bankside,
with its pubs, amusements and brothels, as he is at the palace
of Westminster; this is the conundrum that will occupy
Shakespeare throughout his second tetralogy of history plays
(comprising *Richard II*, *Henry IV 1*, *Henry IV 2* and *Henry V*).
As we saw in our introduction it is this social and economic

diversity, the close juxtaposition of such extremes, that in fact characterizes early modern London itself and which makes the city so exciting for the playwright.

In this chapter we will focus on the wide-reaching, capricious and highly changeable political life of Shakespeare's city, concentrating primarily on the neighbourhood of Whitehall and especially the environs of Westminster, the beating political heart of early modern London. John Norden's 1593 map of the neighbourhood (Figure 3) depicts a complex of governmental buildings, law courts and other administrative and ceremonial venues at Westminster. The massive and lavish Whitehall Palace was the primary residence of monarchs in London up until the early eighteenth century. The only part of the building to survive today is the banqueting hall, built between 1622 and 1634 by Elizabeth's successor, James I, who liked to hold Bacchanalian parties in its undercroft (less happily, the hall was also the scene of Charles I's execution in 1649). Gardens, parkland and a tiltyard (for jousting tournaments) are also clearly visible on the map, emphasizing the fact that this was a dwelling place used for the activities that filled the leisure time of early modern courtiers, as well as a working political centre.

Let us begin by looking at another scene from *Richard II* that takes place in a specific London setting and which contains a speech that not only gives us a useful introduction to the political issues dominating both Shakespeare's city and the play itself, but that also happens to be one of the playwright's best known and most brilliant pieces of poetry. The dying words of Bolingbroke's father, John of Gaunt, are spoken at his London home as he awaits a visit from the King of whom he has come to despair. (The historical John of Gaunt died on 3 February 1399 and was buried in London in St Paul's Cathedral, which we will visit later in this book.) Ely House, then a large dwelling just off Holborn, near the modern-day Hatton Gardens, is the location for this scene. Gaunt moved into this mansion after his great palace on the site of the modern Savoy Hotel was burnt to the ground in 1381 by rebels

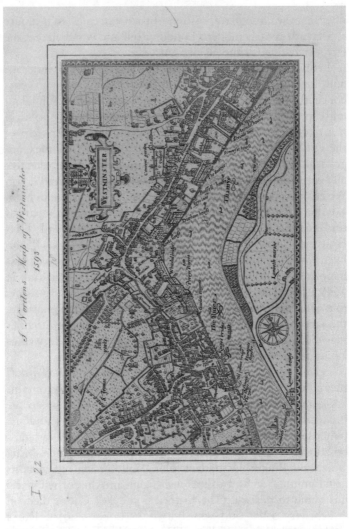

FIGURE 3 *From John Norden,* Speculum Britanniae *(1593) (© The British Library Board, Maps Crace Port. 1.22)*

who believed him to have aspirations towards kingship himself. The rebuilt 'Savoye' is clearly visible on Norden's map of Westminster, just south of Covent Garden (Figure 3). Stow – who reports that 'there was none in the realm to be compared in beauty and stateliness' to Lancaster's house of Savoy – notes that the rebels destroyed all the many precious goods they found in Gaunt's possession, breaking 'plate and vessels of gold and silver' into 'small pieces', which they threw into the Thames. 'They found there certain barrels of gunpowder,' Stow recounts 'which they thought had been gold or silver, and throwing them into the fire more suddenly than they thought, the hall was blown up, the houses destroyed, and themselves very hardly escaped away' (372). His residence destroyed, Gaunt leased from the bishops of Ely their grand London palace, which, Stow tells us, included some 'two cellars, and forty acres of land', a 'chapel', 'a large port, gatehouse, or front towards the street or highway' and a series of 'large and commodious rooms' (326). Given the lavish nature of his London homes, the laudatory tone of much of Gaunt's speech – in which he compares England itself to a 'precious stone' of the kind he owned in great quantities – is perhaps not surprising. But as we will see, his words also reveal his experience of the other side of London life too, the social unrest, fear of conspiracy, envy of others' wealth and wilful destructiveness he had experienced at the hands of the rebels who destroyed the house of Savoy, and whose actions presaged the greater instability to come as Richard's reign progressed.

Gaunt's speech is often cited as defining all that is great about Englishness but in fact, in its full version, presents a highly political critique of Richard's reign and the current state of the country:

> This royal throne of kings, this sceptred isle,
> This earth of majesty, this seat of Mars,
> This other Eden, demi-paradise,
> This fortress built by Nature for herself
> Against infection and the hand of war,

This happy breed of men, this little world,
This precious stone set in the silver sea,
Which serves it in the office of a wall
Or as a moat defensive to a house
Against the envy of less happier lands,
This blessed plot, this earth, this realm, this England,
This nurse, this teeming womb of royal kings,
Feared by their breed and famous by their birth,
Renowned for their deeds as far from home,
For Christian service and true chivalry,
                    [. . .]
This land of such dear souls, this dear dear land,
Dear for her reputation through the world,
Is now leased out – I die pronouncing it –
Like to a tenement or pelting farm.
England, bound in with the triumphant sea,
Whose rocky shore beats back the envious siege
Of wat'ry Neptune, is now bound in with shame,
With inky blots and rotten parchment bonds.
That England that was wont to conquer others
Hath made a shameful conquest of itself.

(2.1.40–54, 57–66)

The speech explores the four key issues with which we will be concerned in this chapter. First, it portrays the realities of political life – for better or worse – medieval, early modern or (for that matter) modern England and particularly, we might argue, the London in which Gaunt speaks, is figured as a 'teeming womb of royal kings', a tightly bound network of allegiances and claims to power, in which each bearer of the crown is determined by 'their breed' and 'birth'. Gaunt's comments about 'Christian service' and 'true chivalry' will begin to seem ironic as the play progresses, given Richard's treatment of him and his son, prompting Shakespeare's audience to question what it really means to be 'Feared' and 'famous'. The England of Gaunt's speech is not the idyll that it first appears; rather it inspires envy, both within and without, riven by conflict and teetering on the edge of a self-defeating civil war. As such, the speech reflects the reality of the political climate of Shakespeare's own day, as much as that of fourteenth-century England, and the play's depiction of the fickle nature of political allegiances, shifting loyalties, petty infighting and outright jealousy offers an unflattering portrait of early modern Westminster, portrayed through the guise of Richard II's court.

Second, we get a symbolic image here of the mechanisms by which members of the court were included or excluded from royal favour in Gaunt's exploration of England's status as an island, surrounded by an ocean that keeps enemies out and others in. This ensures the nation's population and its monarch are almost divinely protected within a 'fortress built by Nature for herself' that is bounded by the 'silver sea', which fulfils 'the office of a wall | Or as moat defensive', he says. But, at the same time, England is cut off, isolated, its people trapped by the same 'triumphant sea' that now seems to subdue them, such that they are 'now bound in with shame'. Just as London's city walls both offered protection and also served to curtail the behaviour of its citizens, or as the court functioned as a physical manifestation of royal favour, by which nobles were either elevated or cast out, embraced or forbidden entry (as will become especially clear in our study of *Henry VIII* in the epilogue to this book), so here the sea that surrounds England manifests some of the contradictions of its political position. This is mirrored in the complex network of interlinked spaces that make up the nation's physical centre of power at Whitehall.

Third, the speech also reflects what may be Shakespeare's most important political insight in *Richard II*, the idea that the fates of its central characters, Richard and Bolingbroke, are interlinked and that the rise of one depends upon the fall of the other. This understanding determines the structure of the drama, as well as one of the most striking features of its language. Throughout *Richard II* Shakespeare is very fond of the use of a rhetorical device known as chiasmus, by which two grammatical clauses are repeated in reverse order, switching their original positions. It appears here when Gaunt bemoans the fact 'That England that was wont to conquer others | Hath made a shameful conquest of itself.' The two lines of verse are mirror images of each other, with the subject and object of their repeated verb, 'conquer', inverted; England becomes the subject of a conquest having previously succeeded in subduing 'others'. Likewise, the 'dear dear land' of 'dear souls' has now become 'dear' in another sense, 'leased out' at what Gaunt implies is too high a rate, 'Like to a tenement or pelting farm' (the class implications of this phrase will also be important later in this chapter). Repetition here turns a word's meaning inside out, just as Richard's life is emptied of meaning by Bolingbroke's exposure of his own vacuousness, what he himself will call his 'hollow crown' (3.2.160).

Finally, while *Richard II* is highly attuned to the often unattractive realities and pragmatic worldliness of political life the play also reminds us of the sanctity of 'This royal throne', and the wondrous quality of 'majesty'. Shakespeare uses unearthly terms here to invoke the quasi-divine status of the anointed monarch, who inhabits 'this seat of Mars, | This other Eden'. This latter phrase is particularly important. As we will explore later in this chapter, one of *Richard II*'s key concerns is with the relationship between the holy office of kingship, which is passed from one monarch to the next, and the body of an individual ruler, upon which the divine right to rule is temporarily bestowed. Rather paradoxically, the English king is part human, part divine; as such, Gaunt's speech suggests, it is fitting that he dwell in a 'demi-paradise'.

Gaunt's eulogy thus reveals some of the central discoveries that Shakespeare's play uncovers about the nature of power and the political workings of his city. In what follows we will explore the four aspects of the play's depiction of early modern politics highlighted by his speech. First we examine the ways in which *Richard II* reflects the vicissitudes of political life in Shakespeare's London, revealing the ever-shifting and often self-serving nature of allegiances between those who aspire to power, quickly forged and just as quickly broken. In the second section of this chapter we look more closely at the workings of royal favour and the mechanisms of inclusion and exclusion by which this is bestowed, or taken away, in the play, an aspect of the drama that we argue reflects the architecture and location of Westminster itself. The structure of power itself as depicted in the play is our focus in the third part of this study, where we explore the rapidity with which political fates are transformed in *Richard II* – as in Shakespeare's London – and the fact that these reversals are often interconnected, the success of one courtly career depending upon the failure of another. In our final section we take up the last idea illuminated by Gaunt's speech as discussed above, exploring *Richard II*'s notorious deposition scene as an inversion of the coronation process in order to cast light upon the ways the play mirrors early modern understanding of the quasi-divine nature of kingship.

Whitehall: Political networks in Shakespeare's London

On 7 December 1595 the MP Sir Edward Hoby wrote to Sir Robert Cecil, the Queen's Secretary of State, inviting him 'to visit poor Canon row', where 'a gate for your supper shall be open: & K. Richard present him self to your view' (quoted in Forker's introduction to his Arden Shakespeare edition of the play, 114). Hoby had risen at court under Cecil's father, Lord Burghley, serving on several important parliamentary committees, but had more recently fallen from favour, being briefly placed under house arrest after insulting the privy councillor Sir Thomas Heneage. The invitation he extends to Cecil could well be interpreted as an attempt to secure the support of one of the most important of Elizabeth's advisors, and thus a shrewdly political move. The location to which Cecil is invited also speaks of Hoby's political ambitions; his dwelling has been chosen to place him as close to the political action of Shakespeare's city as is possible. Canon row, a series of townhouses in the heart of Whitehall, directly abutting Westminster Hall and the Star Chamber, can be seen along the riverfront running between the 'King's bridge' and 'Garden stairs' on Norden's map (Figure 3). The choice of entertainment on offer may also be revealing: some critics believe that Hoby's letter refers to a performance of Shakespeare's *Richard II*, and think that the play may have been first performed in this private Westminster residence. While no direct evidence exists confirming that Hoby refers to Shakespeare's play here (we do not know when or where the drama was premiered), we do have reason to believe that early modern politicians would have been particularly interested in *Richard II*. The play's ever-shifting network of allegiances mimics those encountered in their daily lives at court and in Elizabeth's parliament, where the rapidly changing fortunes of a figure such as Hoby (who would return to royal preferment under James I) is indicative of the vacillations faced by her government as a whole.

Opening with a confrontation at Windsor between Bolingbroke and the Duke of Norfolk, Thomas Mowbray, the play initially positions the future challenger of Richard II as primarily concerned with 'Tend'ring the precious safety of my prince', accusing his adversary of being 'a traitor and a miscreant' (1.1.32, 39). Mowbray, for his part, lays the same charge at Bolingbroke's door: 'I do defy him, and I spit at him, | Call him a slanderous coward and a villain' (1.1.61–62). The heated exchange that culminates in Richard's command that the two do battle in hand-to-hand combat 'At Coventry upon Saint Lambert's Day' (1.1.199), repeatedly invokes Bolingbroke's noble blood. Mowbray asks the King to set aside his rival's 'high blood's royalty', imploring Richard to 'let him be no kinsmen to my liege' (1.1.58, 59). Both antagonists are at pains to prove their loyalty to the crown, by blood or otherwise, and the first scene is dominated by their rhetorical attempts to demonstrate this commitment.

As the play proceeds such concerns about loyalty will become pressing as Bolingbroke mobilizes his own allies against the

King's followers. Richard's former supporters gradually join the Lancastrian cause until he is left with just a few favourites, Bagot, Bushy and Green, along with his stalwart political allies the Earl of Salisbury, Bishop of Carlisle, Abbot of Westminster and Sir Stephen Scroop. Such allegiances are particularly important in *Richard II* because they bring with them access to the resources (money and soldiers) of each respective nobleman; the need to establish or maintain networks of power therefore becomes the driving force for the play's action. It is the fear that his followers have deserted him, and the subsequent discovery they have in fact lost their lives fighting his cause, that prompts Richard's first realization that his reign is drawing to a close. In act three, scene two he acknowledges the time has come to 'talk of graves, of worms and epitaphs', confronted by the stark reality that 'Our lands, our lives, and all are Bolingbroke's' (3.2.145, 151). The Duke of York, who successfully navigates the tumultuous events of the play, shifting his allegiance from one king to his successor while privately assuring Richard of his ongoing sympathy, is perhaps the most visible representation of the need to fit oneself to the changing political climate of the court. Richard's downfall is completed, he must realize, when Scroop reports later in the same scene:

Your uncle York is joined with Bolingbroke,
And all your northern castles yielded up,
And all your southern gentlemen in arms
Upon his party.

(3.2.200–203)

York's changing allegiances seem to mirror, or even bring about, the loss of support Richard sustains across the country as a whole, as both north and south go over to Bolingbroke's side and his own network of support shrinks ever smaller.

Shakespeare's acute rendering of the vicissitudes of political life, including the need to respond with subtlety and care to shifting power dynamics amongst the ruling class, as well as his emphasis upon the necessity of loyal supporters in maintaining a secure power-base may partly reflect his own experiences of such matters in early modern London. His position as a poet and a playwright in the city depended to a large extent on the protection of certain nobles in the face of a constant stream of challenges from the city authorities, puritan opponents of the theatre, the plague closures, rival companies, legal disputes and demands to conform to a febrile, newly reformed national church. Just as Bolingbroke depends upon Richard's former supporters forsaking the king and flocking to his own cause, so Shakespeare himself had to court the nobility (including the reigning monarch) as he sought patronage for his writing. Protection, credibility and even hard cash were initially provided to the playwright by Henry Wriothesley, third Earl of Southampton, to whom his narrative poems, *Venus and Adonis* (1583) and *The Rape of Lucrece* (1594) had been gratefully dedicated. Shakespeare would then be more securely supported by the Lord Chamberlain, Henry Cary, Baron Hunsdon, who in 1594 formed the playing company with whom he would be profitably associated for the rest of his career, as a writer, actor and later shareholder. The date of the formation of the Lord Chamberlain's Men, and Shakespeare's recent experiences with Southampton (a politically and personally volatile figure, as we will see later in this chapter) together form a particularly important context for *Richard II*, a play written with the politics of patronage and the importance of support networks amongst the nobility foremost in Shakespeare's mind.

Inclusion and exclusion: Court politics and royal favour

Throughout *Richard II* this preoccupation with maintaining royal or noble favour, in all its magnitude and fickleness, is physically represented by the recurring motif of banishment, which we will discover is also important in his much later history play, *Henry VIII*. Characters including Bolingbroke and Richard themselves (as well as Mowbray, and the Queen) are frequently exiled from the court, a potent symbol of loss of political status in Shakespeare's London as much as it was in the medieval England of the play. The poet Sir Philip Sidney had been forced to withdraw from court in 1579, for example, having written an ill-advised letter opposing the Queen's mooted marriage to the Duke of Anjou and subsequently engaged in an equally misguided row with the earl of Oxford over a game of tennis (his absence did at least provide him with the opportunity to compose his *Old Arcadia*, with which Shakespeare was very familiar). Sidney's return to court was only welcomed after he gifted Elizabeth a diamond encrusted whip at the start of 1581 as a symbol of his submission. Richard II, whom Shakespeare appears to deliberately parallel with the Queen (as touched upon later in this chapter), likewise sets his own demise in motion when he banishes Bolingbroke and Mowbray for six years and for life, respectively, saying to the latter, 'The hopeless word of "never to return" | Breathe I against thee, upon pain of life' (1.3.152–53).

So bleak is the prospect of banishment, of never speaking his mother tongue again, that Mowbray compares his fate to its apparent opposite, imprisonment: 'Within my mouth you have engaoled my tongue, | Doubly portcullised with my teeth and lips,' he says (1.3.166–67). The idea that exile – casting out – might be a form of enclosure – or locking in – is a curious paradox that recurs on a larger scale in what happens to Richard himself. If his (albeit voluntary) exile to Ireland traps him into behaviour that will be his undoing, Richard's later imprisonment in the Tower will ultimately free him from the bonds of his office. In one of the play's most remarkable speeches the embattled monarch imagines the crown and even his body as a kind of prison:

> For within the hollow crown
> That rounds the mortal temples of a king
> Keeps Death his court; and there the antic sits,

Scoffing his state and grinning at his pomp,
Allowing him a breath, a little scene,
To monarchize, be feared and kill with looks,
Infusing him with self and vain conceit,
As if this flesh which walls about our life
Were brass impregnable; and humoured thus,
Comes at last and with a little pin
Bores through his castle wall, and farewell, king!

(3.2.160–70)

In Richard's sustained imagining a personified Death toys with his prisoner, the king, 'Allowing him a breath,' but equally able to snatch life away with a mere pinprick. The 'brass impregnable' crown that has seemed to protect the monarch's quasi-divine state is compared to the body that 'walls about our life', each equally restrictive because each offers nothing more than a temporary illusion of endurance. Just as life and kingship are fragile, both a mere performance or 'a little scene' (to return to that favourite trope of Shakespeare's), so those things that first appear to sustain them can in fact function as a prison, drawing out mortal suffering to the point that death or deposition come to seem welcome.

Richard's comparison of the 'hollow crown' to a court is remarkable in another sense, too, for this underlying notion that what seems to protect can really imprison also reflects the architecture of the physical space inhabited by English monarchs. Anne Barton discerns a pattern of concentric circles centred around the Queen herself in the structure of Whitehall and the other royal palaces of Elizabeth's reign. The Palace at Westminster 'housed the sovereign's person, in a series of carefully graded spaces', she writes, 'extending outward from the intimacy of the Bedchamber and various withdrawing chambers, access to which was denied to all but a select few, to the somewhat more populous but still elite Privy Chamber'. As Barton continues, next came 'the Presence Chamber, where the monarch could sometimes be viewed – by those with any right to be present at court at all – receiving ambassadors and other guests, or dining in state, the Great Chamber, and finally, a Hall' (123). In fact, Barton's description could be extended yet further. Westminster was constructed on land reclaimed from the Thames estuary, and had in Anglo-Saxon times been effectively cut off from the rest of London by river inlets (the area was known at this period as Thorney Island). During Elizabeth's rule traces of these waterways remained; John Stow describes the 'Long Ditch' that 'almost insulates the city of Westminster' in his account of Shakespeare's London (378). He also notes that the water level was still high enough in medieval times for the neighbourhood to flood, recounting that in 1236 the Thames overflowed its banks 'and in the great palace of Westminster men did row with wherries in the midst of the hall' (387). The Elizabethan Whitehall Palace remained effectively moated, its inhabitants both sheltered and also contained by the multiple layers of its walls and the remnants of this river, which continued to isolate it from the rest of the city. Shakespeare was acutely conscious of the layout of Westminster and the intricate workings of the court, at both a symbolic and a practical level; his playing company was frequently called upon to perform there. *Richard II* reveals this familiarity with the court's enclosed nature, with each successive layer of increasing grandeur and exclusivity serving to cushion the King artificially from having to confront the greatest danger of all: his true self.

'Ascend his throne | Descending now from him': Chiasmus in *Richard II*

The gradual unpeeling of these layers and need to confront the reality of who and what he is forms the central dramatic trajectory of the character Richard II, a protagonist who anticipates King Lear's eventual journey towards self-discovery and with it an awakening of human empathy (as we see in

Chapter 6). *Richard II* contains at its centre a pair of key scenes in which this process reaches its fulfilment, and to which we turn now in the next section of this chapter. When Richard surrenders at Flint Castle (3.3) he literally descends from the highest throne of kingship, forced by Bolingbroke's allies to come down from the battlements where he first appears to them (for which the Globe's Upper Gallery may have served in early modern productions) into the base court. This is mirrored in the play by the new King Henry IV's ascent of the throne before parliament at Westminster Hall (4.1). 'Ascend his throne, descending now from him,' urges the Duke of York (4.1.112). In a further iteration of the rhetorical device of the chiasmus, which we have already identified as an important feature of the play's form and language, Shakespeare has carefully designed this structure to balance the fall of Richard with the rise of Bolingbroke. Another important example of this also occurs in the Flint Castle scene, when Bolingbroke insists, 'My gracious lord, I come but for mine own,' to which Richard replies, in an inversion of what has just been said, 'Your own is yours, and I am yours and all' (3.3.196–97). Thus the language of the play displays at a local level the same organizational principles, the same fondness for doublings and reversals, which its larger structure also embodies.

Reluctant to give up the crown to his cousin, Richard compares it to 'a deep well':

That owes two buckets, filling one another,
The emptier ever dancing in the air,
The other down, unseen and full of water.
That bucket down and full of tears am I,
Drinking my griefs whilst you mount up on high.

(4.1.184–89)

Standing in the middle of Westminster Hall, Richard employs a metaphor that draws upon the daily lives of those he addresses; the Norden map (Figure 3) clearly shows 'a deep well' just outside of the building, which those assembled to see him uncrowned would have passed on their way inside. That Shakespeare uses such a quotidian image to convey the mystery of kingship is typical of his dramatic technique, as we saw in Chapter 1, where he employed the same understated image to portray the horrific violence done to Lavinia. Throughout this study, we will witness the playwright rendering the most exceptional of states more vividly by firmly placing them within the common experiences of his first London audiences. The contrast between what is being described here and the register in which Richard speaks (the enormity of the dethroning of a king reduced to the scope of what can be held in 'two buckets', one of them empty) is in turn a measure of the contrasting fates of the two kings portrayed in this scene. Comparing himself to the lowlier of the two buckets, 'full of tears' and 'Drinking my griefs', Richard makes clear that Bolingbroke's ascent, 'dancing in the air' and 'up on high', can only be achieved at his own personal cost. As such, in keeping with the delicate negotiation of the transfer of power throughout the scene in Westminster Hall, Richard continues to assert his own importance while seeming to resign himself to obscurity. If he maintains the authority to make a king – if Bolingbroke's ascent is dependent upon his acquiescence – then in some senses Richard might yet be thought the more powerful man here, Shakespeare suggests fleetingly.

Forker picks up on this same point, noting that the two men are shown in a 'double light' throughout this scene and its precursor at Flint Castle. Both Richard and Bolingbroke 'are to some extent victims of self-delusion', he writes in his Arden introduction. 'Richard remains unable or unwilling to confront the flaws of character and policy that have brought him to his unhappy pass,' while 'Bolingbroke seems equally unable to acknowledge (perhaps even to himself) the thirst for sovereignty that underlies his self-restraint and calculated realism' (32–33). By complicating the characters and relative moral values of his two anti-heroes in this way, Shakespeare prevents his audience from straightforwardly shifting their sympathy from one king to the next. In the same way, characters in the play are not permitted to simply change their political affiliations (we have already discussed the complex case of the Duke of York, for instance). Instead he holds his characters, and his audience's sympathies, within a carefully woven net of differing allegiances, constantly shifting in response to the ever-changing political circumstances. If *Richard II* was performed at Westminster on that night in 1595, then its events would in this respect have felt all too familiar to the MPs and royal councillors in the audience.

Lest the interdependency of the twin fates of Richard and Bolingbroke go unnoticed by his audience, Shakespeare uses a striking flashback scene to reiterate the connection between them, in which the Duke of York tells his wife about 'our two cousins' coming into London' some weeks previously (5.2.3). Conflating the events of what are two separate days in Holinshed into a single re-entry into the city, Shakespeare again emphasizes the complex connections between the destinies of Richard and Bolingbroke. The Duke notes that 'rude misgoverned hands from windows' tops | Threw dust and rubbish on King Richard's head' (5.2.5–6); his account makes clear that the former monarch is subjected to the most undignified treatment at the hands of Londoners while Bolingbroke is welcomed with adulation:

> Mounted upon a hot and fiery steed,
> Which his aspiring rider seemed to know,
> With slow but stately pace kept on his course,
> Whilst all tongues cried, 'God save thee, Bolingbroke!'.
> You would have thought the very windows spake,
> So many greedy looks of young and old
> Through casements darted their desiring eyes
> Upon his visage, and that all the walls
> With painted imagery had said at once,
> 'Jesu preserve thee! Welcome, Bolingbroke!'

(5.2.8–17)

Once again, the descent of Richard is contrasted with Bolingbroke's ascent. In a reversal of the coronation procession in which new monarchs parade through London from the Tower to Westminster, where they will be crowned, Shakespeare has Richard dragged through the city's streets in the opposite direction, on his way to prison (we might recall here similar treatment of early modern religious martyrs, as witnessed in Chapter 1). By drawing attention to the citizens pelting their former king with 'dust and rubbish' from above, Shakespeare positions him in the most abject and lowly state while Bolingbroke's elevation is highlighted, 'Mounted' up on an impressive horse. The streets and buildings of London itself are anthropomorphized here, the 'very windows', 'casements' and 'walls' seeming to speak and even see. The city that once celebrated Richard's own coronation now greets his usurpation with similar jubilance, London proving as fickle to the deposed King as his noble supporters proved to him.

Richard uncrowned: Westminster hall and the king's two bodies

In the final section of this chapter we will address the deposition of Richard in more detail, exploring the ways in which Shakespeare's play reverses the conventions of early modern coronations in the ceremonial uncrowning of the former king that begins with this inversion of the traditional procession through the streets of London. Against his will, Richard is brought to Westminster hall: 'Alack, why am I sent for to a king,' he asks, 'Before I have shook off the regal thoughts | Wherewith I reigned?' (4.1.163–65). In the dramatic climax of *Richard II* he will be formally called upon to give up the crown in favour of Bolingbroke, who is about to become King Henry IV. Known as the 'deposition scene', the staging of this moment was considered so controversial in Shakespeare's lifetime that it was left out of the first printed quarto text of the play. One of the other most notable aspects of the scene is its highly ritualistic nature. Shakespeare portrays Bolingbroke as wanting to be sure everything is done properly 'So we shall proceed | Without suspicion' (4.1.147–48). Richard's position is already hopeless, and it would be perfectly possible for Bolingbroke simply to seize the crown by this point in the play as most of the nobility of the country supports him, not Richard. But it matters to Bolingbroke that Richard be made to come to Westminster hall and to hand the crown over to him 'in common view', a pun on the role of the House of Commons, which in English political life sanctions the decisions of the monarch (4.1.146). He wants his actions to be ratified before this audience, in this particular place.

The location for the deposition scene is also important because it was Richard II himself who had funded the building of Westminster hall (in the form in which it survives today), part of the old palace that the King used as his primary London residence. 'This great hall was begun to be repaired in the year 1397 by Richard II,' notes Stow, 'who caused the walls, windows, and roof to be taken down, and new made, with a stately porch, and diverse lodgings of a marvelous work, and with great costs' (388). This ominous allusion to the financial incontinence that will bring the 'prodigal prince' Richard II such trouble in Shakespeare's play is further amplified in Stow's accounts of the lavish feasts and entertainments put on in the hall under his reign. The chronicler describes one particularly extravagant Christmas celebration in 1398 that the King attended in a specially made gold and pearl gown (worth the astronomical sum of three thousand pounds) and 'whereunto resorted such a number of people, that there was every day spent twenty-eight or twenty-six oxen and three hundred sheep, besides fowl without number' (388).

The hall lies just metres away from Westminster Abbey, in which English monarchs are traditionally crowned, and many critics have pointed out the way that Richard's speech on (reluctantly) giving up the crown is a reversal of the processes a monarch undergoes at his investiture:

Now mark me how I will undo myself:
I give this heavy weight from off my head,

>   [*Gives crown to Bolingbroke.*]

And this unwieldy sceptre from my hand,

[*Takes up sceptre and gives it to Bolingbroke.*]

The pride of kingly sway from out my heart;
With mine own tears I wash away my balm,
With mine own hands I give away my crown,
With mine own tongue deny my sacred state,
With mine own breath release all duteous oaths.
All pomp and majesty I do forswear;
My manors, rents, revenues I forgo;
My acts, decrees, and statutes I deny.
God pardon all oaths that are broke to me;
God keep all vows unbroke are made to thee.
Make me, that nothing have, with nothing grieved,
And thou with all pleased, that hast all achieved.
Long mayst thou live in Richard's seat to sit,
And soon lie Richard in an earthy pit!
'God save King Henry', unkinged Richard says,
'And send him many years of sunshine days!'

(4.1.203–221)

The last six lines of Richard's speech play with the exchange of power between him and Bolingbroke, contrasting their differing fates in another illustration of the kind of structural chiasmus employed repeatedly throughout the play. Shakespeare uses rhyme here to highlight this idea, offering a series of paired lines – rhyming couplets – that describe in turn what will happen to each of them ('me' – 'thee'; 'grieved' – 'achieved'; 'sit' – 'pit' and 'says' – 'days'). The verse here is perfectly balanced, its very form charting Richard's fall and Bolingbroke's rise. From the opening line – 'mark me how I will undo myself' – the main body of this speech is concerned with the question of how far Richard himself is defined by his kingship. Does he have an identity outside of that of being king? What does it mean to be 'unkinged Richard', no longer Richard II? In what we have already described as a reversal, or even parody, of the coronation process, Richard hands back the sceptre and the crown, perhaps the single most potent symbol of kingship in the play. Richard's language here also replicates some of the ceremonial formality of the Whitehall coronation ceremony in the formulaic series of lines beginning 'With mine own . . .' (ll.207–210). He here employs another rhetorical device, anaphora, in which each line begins in exactly the same way, and has exactly the same grammatical structure. This form of repetition recreates – and undoes – the ceremony that invested him with royal power, the coronation that had confirmed him at the heart of England's political networks as they converge upon the palace of Westminster.

In the final part of this chapter we wish to take up a key political idea from Shakespeare's England that is referred to in Richard's speech. In a particularly important phrase the deposed monarch alludes to the 'sacred state' of kingship. Richard (and indeed Shakespeare) lived in an age when the English believed their monarch to rule by divine right, tracing a direct connection between the reign of God in heaven and that of the king or queen in England (Queen Elizabeth II is still de facto head of the Church of England in this way). Perhaps the single most important part of the coronation ceremony is the moment at which the new monarch is anointed with holy water (what Richard refers to in his speech as 'balm'), symbolizing the transference of divine power into the new king or queen. It is this belief in the 'sacred state' of the monarch, as Richard calls it, which makes the idea of deposing a crowned king so traumatic in this play.

We should also note though that Richard does not seem to believe he will die instantly upon losing his God-given power to rule. Rather he will still be left 'With mine own tongue', with a voice that he can use to 'deny my sacred state'. In other words, his physical life may continue after his kingly life is extinguished. This is an allusion to an important aspect of how kingship was understood in the medieval and early modern periods, an idea that has come to be known as the concept of the King's Two Bodies. According to this theory of monarchy, kings and queens have both their ordinary, physical body, but also another spiritual, royal, divine body. We might think of this latter entity in the terms of the 'body politic', of whom the monarch is figured as the head, and all the people who make up a nation the rest of the body. It is the idea of this sacred function of the monarch as head of the body politic that allows the famous proclamation, 'The King is dead! Long live the King!' How, we might ask, can the king be both dead and alive at once? The answer lies in the fact that while the previous king's physical, earthly body has died (or been forcibly separated from the crown, in the case of Richard II), the spiritual body of kingship has already passed over into the new ruler, in medieval and early modern understanding. This divine body, or body politic, cannot die. The theory of the King's Two Bodies was articulated in detail by Edmund Plowden in his legal reports published in French in London in 1571. The issue had come into focus upon the succession of Edward VI, then still a minor (he was only ten when Henry VIII died in 1547). When certain of his decisions were challenged on the grounds of his age, lawyers had made the case that it did not matter that the King's natural body was underage, his political body was nevertheless fit to rule.

The historian Ernst Kantorowicz wrote an influential account of this theory, publishing his still highly regarded *The King's Two Bodies: A Study in Mediaeval Political Theology* in 1957. Kantorowicz pays particular attention to the ceremonial function of the coronation in Westminster as the moment at which a successor's body became formally invested with the power of the body politic. Elizabeth I's coronation on 15 January 1559 was a particularly grand affair, beginning the previous day with a procession of the new queen through the streets of London. The procession stopped at five different key locations in the city en-route in order to enjoy a series of pageants put on for the royals (these were usually highly symbolic displays celebrating the powers of monarchy). In

Shakespeare's lifetime – as in the fourteenth century when the historical Richard II reigned – it was considered particularly important that the monarch be made visible to the people, that the population at large could see for themselves the physical manifestation of the divine right to rule (body politic) in the actual person (body natural) of the king or queen.

Not coincidentally, this physical body would be dressed extremely elaborately, to reflect the dignity of this spiritual role. Queen Elizabeth I famously loved clothes; Richard is likewise accused of being vain about his appearance in Shakespeare's play, as when he asks for a mirror in the deposition scene (a moment not in any of Shakespeare's sources). This possible parallel was played upon by a recent RSC production of *Richard II*, in which Jonathan Slinger played the title role in a costume designed to resemble Elizabeth's iconic appearance. The extent to which Richard considers his identity to be predicated on how he looks is also suggested by the old Duke of York's rather bitter comment to the dying John of Gaunt that the King is unwilling to listen to advice, unless it is about the latest trends, heeding only 'Report of fashions in proud Italy, | Whose manners still our tardy-apish nation | Limps after in base imitation' (2.1.21–23). Before television, newspapers or the internet, displaying the royal personage to the people meant embarking on a kind of extended procession known as a progress; those regularly undertaken by Elizabeth I each summer usually lasted around 10 weeks (although they never got very far, impeded by the logistical difficulties of moving with her huge retinue). Historian Patrick Collinson has emphasized the way this impressed upon citizens their sense of connectedness to the monarch, of being part of the network that makes up the body politic, observing in his entry for the Queen in the *Oxford Dictionary of National Biography* that 'Elizabeth in procession may well have been a familiar sight in and around London, as she moved from one palace to another, by road or river, and displayed herself ceremonially when she returned to Whitehall to keep Christmas.' It is this phenomenon of showing the

FIGURE 4 *Jonathan Slinger as Richard II, RSC Histories Cycle (2008) (Ellie Kurttz © Royal Shakespeare Company)*

monarch to the people that Shakespeare plays upon at the end of *Richard II*. In a parody of the type of progress undertaken by Elizabeth I described by Collinson here, the new King Henry IV parades the former Richard II, now his prisoner, through the streets of London to the Tower (although Bolingbroke then changes his mind at the last minute, deciding the symbolism of imprisoning his predecessor there is unwise, and therefore send him instead to Pomfret Castle in Yorkshire, where he will later be assassinated). In another juxtaposition of the downfall of Richard with the rise of Bolingbroke, this mockery of a coronation procession in reverse takes place just after plans for the crowning of the new king have commenced; 'On Wednesday next we solemnly set down | Our coronation,' says the future Henry IV (4.1.319–20). As one monarch comes to the end of his reign, another takes his place, and so the cycle that persists throughout Shakespeare's history plays repeats itself again. Some years later the playwright would himself live to witness the elaborate coronation procession of James I through the city of London, enjoying the patronage of the new monarch as his company became the King's Men. Upon the death of Elizabeth I in 1603, Shakespeare would hear cries through the streets: 'The Queen is dead. Long live the King!'

3

Class in Shakespeare's London:

Romeo and Juliet (1595–6) and The Strand

Introduction

Two households, both alike in dignity,
In fair Verona, where we lay our scene,
From ancient grudge break to new mutiny,
Where civil blood makes civil hands unclean.
From forth the fatal loins of these two foes
A pair of star-crossed lovers take their life...

(1.0.1–6)

One of the few surviving prologues to a Shakespeare play, the opening lines of *Romeo and Juliet* offer the play's iconic image of 'star-crossed lovers'. However, before introducing the plight of his tragic couple, Shakespeare's prologue presents a detailed image of the world in which his lovers will exist. They are first introduced as members of 'Two households' who we are told are of equal 'dignity' or status. The 'ancient grudge' between the Montague and Capulet families is well known to audiences of the play as a cause of Romeo and Juliet's tragic end. Less attention is given to the feud as it is described in the prologue's fourth line: 'Where civil blood makes civil hands unclean.' The word 'civil' in this instance is synonymous with 'citizen', which in Shakespeare's time was less a marker of national identity than of having attained a level of respectable, professional status directly linked to obtaining a particular degree of legitimacy within a trade. By constructing a world of family, civic and vocational identities, the first four lines of the prologue situate Romeo, Juliet and their play within these three types of institution, which lay at the centre of early modern urban society.

When we think of 'class' we usually talk about economic distinctions such as rich versus poor. However, the social culture of early modern London is far more diverse than this simple dichotomy allows. As the capital of government and trade, Shakespeare's London was a melting pot of people from every conceivable walk of life, from the poorest vagrant, to tradesmen, gentry and even the Queen herself. Act one, scene one of *Romeo and Juliet* depicts a world similarly inhabited by people from a variety of backgrounds and social groups. What begins as a private quarrel between servants of rival masters soon includes gentlemen, citizens of Verona and finally a prince. In this opening confrontation (examined in detail later in this chapter), battle lines are quickly drawn and the audience realizes that Verona is a place where knowing who everyone is goes beyond simple familiarity and the determining of friend or foe is necessary for survival.

Shakespeare and his contemporaries also lived and worked in a system intently focused on regulating behaviour through defined parameters of identity, which governed activities, friends, accommodation and even clothing. The idea that a person could be judged by their apparel, job, family or neighbourhood is not unfamiliar to modern society, however in Shakespeare's time many of these rules were made by the government through either the crown or parliament. There were statutes of apparel or 'sumptuary laws' that required people to wear clothing and accessories whose cost coincided with their status. For example, only the monarch, members of their immediate family and those bearing the titles of duke, marquis or earl could wear the colour purple, cloth of gold, or furs made of sable. Other statutes prohibited people below a certain status from carrying swords, daggers or rapiers. There were even rules controlling the movements of certain people. Groups who contested authority such as the recusants (individuals who refused to attend Church of England services, whom we encountered in Chapter 1) were prohibited from travelling further than five miles from their homes without a license by an act in 1593 (Dillon, 104–5). Unemployed, so-called 'masterless men' and vagrants found outside their hometown or parish could be arrested and sent back to their designated place of residence to be punished.

In addition to such government regulations, the social, civic and professional institutions mentioned in the prologue also operated under clear rules (official or implied) that similarly shaped the lives of early modern Londoners. For instance, a first-born son could expect to inherit the largest portion of his family property be it a tailor's shop, an earldom, or even a kingdom. Chapter 2 and our Epilogue discuss Shakespeare's interest in royal succession and inheritance in *Richard II* and *Henry VIII*, but these issues were equally important to the working classes. Achieving status as a citizen or freeman, a recognized member of one of the professional organizations or 'guilds', entitled one's business to protection from outsider competition and gave the businessman a say in the development and management of the larger market. A 'citizen' of London not only participated in the cultural and social life of the city, but also more formally contributed to its management, including looking after its poor. These kinds of restrictions and preordained pathways were influential in determining the trajectories and subsequent identities of early modern residents of London as individuals and as members of particular groups. In the world of *Romeo and Juliet*, identity is likewise of vital importance. For the Montagues and Capulets generally, it dictates both one's family and choice of friends. Shakespeare simply but effectively illustrates this in the way characters regularly identify each other first and foremost by their family affiliation: 'By my head, here comes the Capulets' (3.1.34). These familial connections in turn determine where characters could and could not safely travel (Verona's streets, a Capulet feast, an enemy's garden, for example). In addition, the power to identify by naming and renaming, as when Juliet asks Romeo to resist family and social convention and 'refuse thy name' (2.2.34), is integral to a character's truly knowing themselves and their place in the world. In this chapter, we will therefore look beyond 'class' as an economic distinction and instead think about the various groupings of early modern society as a system defined by boundaries of belonging. We will look at how difference and affiliation are expressed through spaces and language in the play. We will also consider how particular socio-economic groups are portrayed in *Romeo and Juliet* and ask what relation this may have to the social complexities Shakespeare saw in the city around him. To begin, we explore the intermingling of classes in one of the epicentres of social and economic activity in Shakespeare's city: its busy streets. In early modern London, there was perhaps no more dynamic meeting place for all manner of men (and women) than the Strand, our focus here. A close reading of the portrayal of class in the well-known 'Queen Mab' speech will then reveal what the speech might tell us about inter-class relations in Shakespeare's London. We will conclude by considering the role of names and naming in *Romeo and Juliet*, and in the ever-expanding city in which Shakespeare lived and wrote.

In Shakespeare's time as now, 'the Strand' referred to the major street running along the north bank of the River Thames from the edge of the Palace of Whitehall to the walls of the City itself. Shakespeare would have known the boundaries of the Strand by two landmarks. At the Westminster end (an area we explored in Chapter 2) was Charing Cross, at the centre of which stood one of the 'Eleanor Crosses' – stone monuments marking the sites where the body of Eleanor of Castile, wife and consort to King Edward I, paused during its funeral procession. The Strand continued parallel to the Thames until it met the Temple Bar, one of the gatehouses where people passed through the City walls. Today, the Strand still runs alongside the Thames but many of the landmarks have changed: the Eleanor Cross has been removed (a replica now stands in the entry way of Charing Cross station) and replaced by a busy traffic roundabout and the iconic monument of Lord Nelson guarded by four massive lions in Trafalgar Square, while the Temple Bar has been substituted for one of the much smaller dragon statues that now mark the modern entrances to the City. However, the Strand is still a bustling street of wide pavements filled with tourists, traders, students and businessmen passing back and forth between the government buildings of modern Whitehall and the City of London.

A convenient conduit between crown, government and City, it is not surprising to discover that then, as now, the Strand was central to the everyday comings and goings of early modern Londoners. As a major thoroughfare, the street was home to numerous inns and taverns that serviced both the working and service classes who lived and worked in the area, as well as travellers passing through to the metropolis. As a member of the company of players who would become the King's Men from the succession of James I in 1603, Shakespeare may have walked the Strand on his way to give command performances to the royal court at Whitehall, perhaps even stopping at one of the many inns for a quick drink and taking the chance to scribble down ideas for his next play.

Today, visitors to the Strand find a homogenous corridor of tall marble buildings filled with all manner of shops, restaurants, pubs, offices and theatres. Walking from the palace of Whitehall to the City, Shakespeare would have seen a street that was more conspicuously divided. On the north side of the thoroughfare were many businesses, particularly those which serviced the needs of the city's elite residents including tailors, goldsmiths and silversmiths (who also made swords), plying their trades and selling their wares out of shops, windows (much like the one Shakespeare's father sold gloves from back in Stratford), or small tables on the edge of the road (Boulton (2000), 188, 202, 205). As was frequently the custom, many of these tradesmen lived with their families and apprentices in rooms above and behind their shops, and the sounds of family life would have added to the general hum and noise of business and travel in the street. The south, or Thames side of the street was quite a different matter. At the time Shakespeare was living and working in London, this side of the Strand was an address much sought after by prominent and fashionable members of Elizabeth I's court for its convenient proximity to the palace. From the middle of the sixteenth century the Thames side of the Strand featured an ever-growing number of large, riverside 'town houses' bearing some of the most illustrious names of the time: York, Salisbury, Arundel, Northampton and Somerset (Merritt, 142). (In Chapter 2 we noted another prominent residence on the Strand, the Savoy Palace). After the Reformation, many of these estates housed some of Elizabeth I's favourites. Robert Dudley the Earl of Leicester and Sir Walter Raleigh both lived on the Thames side of the Strand in the later part of the sixteenth century (Merritt, 143–4). With the exception of the original Somerset House, the remains of which are preserved under the foundations of the one which stands today, most of these houses have since disappeared, the only proof of their existence chronicled in the names of streets running off the modern Strand. In their time, these grand houses stood as testament to the wealth and status of the elite class of gentry and nobles who lived in them. As we will discuss shortly, Shakespeare creates a home of comparable opulence for the Capulets that similarly signals their social status.

Between these two distinct areas lay the Strand itself. Here the tailor (and his household) and the Earl (and his household), as well as stablemen, servants, lawyers and odd-job men spilled out of their professional and familial spaces on either side and into the street where different ranks, families, ages, professions, genders and nationalities mixed freely. The situation was not always harmonious: records document both sides complaining about the lifestyles of their very diverse neighbours. One such incident is recorded in a letter sent to Elizabeth I's secretary, Sir Robert Cecil, whose correspondent laments that a certain group of carpenters and labourers 'do annoy the neighbours very dangerously and in fashion too unreverent to be reported to you' (Merritt, 196, n.77). In 1605 a tailor living on the north side of the Strand complained 'that his view of the Thames would be impeded' by Sir Walter Cope's new building on the south side, to which Cope responded rather snobbishly that the tailor's view would be 'of sufficient prospect for a man of his quality' (Merritt, 195). Visitors to the Strand today have to work as hard as the tailor to see the Thames from the street because the view is now almost completely obscured by buildings. The discomfort of negotiating and confronting boundaries of social space amongst people with different agendas and backgrounds was a part of metropolitan living that would be as familiar to Shakespeare and his contemporaries as to city-dwellers today. The streets and public spaces of *Romeo and Juliet* thus play a central role because they both mirror and perpetuate the social conflict at the heart of the play. As we will see, when the Montagues and Capulets enter these unrestricted areas they too are forced to confront different classes and social groups, resulting in the play's well-known scenes of street violence and the deaths of Mercutio and Tybalt.

Walls, gardens and plate: Objects and spaces of class

John Norden's 1593 'bird's-eye' view of Westminster from his book *Speculum Britanniae* (Figure 3) offers a contemporary view of the Strand ('The Strond') at this time. On the north side is a line of the small, multi-storey buildings that accommodated the shops and homes of tradesmen. The Thames side shows a series of large estates each containing a substantial house or series of smaller buildings and a sizeable garden. Many of these gardens overlook the river, offering an easy route to the palace and the monarch's court for business, pleasure, or even – if need be – escape. From the street, these properties created an uninterrupted barrier of gated walls and structures that obstructed a passer-by's view of the river and the homes inside, giving privacy to its residents. In this light, the south side of the Strand can be seen as an exclusive space reserved for the elite who reside there. We can go a step further and say that the gates and walls of these residences actually reinforce the status of anyone living in them by portraying them as separate from and inaccessible to, the general population. A play whose action is similarly premised on a division of households, *Romeo and Juliet* also contains spaces where access is restricted to a privileged few. However, unlike the remote and elite houses on the Strand from which most early modern Londoners were prohibited, Shakespeare's play brings us into these exclusive spaces, offering us a taste of early modern luxury, and a sense of how such spaces developed and reinforced ideas of class and status.

The most meticulously constructed private space in *Romeo and Juliet* is the Capulet home. Act one, scene five provides a glimpse into life in the Capulet household during the preparations for a large feast. The details surrounding this event in the play give us insights into life inside these elite homes, as well as the economic status of the Capulets. To begin with, the very fact that their home contains a 'great chamber' (1.5.13) in which to hold such an event already suggests that the Capulet dwelling has more in common with the grand townhouses on the Thames side of the Strand than the more modest, functional homes on the north side. Additional indicators of the Capulets' status are the people and items displayed in its interior. The scene begins with a group of household servants making last minute preparations:

HEAD SERVINGMAN	Where's Potpan, that he helps not to take away? He shift a trencher, he scrape a trencher!
	[. . .]
HEAD SERVINGMAN	Away with the join-stools, remove the court-cupboard, look to the plate. Good thou, save me a piece of marchpane and, as thou loves me, let the porter let in Susan Grindstone, and Nell, Antony and Potpan.
2 SERVINGMAN	Ay, boy, ready.
HEAD SERVINGMAN	You are looked for, and called for, asked for, and sought for, in the great chamber.
3 SERVINGMAN	We cannot be here and there too. Cheerly, boys, be brisk awhile, and the longer liver take all.

(1.5.1–2, 6–15)

This brief scene is remarkable first for how many servants are involved. In addition to the four servingmen who speak in the scene, four further servants are mentioned working behind the scenes: Susan Grindstone, Nell, Antony and the lazy Potpan. These are not the only members of staff working in the Capulet household, however; the play begins with the opening dialogue of Samson and Gregory, two more Capulet servants and there is also of course Juliet's nurse who, in act two, scene four, is attended by Peter, another servant. In short, the Capulets have a house maintained by at least a dozen servants (and these are just the ones with names and speaking parts in the play). In the same way the Chorus in *Henry V*, examined in our introduction, urges us to 'Work, work your thoughts' to turn a handful of actors into an entire army so we can 'see a siege' (3.0.25), scenes like this domestic hustle and bustle before the Capulet feast conjure the impression that the family is attended by a large household staff.

This scene also draws attention to how the Capulet house is furnished. The head servingman's command for the servants to move the 'join-stools', 'court-cupboard' and 'plate' both contributes to the stage business of preparing for the upcoming party and simultaneously offers an inventory of specific items in the Capulet home. While the quality of these items is not self-evident to modern audiences, René Weis notes in his Arden edition of the play that such furnishings would be recognized as luxurious by early modern standards (166 n.6). The 'join' or 'joint stool' was so called because it was made by a professional joiner and not cobbled together by an odd-job man. The use of the name not only signifies its superior quality but also indicates that the Capulets could afford well-crafted furniture. The 'court-cupboard' can be seen in a similar light. A place to display rather than simply store the Capulets' 'plate', the cupboard suggests not only that they had room for such non-essential furniture but also that their tableware was worth showing off to visitors. In fact, in the second half of the sixteenth-century plates were replacing the traditional wooden trenchers from which people previously ate their food (Weis, 166 n. 7). Possessing and exhibiting their plates in this way helps establish an image of the Capulets as a well-off family who could afford to fill their house with the newest luxury items. Depending on the production of Shakespeare's play, the parade of servants and goods in this scene may only be a prelude to the display of wealth in the party that follows. However, the scene alone is enough to suggest that the Capulets were well off. More than that, this scene gives modern audiences a sense of what kinds of items early modern Londoners might expect to see in a wealthy household like the Capulets' home or a residence on the Thames side of the Strand.

The Capulet feast gives us a further glimpse of how interior furnishings and spaces in *Romeo and Juliet* might suggest wealth. Act two, scene two, best known as the 'balcony scene' (despite Shakespeare himself making no mention of such a space), shows how the exteriors of the Capulet home can reinforce ideas of class and boundaries. Romeo's allusions to Juliet as the 'sun' and 'being o'er my head' (2.2.3, 27) give the impression that in this scene he encounters Juliet in an 'aloft' (2.2.9.1) space. A likely source for Shakespeare's play, Arthur Brooke's poem *The Tragical History of Romeus and Juliet* (1562), suggests that Romeo discovers Juliet at 'her leaning place' and 'window' (Bullough in Brooke (1964) 297–8, ll.453, 468), spaces perhaps similar to the large windows depicted on many of the Thames-side Strand houses on Norden's map. When describing his first glimpse of Juliet in this scene, Romeo similarly mentions a window in his well-known line 'what light through yonder window breaks' (2.2.2), aligning Shakespeare's image with the grand houses known to Londoners at the time. Be it from window or balcony, Juliet has a view of a private green space:

> The orchard walls are high and hard to climb,
> And the place death, considering who thou art,
> If any of my kinsmen find thee here.

> (2.2.63–5)

Juliet's description reveals that Capulet has more than a modest patch for a few flowers and vegetables: he has room for fruit trees and his gardens represent the kind of large open space Norden indicates was attached to several of the Strand's great houses. Our emerging portrait of the Capulet residence as a large, finely furnished home with multiple floors and a large private garden confirms one family servant's description of his master as 'the great rich Capulet' (1.2.80). The depiction of the Capulet home's exterior goes beyond identifying a wealthy family, however. From her elevated position, Juliet is placed physically out of Romeo's reach in a home built by, and representative of, her family and their status. The Capulet mansion thus acts as an extension of the play's central feud, by reinforcing the separation of the lovers along the familial boundary lines that divide them.

Another feature that the Capulet and Thames-side Strand houses share are boundary walls. We know from Juliet's own description that the orchard walls are not only high but also 'hard to climb' and none-too-subtly devised to forcibly keep out those who are not freely admitted to the Capulet estate. One might commonly see these kinds of high walls on the exterior or street-side of an affluent early modern London property, as a way to deter unwanted outsiders. However, Norden's map shows that the boundary walls of the houses on the Thames side of the Strand also serve to establish property lines between neighbours. In short, they are as much about distinguishing the land of one wealthy landholder from another as keeping the lower classes out, reflecting rivalries amongst households 'alike in dignity' that are reminiscent of the feuding Montagues and Capulets. As a Montague, Romeo is exactly the kind of outsider the Capulets' walls are built to exclude. His status is bluntly confirmed by the Chorus' remark that 'Being held a foe, he may not have access' (2.0.9). Literally from the wrong side of the wall, Romeo cannot enter via a traditional entrance and though he claims it is by 'love's light wings' that he o'erperch' the wall (2.2.66), there is little doubt that some awkward climbing was involved. The dividing wall creates an easy visual figuration of the separation of the two lovers founded in their family ties. However, we cannot ignore the fact that Romeo eventually does manage to overcome the exterior and interior boundaries of the Capulet estate – first publicly at the Capulet feast, then in the private garden and eventually in the most exclusive interior space of Juliet's bedroom. In an environment where lines of loyalty are strictly drawn, the play subtly points out that physical walls may be 'hard' to climb but are not impossible to overcome. The marriage of Romeo and Juliet (2.6) similarly challenges the familial boundaries set up by Montague and Capulet, and the reconciliation of the two families after the lovers' deaths will suggest their complete dissolution. Thus Shakespeare shows how these seemingly immovable familial and social boundaries are ultimately as surmountable as the orchard walls.

It is also worth noting that while Shakespeare is careful to place Juliet in a home that identifies her with her wealthy Capulet family, Romeo – and indeed the entire Montague family – are afforded very little space in the play. Romeo is never shown at 'home', instead he loiters in the street or in a garden. Perhaps as a result, he is repeatedly seen 'breaking into' spaces that are not his, such as the Capulet feast, Juliet's bedroom and even the Capulet family tomb. In particular, Romeo's infiltration of the Capulet feast in a masked disguise in act one, scene four is suggestive of another early modern form of theatre. Masques, a dramatic form we will encounter in several chapters in this book, and which Shakespeare draws upon elsewhere in his writing, consisted of highly choreographed and musical performances that drew on classical sources and featured gods, goddess, witches and other fantastical characters rendered through the use of elaborate and expensive costumes. These performances were usually staged at the royal court but also in the homes of aristocrats. By adopting the anonymity of costumed performance and festively parading through the streets with instruments and torches (1.4), Romeo and his friends are similarly able to cross the boundaries of public and private space to enter the Capulet home. The anonymity of wearing a mask provides an alternative identity that enables Romeo to travel freely between the public and private spaces of street and estate, and will ultimately lead to his first encounter with Juliet.

The opposite of the highly exclusive Capulet home, the streets of Verona are a space where Montague and Capulet alike are entitled to claim their place. The two scenes of major confrontation between the families (1.1 and 3.1) are not given specific locations in the play, yet both begin with characters conversing en-route somewhere. As Benvolio explains, the street is known as a place for uncomfortable, volatile encounters:

I pray thee, good Mercutio, let's retire;
The day is hot, the Capels are abroad,

An if we meet we shall not scape a brawl,
For now, these hot days, is the mad blood stirring.

(3.1.1–4)

A space where all are free to meet, the streets of Verona are a pressure-cooker in which individuals actively seek out foe as well as friend. While the street is a significant site of conflict in the play, as a space outside of the designated areas marked out by the Capulet (and the undisclosed Montague) estates, the unrestricted nature of such thoroughfares also allows members of the two groups to meet for more productive reasons. In act two, scene four the Nurse is able to speak with Romeo about the arrangements for his marriage to Juliet in a public space populated by Montagues and Capulets (although they do so amidst the mockery of Mercutio and his friends). In comparison to the exclusive, restrictive homes of Verona, the streets in this play might remind us of the forests in *As You Like It* or *A Midsummer Night's Dream*, where individuals hemmed in by their structured societies escape to the forest where they may mingle with whoever they choose, regardless of rank or family obligation. Likewise, the streets in *Romeo and Juliet* offer another opportunity for the supposedly rigid boundaries of class and family to be transgressed.

Master, servant and Queen (Mab)

We have seen how different physical spaces can define social groups and status in *Romeo and Juliet* and on the early modern Strand. Now we will look at Shakespeare's portrayal of two of these groups, masters and servants, in the play. While history regularly records the events and lifestyle of the early modern gentry, the day-to-day existence of London's servants is less easy to trace. However, these residents are no less important to our understanding of the cultural make-up of Shakespeare's London and the diverse neighbourhood of the Strand. In addition to the population of domestic servants who maintained the homes and lifestyles of the upper classes there were additional 'serving classes' who contributed labour and support to various industries. One of the most prominent groups within this sector of the workforce was that of London's apprentices. In the 1590s roughly 10 per cent of London's population were indentured to masters of various trades (MacGregor, 108). Apprentices typically began their service around the age of fourteen and would train with their masters for approximately seven to nine years. Living and working in the city, apprentices were an integral part of the highly regulated trade labour force as well as frequent partakers in London entertainments that included theatres like the Globe, making apprentices a prominent presence in the day-to-day culture of the city. At the time Shakespeare was writing *Romeo and Juliet,* apprentices were also a source of anxiety in London. In June of 1595 a crowd of apprentices staged animated protests in Southwark and at the Tower against the prices of fish and butter. One episode culminated at the grand house known as Crobsy Place in Bishopsgate, where a hangman's scaffold was constructed before the front door of its current resident: John Spencer, the Mayor of London (Sharp, 44–47). The riots resulted in five apprentices being tried and hung for treason. Closer to home for Shakespeare, apprentices also caused trouble in and around playhouses that were, Ian Munro argues, 'stigmatized as a breeding ground for social unrest and riotous behaviour' (43). It would not be surprising then if apprentices and large animated groups of disenfranchised young men that were a familiar sight in Shakespeare's London and its playhouses became in the playwright's imagining the bands of young Montagues and Capulets who disturb Verona's streets in *Romeo and Juliet.*

We should, however, remember that while there are many servants in the Capulet household, Shakespeare does not depict apprentices in these scenes. Servants are identified as 'servingman' or 'man' and appear to carry out household tasks readily associated with domestic or household duties rather than trade work. But most remarkable is the overall character of the servants in this play. Far from discontented masses, the servants going about their various duties in *Romeo and Juliet* do so with a generally upbeat air of household chaos (1.3.101–4, 4.4.13–20, 4.5.100–41). Even when they are fighting, as in the opening skirmish of act one, scene one, where the Capulet servants Samson and Gregory engage two approaching men from the house of Montague, their reasoning has little to do with economic or class grievances but is more focused on the family rivalry and demonstrating their wit:

> SAMSON   A dog of the house of Montague moves me.
> GREGORY To move is to stir, and to be valiant is to stand; therefore, if thou art moved, thou runn'st away.
> SAMSON   A dog of that house shall move me to stand. I will take the wall of any man or maid of Montague's.
>   [. . .]
> GREGORY The quarrel is between our masters and us their men.
> SAMSON   'Tis all one.
>
>   (1.1.7–11, 18–20)

Samson and Gregory are eager for a fight, yet their assertion that the feud 'between our masters and us their men' is 'all one' suggests a unity between serving classes and those they wait upon that runs counter to the friction Shakespeare was seeing in the city around him. This harmonious linking of master and servant continues in scenes such as act four, scene two, where Capulet exchanges pleasant banter with a servingman during preparations for Juliet's wedding to Paris, and in act one, scene two, where Romeo helps an illiterate but good-humoured Capulet servant who cannot read the list of guests he is supposed to invite to his master's feast. Servants in these scenes bring to mind the convention later seen in elaborate stage productions of opera or ballet, where peasants and servants fill the stage to provide congenial background activity and the occasional comic interaction with the typically upper class principle characters. One only has to think of the entertaining antics of Falstaff and his Eastcheap companions at the Boar's Head Tavern in the *Henry IV* plays or the adventures of Bottom and his friends (often referred to by their vocational status as 'Mechanicals' in *A Midsummer Night's Dream*) to see that Shakespeare also uses such characters to infuse his plays with light, comic moments. For this reason, it is difficult to align the generally congenial, loyal servants of the Capulets and Montagues with the disruptive apprentice rioters of the 1590s crisis. However, there is one place in the play where Shakespeare applies this image of the 'congenial servant' to a more serious social purpose.

The 'Queen Mab' speech in act one, scene four is often anticipated in performance as a highlight for the bravado talents of the actor playing Mercutio. The speech is renowned for its rustic, natural images of woodland creatures and the tiny folk fairy Queen Mab, which seem somewhat incongruous in the midst of a play set in an urban landscape. Looking at the Queen Mab speech with an eye towards representations of servants and masters, class and identity, another pattern emerges, however:

O, then I see Queen Mab hath been with you.
She is the fairies' midwife, and she comes
In shape no bigger than an agate stone
On the forefinger of an alderman,
[. . .]
Her chariot is an empty hazelnut
Made by the joiner squirrel or old grub,
Time out o'mind the fairies' coachmakers;
[. . .]
Her wagoner a small grey-coated gnat,
Not half so big as a round little worm . . .

(1.4.53–6, 59–61, 67–8)

On closer inspection, Shakespeare's forest tale of agate stones, hazelnuts and gnats can be read as an idealized portrayal of tradesmen and women. Mab herself is described as a 'midwife', her chariot – an allusion to the coaches that were becoming a frequent sight on London streets – is the work of a squirrel, who Shakespeare is careful to identify as a joiner or wood-worker, and Mab is driven by a gnat who is designated as a 'wagoner' whose 'grey-coated' livery further marks his status as professional tradesman.

This fanciful depiction of the early modern working class has its counter-point in the second half of the Queen Mab speech, where we hear that 'in this state she gallops night by night' (1.4.70). Mab rides:

> O'er lawyers' fingers, who straight dream on fees;
> O'er ladies lips, who straight on kisses dream,
> Which oft the angry Mab with blisters plagues,
> Because their breaths with sweetmeats tainted are.
> Sometime she gallops o'er a courtier's nose,
> And then dreams he of smelling out a suit;
> And sometime comes she with a tithe-pig's tail,
> Tickling a parson's nose as 'a lies asleep;
> Then he dreams of another benefice.
> Sometime she driveth o'er a soldier's neck,
> And then dreams he of cutting foreign throats,
> Of breaches, ambuscados, Spanish blades,
> Of healths five fathom deep [. . .]

(1.4.73–85)

Courtiers, lawyers, gentle ladies, a well-off parson and a soldier who dreams of expensive Spanish blades rather than bows and arrows (the weapon of the working classes) can all be found in this half of Shakespeare's tale of Queen Mab, characters that represent more elite members of society. However, the divisions within this speech go beyond social status. The tradesmen in the first half of the speech, depicted as woodland creatures of

Queen Mab's realm, are presented amiably going about their tasks in an idyllic representation of the working class not unlike that of the servants of the Capulet household. The gentry in the second part of the speech are a different matter. Here we get a series of less savoury portraits: lawyers dreaming of fees and soldiers dreaming of enormous 'healths' (drinks) that are 'five fathoms deep'. Even less enticing are the parson, who contradicts the clergy's vow of poverty by hungrily craving additional wealth, and the lady whose use of 'sweet-meats' suggests bad breath that could be indicative of venereal disease. The use of the term 'sweet-meat' as slang for 'whore' at the time casts further doubt upon the morality of this particular woman (Weis, 163 n. 75–6). The Queen Mab speech thus positions an idealized portrayal of wholesome tradesmen against a parade of despicable, vice-ridden members of the upper class who share an insatiable greed for more of whatever they crave.

Shakespeare's pointed comparison of the rustic tradesmen and the vice-ridden elite may also have had an even more topical relevance in 1590s London. At the time it was generally agreed that the wealthy, ruling classes in government had a social obligation to regulate markets in moments of crisis in order to make sure that the poor were provided for (Archer, 6–7). This responsibility was documented in a series of statutes known as the Book of Orders, which required the government to step in at times of economic distress. In the case of a food shortage such edicts required merchants to sell their reserve stocks of wheat and other necessary goods to the city at low rates for dispersal to the poor. A key complaint of the London apprentices in the butter and fish riots of the 1590s was that after four successive bad harvests merchants continued to sell these items at unfair prices (Sharp, 43–44). Scholars like Ian Archer who study these riots see such acts of disorder as 'part of the process of interaction between rulers and ruled' and as concerted efforts by the public to send a message to the government at Westminster, urging prosperous merchants and suppliers to do their duty and provide for the city's struggling residents (7). In the Queen Mab speech, Shakespeare might be seen as cautiously favouring the position of the working classes, in this case by painting a picture of the quaint, hard-working tradesmen juxtaposed against a gentry more focused on their own pursuit of wealth and pleasure.

The failings of the gentry depicted in the Queen Mab speech also encourage us to take a closer look at the ruling classes throughout *Romeo and Juliet*. For example, while his servants are presented as a generally contented workforce Lord Capulet is perhaps not the most insightful master. His disengagement from the service class in his own home is revealed in act one, scene two when he gives an illiterate servant a list to read. More seriously, the selfish insistence of the two patriarchs on holding to a disagreement that even they cannot remember the cause of is responsible for causing civil instability throughout an entire town, as well as the death of their two only children and the destruction of their family lines. For this reason, it may not be a coincidence that Mercutio, who is friends with Romeo but also manages to be invited to the Capulet party, is given this speech, which challenges the morals and motives of the upper class while favourably depicting the lower. As a character who seems to stand outside the traditional boundaries of Capulet and Montague, servant and master, he is perhaps most qualified to observe and comment on the actions of both. He will, of course, die cursing the two families: 'A plague a' both your houses!' (3.1.108)

In a decade where volatile apprentices and disgruntled poor were causing unease amongst the upper classes, why does Shakespeare include such a contradictory and potentially controversial speech in his play? To glimpse one possibility we can go back to Shakespeare's roots. The combination of woodland imagery and tradesmen found here evoke Shakespeare's childhood home of Stratford-upon-Avon. A small village in Warwickshire nestled near the forest of Arden, Shakespeare grew up amongst scenery more like Queen Mab's realm than the streets of Verona or London. And while Shakespeare was granted the right to bear a family coat of arms and to use the title 'Gentleman' in 1596, the very same year he was probably writing *Romeo and Juliet*, he spent his life the son of a tradesman of the sort who occupied the north side of the Strand. Trying to write amongst the noisy, dirty streets of London while surrounded by the opulence of nobles like those living on the Thames side of the Strand, may have conjured up nostalgic longings in Shakespeare for the quieter existence he had known amongst the tradesmen of country village life.

What's in a name?

As we have seen, Shakespeare's Verona is a highly structured world in which identities are grounded in different social and familial groups. It is not surprising therefore that Romeo and Juliet's declaration of love in act two, scene two's 'balcony scene' explores the use and meaning of names as they embody such allegiances. From the opening scene's pitting of those named Montague against those named Capulet, the play's actions are driven by its characters' names. Within a monarchical system predicated on family succession the giving and, particularly, the taking away of names and titles held great importance amongst early modern members of the elite. In Shakespeare's time, older members of the court might have remembered Thomas Howard the Duke of Norfolk being expelled from the Order of the Garter in January 1572, in a ceremony at which his banner of arms, helm and crest were cast into the ditch of Windsor Castle. In the last chapter, we saw how Shakespeare stages perhaps the most important stripping of a title in English history in his envisioning of the deposition of King Richard II. Shakespeare witnessed firsthand the pursuit of social status in his father's failure to secure the right to a family coat of arms, and with it the respectability that came with being able to use the title 'gentleman'. In 1596 Shakespeare successfully renewed the petition on behalf of his family, including his aged father. It may be the tremendous

value placed upon names and titles both by early modern
society at large and in his own life that led Shakespeare to begin
the balcony scene by playing upon the idea of erasing names.
The opening of their dialogue, spoken by Juliet – 'Deny thy
father and refuse thy name' (2.2.34) – implies that the two
actions are one and the same. Romeo, it seems, cannot reject his
father and keep his name, or vice versa. Romeo's response –
'Call me but love and I'll be new baptized' (2.2.50) – implies
that a solution might be reached by simply taking on a new
title. However, the lines that follow show that it is not so easy
to sever the ties between a person and their name:

> JULIET   What man art thou that thus bescreened in night
>   So stumblest on my counsel?
> ROMEO   By a name
>   I know not how to tell thee who I am.
>
> (2.2.52–4)

Having rejected his family-given first name, Romeo is now at a
loss to answer Juliet's question, 'who are you?' His inability to
respond not only reveals the universal complexity of this
question, it also shows us how, until this moment, Romeo has
seen himself primarily as a part of his family. His sense of
identity is so linked to this role that when the label is removed
he struggles to see what is left. In early modern London
Romeo's predicament may have resonated with the city's
inhabitants who were forced to come to terms with the
overpowering anonymity of a large and ever-growing city.

Juliet, however, offers a potential answer to this dilemma
for both Romeo and Shakespeare's first audiences in a new
'nameless' form of recognition:

> My ears have yet not drunk a hundred words
> Of thy tongue's uttering, yet I know the sound.
> Art thou not Romeo, and a Montague?
>
> (2.2.58–60)

Knowing simply by the sound of his voice that the man in her garden is the same one she spoke with earlier at her family's feast, Juliet takes the first step in the pairs' attempts to build an identity free of their family names and associations. Juliet, who many scholars believe is the more mature of the lovers, becomes the architect of a new self-styled identity. In what Stephen Greenblatt would describe as an act of 'self-fashioning' she begins a process of recreating herself that would have resonated with those (including possibly Shakespeare) who came to the city hoping to create a new identity ((2005), 1). Juliet schools Romeo in their new philosophy when, having found insufficient things on which to swear his faithfulness, she points out that he need only 'swear by thy gracious self' (2.2.113). Instead of names and labels given by external sources such as family and society, Juliet proclaims that they need look no further than themselves to discover their true identities. The power of this internal knowledge is best shown when Juliet describes her own devotion to Romeo:

My bounty is as boundless as the sea,
My love as deep; the more I give to thee,
The more I have, for both are infinite.

(2.2.133–5)

Asserting that committing the internal self is more powerful than a union based on the giving or accepting of names, Romeo and Juliet propose a path that will supersede the boundaries of social and familial affiliation that dominate Verona and early modern London alike.

However, we know that this alternative union will not last. Their dialogue immediately takes a turn that contradicts the couple's philosophy and foreshadows their impending tragedy. Hearing her nurse calling, Juliet cries 'Anon, good Nurse! – Sweet Montague, be true' (2.2.137). After all their efforts to redefine their love and themselves outside the constraints of their feuding families, Juliet's uttering of the very name they have worked to dispel marks the beginning of the end for their new identities (and indeed their love affair). Juliet's use of 'sweet Montague' (2.2.137) is only the first in a number of uses of proper names in the passage that follows. She also calls him 'dear Romeo' (2.2.142) and by the end of the scene Juliet is wishing to make herself hoarse 'With repetition of my "Romeo"' – another name given to him by, and therefore associated with, his family (2.2.163). The re-appearance of both names might suggest an attempt to appropriate the lovers' former identities into their new union. However, the success of this renaming is called into question by the mounting obstacles faced by the couple as the play reaches its crescendo. For instance, in act three, scene one, Romeo cannot be Juliet's husband and Capulet's son-in-law in the public square where the two families repeatedly meet in conflict. Instead, he is quickly drawn into the fight when he kills Tybalt. Likewise, Juliet cannot sustain her new identity as Juliet, wife of Romeo in act three, scene five without contradicting her father's wish that she marry Paris. In both cases, names cannot be separated from their original social context. In short, Romeo and Juliet are still restricted by the boundaries of their family identities; Shakespeare may be happy to let Juliet dream that 'a rose | By any other word would smell as sweet' (2.2.43–44), but the reality he imposes upon her is far more rigid.

While (in this life at least) Romeo and Juliet fail to rise above the restrictions placed upon them by their feuding families it is their attempt to do so that is chronicled and celebrated by Shakespeare's play. In this way, *Romeo and Juliet* dramatizes the difficulties of trying to move within such a world, let alone change or improve one's position in such a system. This is another situation with which Shakespeare would have been familiar. As we saw in our introduction, Shakespeare left his father's glove shop and the rural village of Stratford-upon-Avon for London and in a matter of years reinvented himself as a writer, gentleman and shareholder in London's most eminent playing company, enjoying the attention and patronage of King and court. However, William

Shakespeare, Gentleman, would never entirely shed his rustic beginnings. His lack of university education provoked resentment amongst the higher educated playwrights or 'university wits' who, as we noted in our introduction, saw him as a country upstart with pretensions beyond his proper place. The Queen Mab speech shows how Shakespeare's family background and experiences in London infuse his writing with an empathy for the tradesmen and servants of the working classes, placing them at the heart of the infrastructure of society. While Shakespeare's past informs his work, the playwright's new environs amidst the power, social hierarchies and excesses of the city elite encountered in places like the Strand are also reflected in the streets of Verona. In this way, Shakespeare's portrayal of class in *Romeo and Juliet* is a poignant self-portrait of the writer and, more broadly, a likeness of the city in which he wrote.

4

Law in Shakespeare's London:

The Merchant of Venice (1596–8) and the Inns of Court

Introduction

On 11 May 1612 Shakespeare would climb the stairs from Westminster Hall (a place we visited in Chapter 2) and enter the Court of Requests. He had been summoned there in order to give his testimony in a legal case relating to his time as a lodger in Silver Street, a road in Cripplegate ward noted for its 'divers fair houses' by John Stow (259). The case in question was a family dispute, in which a Mr Belott sought damages for a dowry of £60 he believed he was promised but never paid when he married the daughter of Shakespeare's former landlord Mr Mountjoy in 1604. Shakespeare affirms that he knows both men, and that Belott had been promised a 'portion' (or dowry) but claims that he cannot remember how much; he also adds intriguingly that he had been asked by the girl's mother, Marie Mountjoy, to 'persuade' Belott to marry her daughter. A court clerk took down what was said, thereby preserving the only instance of Shakespeare's own speech to survive from his lifetime; the transcript of his testimony can be seen here. 'We know the thousands of lines he wrote in plays and poems,' writes Charles Nicholl, 'but this is the only occasion when his

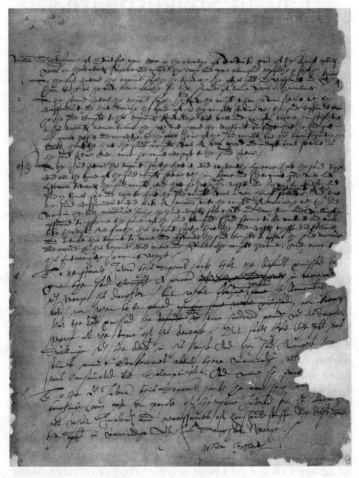

FIGURE 5 *Shakespeare's testimony in the Mountjoy case (11 May, 1612) (by kind permission of The National Archives)*

actual spoken words are recorded' (3). The fact that this legal document is our sole remaining trace of Shakespeare's own voice is indicative of the highly litigious nature of Elizabethan society and such interactions with the law seem to have been commonplace for early modern Londoners. The play we focus on in this chapter, *The Merchant of Venice* (1596–8), is deeply informed by Shakespeare's dealings with the law and the different kinds of legal practices taking place in his city, with which his first audiences would have been familiar.

In *The Lodger: Shakespeare on Silver Street* Charles Nicholl quotes another witness in the Mountjoy case, who says that the couple in question was 'made sure by Mr Shakespeare', and recalls them 'giving each other's hand to the hand' (5). It seems that Shakespeare may have performed the ceremony of troth plighting or hand-fasting – formally betrothing the couple – contracting them in their commitment to marry. His participation in this ceremony may explain the centrality of the same ritual to the plot of another of Shakespeare's plays, *Measure for Measure* (1603–4), which was written while the dramatist was living with the Mountjoys. However, we know that Shakespeare's interest in the legally binding rituals surrounding early modern betrothal predates this moment, and the rituals preceding marriage also take centre stage in *The Merchant of Venice*.

Often seen as a tragicomic drama, *The Merchant of Venice* follows the fortunes of Bassanio, a Venetian lord who hopes to marry a young lady named Portia. This has prompted him to borrow money from the Jewish moneylender Shylock, which he then finds himself unable to repay, thus endangering his friend the merchant Antonio, who has guaranteed the loan. This is not the only contract with which Bassanio becomes embroiled during the course of the play. He also becomes involved in the legal issues surrounding Portia, who is bound by the terms of her father's will to follow an elaborate betrothal ritual in which her suitors must pick from one of 'three chests, of gold, silver and lead, whereof who chooses his meaning chooses you' (1.2.28–30). The terms of this 'lottery' (1.2.28) are spoken of throughout the play in legal vocabulary that reminds us of the unbreakable nature of the contract governing any man's attempt to woo Portia. For example, Portia's servant Nerissa dismisses one suitor, a 'Scottish lord', for having 'borrowed' from an Englishman, swearing 'he would pay him again when he was able'. She is particularly scathing of the fact he has allowed a Frenchman to become 'his surety and sealed under for another', in a comic inversion of Antonio's securing of Bassanio's loan (1.2.75–78). Nerissa speaks with the convoluted formality of the law courts, employing procedural jargon – rather unnecessarily – to tell Portia that all existing wooers have given up. 'They have acquainted me with their determinations, which is indeed to return to their home and to trouble you with no more suit,' she says. She even adds a qualification befitting any legal contract: 'unless you may be won by some other sort than your father's imposition, depending on the caskets' (1.2.95–100). By equating the 'suit' of those who would win Portia with the pleas of those who would seek justice in the law courts of Shakespeare's London Nerissa emphasizes the unromantically transactional nature of this process. This is also mirrored in Portia's own assessment of her predicament: 'Is that not hard,' she asks, 'that I cannot choose one, nor refuse none?' (1.2.24–25). The choice of who she will marry has been removed from her by the terms of her father's will, a matter to be determined by the jurisdiction of the law rather than by love, it seems.

When Bassanio – whom Portia herself considers a genuinely deserving match – finally triumphs, he does so not by attempting to sidestep the legal specifications of this document, but rather by succeeding within them. When faced with the choice of caskets, he reasons that 'outward shows' are often 'least themselves', and that 'ornament' is deceptive (3.2.73, 74). In what becomes their betrothal scene, with all the legal force of the hand-fasting Shakespeare would witness in Silver Street, Bassanio invokes the legal fictions that govern the rhetoric of the courts in order to justify his choice of the lead chest: 'In law, what plea so tainted and corrupt, | But, being seasoned with a gracious voice, | Obscures the show of evil?' (3.2.75–77). Even the most unedifying case can be made palatable if pleasingly presented, he suggests. Throughout the negotiation Bassanio is eager to stress that he will follow the letter of the law, saying that he has 'come by note to give and to receive', with the expectation that both sides of the contract will be upheld and he will receive the promised reward (3.2.140). The legal terms in which this trial is conducted are rendered yet more explicit when Bassanio asks Portia to make the success of his choice official, confessing himself 'doubtful whether what I see be true, | Until confirmed, signed, ratified by you' (3.2.147–48). The same processes required to seal a legal document will here be the means of entering into a legally binding contract to marry (although Portia responds, less conventionally, with a kiss).

This chapter will be concerned with the role of the law in Shakespeare's city and in his play, with particular attention to the famous trial scene with which *The Merchant of Venice* climaxes. The Inns of Court, institutions providing legal education during Shakespeare's lifetime, provide the geographical focus for our study of the play, which considers not just the place of the law in early modern London, but also suggests that the Inns themselves embody the collision of values that underwrites the play. Shakespeare's connections to the Inns have been long established. We know from the diaries of law student John Manningham that one of his most popular comedies, *Twelfth Night*, was first staged in Middle Temple Hall in February 1602 (the year that the dramatist moved to Silver Street), for example (see Keir Elam's introduction to the Arden edition of the play, 3). We will be using what we know about the constant presence of the law and its associated vocabulary in Shakespeare's city to help us better understand *The Merchant of Venice*, a play that presents a conflict between several different kinds of legal values, and between the operation of differing legal practices. It is a commonly held idea that the play stages a straightforward clash between the Jewish and Christian value systems. We will suggest instead that as one of Shakespeare's most litigious plays *The Merchant of Venice* can more productively be read as an exploration of some of the contrasting legal systems operating in Shakespeare's London, which thereby illuminates the workings of justice in early modern society.

Shakespeare and the law

The Merchant of Venice was first published in 1600, but the play is likely to have been written a few years before that, sometime between the summer of 1596 and July 1598. This date is important because during that time the members of Shakespeare's acting company, then the Lord Chamberlain's Men, were struggling with the fact that they did not have an official home in London. As charted in our introduction to this book, the players were initially associated with the Theatre, in Shoreditch (they would not take up residence at the Globe until 1599). By 1596, however, the Lord Chamberlain's Men had lost their lease at the Theatre, and instead were forced to enter into a highly disadvantageous legal bond with Francis Langley, the owner of the Swan theatre, on Bankside. Langley stipulated that in exchange for the right to perform at the Swan the company would stage no plays at any other venue; if they broke this promise of exclusivity they would have to forfeit £100, then a huge sum of money. This was quite an unusual arrangement, albeit one that was to become increasingly common in the day-to-day running of the theatres; Philip Henslowe (who we encountered in Chapter 1) started employing bonds in running his own company not long after this time. As he began to write *The Merchant of Venice* Shakespeare thus had direct personal experience of what it meant to sign a bond that legally committed him to an arrangement that would ultimately prove extremely detrimental to his own well-being.

This personal dealing with the law may have inspired the agreement between Bassanio and Shylock that provides the impetus for the play's dramatic action. The negotiation highlights the difficulties inherent in entering into legally binding contracts with others, and particularly the question of what fair recompense might be under the terms of such a deal. As we have seen, Shakespeare was writing this scene while engaged in a bond that he and his players may have felt to be singularly unfair – the owners of the Swan stood to make money out of the Lord Chamberlain's Men if they did perform plays for them, and also if they failed to perform. As we will see further in our penultimate chapter (on *Timon of Athens*), Shakespeare was in this way deeply enmeshed in the day-to-day commercial life of his city, a fact that may have reinforced his decision to set this play in Venice, then known as Europe's most important trade hub. A concern with the workings and – particularly – the equality of financial transactions is suggested here in the problematic contract proposed by Shylock. If Bassanio fails to keep up his side of the bargain his guarantor Antonio will have to pay a particularly high and some might say unfair price, much like Shakespeare at the Swan.

> SHYLOCK Go with me to a notary, seal me there
> Your single bond, and, in a merry sport,
> If you repay me not on such a day,
> In such a place, such sum, or sums, as are
> Expressed in the condition, let the forfeit
> Be nominated for an equal pound
> Of your fair flesh, to be cut off and taken
> In what part of your body pleaseth me.
> ANTONIO Content, in faith: I'll seal to such a bond
> And say there is much kindness in the Jew.
> BASSANIO You shall not seal to such a bond for me;
> I'll rather dwell in my necessity.
> ANTONIO Why, fear not, man, I will not forfeit it;
> Within these two months, that's a month before
> This bond expires, I do expect return
> Of thrice three times the value of this bond.

(1.3.140–55)

Shylock speaks the language of contract law here, seeking repayment of 'such sum, or sums, as are | Expressed in the condition', a phrase that seems to imply the terms of the loan are being set in writing, to be witnessed by a 'notary', a clerk or secretary with the authority to draw up legal documents. The legal language of the notorious 'bond' that Shakespeare's characters 'seal' is echoed repeatedly through this passage, each of the characters here testing out the precise meanings of these words as if mimicking the discourse of the court-room in which lawyers pay forensic attention to one another's terms. If Antonio fails to repay Shylock he will 'forfeit' a pound of his own flesh, we learn here. Bassanio expresses his horror at the nature of this agreement in his pun on the word 'equal', meaning 'exact', but also causing Shakespeare's audience to call into question whether such a deal can ever possibly be equal. The passage raises the issue of what a fair deal might be in other ways too. Antonio boasts that when his ships return from their trade expeditions they will bring in 'thrice three times the value of this bond' – he will more than repay it. Crucially then, in neither scenario is the 'bond' an exchange of one thing for another of the same value. If Antonio 'loses' he will be deprived of something worth far more than the amount borrowed; if he is able to repay Shylock it will be because of an influx of unprecedented wealth brought by a stroke of good fortune equally beyond his control.

Such issues continue throughout the play, which is itself preoccupied at a fundamental level with the question of how to weigh up, or measure, equivalences between things. In one of *The Merchant of Venice*'s key lines we hear of Shylock's supposed reaction upon discovering his beloved daughter Jessica has eloped with a gentleman friend of Bassanio named Lorenzo. 'My daughter! O, my ducats! O, my daughter!', the moneylender reportedly says (2.8.15) – as if he cannot decide which of the losses is the more costly. At the time of writing *The Merchant of Venice* a highly significant legal case was getting underway in Shakespeare's London that can help cast light on the play's preoccupation with securing fair legal recompense. Known as Slade's Case, this trial continued for six years, from 1596 to 1602, and was likewise concerned with the question of what just compensation for a loss suffered might be, and how best to reclaim money that had been promised. Grain merchant John Slade brought this case against one Henry Morley, whom he claimed had promised to buy a crop of wheat and rye (valued at £16) from him and had failed to keep to this agreement. Led by one of Queen Elizabeth's foremost legal experts, Edward Coke, lawyers enforced the contract and exacted payment from Morley by using a concept called *assumpsit*, a means for recovering damages where a contract had been broken that had previously been employed only in cases involving deceit. As this was the first time *assumpsit* had been used in this way this was a watershed moment in English law, establishing what would become the standard way for resolving cases involving disputed debts. It offered a more flexible and less cumbersome way of dealing with such issues than the previous archaic system, which had required the issuing of a writ of debt, a complex procedure in which even a very minor error could result in the whole case being thrown out. By foregrounding the processes by which financial contracts are made, disputed and eventually settled, Shakespeare thus places the day-to-day financial and legal concerns of his fellow Londoners at the centre of his play.

Inns of Court

Such cases – and indeed such language – would have been particularly familiar to early modern London's many law students, young men who flocked to the city's Inns of Court where they sought not only training in the law but also a broader education. After Oxford and Cambridge these were the primary educational establishments in the country; in 1615 the master of the revels George Buck would call them the nation's 'third university' and they have been popularly known as such ever since. Lying halfway between the City of London and the court at Westminster, with strong connections to the commercial and political worlds of both, the Inns of Court maintained their own separate jurisdictions within Shakespeare's city, operating within it but also maintaining their distinctive corporate and legal identity. The Inns survive in the same locations today (although all but Middle Temple were badly bombed during World War II) and all barristers practicing law in the UK must still belong to one of the Inns. Such institutions taught their scholars to play music and to dance as well as training them in academic subjects. 'This was a university in the modern sense,' writes J.H. Baker, 'a place to grow up, to learn about life, to make useful contacts, even to misbehave a bit' (10). Students lived and ate with their masters there and undertook social occasions together, such as the annual Christmas festivities or revels.

Shakespeare did not himself study at the Inns, but he was closely involved with them and shared many traits characteristic of their students, such as a fondness for nimble arguments and virtuosic playing with words. His major patron in the early 1590s, Henry Wriothesley, third earl of Southampton, was one of the leading figures at Gray's Inn after being admitted there in 1589. We know that the glamorous Southampton, who contemporaries complained did not have much time for the actual study of law itself, was present during the holiday seasons for festivities and plays. It may have been at one such occasion that he came into contact with Shakespeare, who had many friends at the Inns. Shortly before he wrote *The Merchant of Venice*, Shakespeare's *The Comedy of Errors* had been given its first performance as part of the Gray's Inn Christmas revels on 28 December 1594. So chaotic and debauched was the evening that ensued that it became known as '*The Night of Errors*', according to the records of the occasion, the *Gesta Grayorum*, published in 1688; it is worth remembering here that the word 'revel' shares its etymological root with 'rebellion'. Another performance at the Gray's Inn revels of that year seems to have provided Shakespeare with inspiration for the masque of Muscovites that appears in 5.2 of his early comedy, *Love's Labour's Lost*, written around this time (Hibbard, introduction, 45–47). One of the play's main characters, the student Berowne, displays rhetorical sophistry and witty wordplay that would not have been out of place at the Inns of Court.

Indeed, some critics have even suggested that Shakespeare found a proto-type for Berowne's compulsive punning in the young John Donne, who was admitted to Lincoln's Inn on 6 May 1592, and who wrote many of his bawdiest, most sexually explicit poems in order to impress his classmates there; later Donne became a clergyman and eventually Dean of St Paul's. Donne provides us with a useful illustration of how the experiences of students at the Inns of Court pervaded the way that they thought and wrote. 'Although Donne was never called to the bar, nor practised the law professionally,' writes David Colclough, 'its language and modes of thought remained crucial to him throughout his life, and lend much of his writing its distinctive character'. In his first satire, Donne describes what he finds as the somewhat oppressive environment at the Inns, calling his dwelling there a 'standing wooden chest', a 'prison' in which he is 'coffined' (ll. 2, 4). The speaker of the poem laments those legal scholars who 'fawn' upon any passing 'velvet justice with a long | Great train of blue coats, twelve or fourteen strong' (ll. 22–23). He lists the aged and distinguished population of the Inns from whom he longs to flee, dreaming of a romantic escape:

> Here are God's conduits, grave divines, and here
> Nature's secretary, the philosopher,
> And wily statesman, which teach how to tie
> The sinews of a city's mystic body;
> Here gathering chroniclers, and by them stand
> Giddy fantastic poets of each land.
> Shall I leave all this constant company,
> And follow headlong, wild, uncertain thee?

$$(ll.5-12)$$

Donne mockingly belittles the 'grave divines' by figuring them as 'conduits', in one meaning (already encountered in our previous chapters) water pumps visible on many of early modern London's street corners. He similarly diminishes 'the philosopher', reducing him to the status of a 'secretary' merely recording nature like the courts' many clerks. The political world of the Inns is alluded to in the 'wily statesman' whose elaborate theorizations of how power is structured glance at the theory of the King's Two Bodies also described in our second chapter, juxtaposing a misapplied idea of the 'mystic body' of the city's fathers with the highly physical image of knotted sinews, at an implied cost to the former. Even historians, or 'chroniclers', are no better than the 'Giddy fantastic poets' who stand beside them – or perhaps Donne is suggesting here that poets are equal in stature to these learned and august figures. As Sarah Knight has written of this poem, 'Donne's speaker initially aligns himself with the academic life of the Inns,' only to take up instead the spirit of 'misrule' that dominated their revels. 'The poem illuminates the overlapping worlds inhabited by residents at the Inns,' she writes, 'who were ensconced within these institutions of learning but also situated within the city, subject to its cultural influence and social distractions' (217). While the effects of the Inns upon shaping Donne's distinctive poetry is beyond doubt, his response to the institutions themselves remains highly ambiguous.

We might say that Donne embodies the way in which the Inns served as transitional spaces in the lives of the young men who passed through them, stopping places on the pathway to their professional lives, bridging the distractions and enjoyments of youth and the more adult concerns of commerce, power and the law that would occupy England's gentlemen upon their return to the estates they would administer and govern in later life. The distinctive juxtaposition of the life of the scholar and that of the debauched reveller encountered at the Inns of Court, where terms of study were punctuated by periods of festivity and excess, parallels Jonathan Goldberg's recent interpretation of *The Merchant of Venice* as a play that oscillates between 'fleshly indulgence' and 'lenten abstinence'. Noting its 'unlikely coincidence of carnivalesque extravagance with its deflation', *The Merchant of Venice* constantly shifts between what Goldberg beautifully calls 'inexplicable sadness and precariously founded joy' (428).

One of the play's more exuberant elements is its use of disguise, a prominent feature of the Venetian carnival as much as the Inns of Court revels. Jessica puts on what her lover Lorenzo calls 'the lovely garnish of a boy' in order to elope with him into the night (2.6.46), under cover of the masques that fill the streets of the city. The same revelry drives Shylock to an early bed, remarking 'Let not the sound of shallow foppery enter | My sober house', like a disgruntled senior bencher disrupted by the festivities of the young Inns of Court students (2.5.34–35). Most notable, however, is Portia's decision to disguise herself as the 'lawyer' Balthasar in order to seek a resolution to the legal dispute with Shylock that will free Bassanio to marry her. This is a highly self-conscious theatrical moment, especially when we remember that this female character would have been played by a male actor and thus already disguised, in one sense. By putting on the attire of a lawyer in order to ultimately subvert the processes of the law, Portia engages in a piece of anarchy befitting the topsy-turvy world of the revels, in which one of the Inns' most junior members would be made King of Misrule for the duration of the festivities.

The *Merchant of Venice*'s court-room climax resembles the structure and distinctive rhythms of life at the Inns of Court in another way, too. Young men studying at the Inns were taught the law through practical lessons known as 'moot debates', in which students would be given points of law to debate with one another in a formal way, through mock trials. We might consider the highly ritualized court-room scene in Shakespeare's play as a reflection of this kind of activity at London's Inns of Court, which proceeds by verifying one point of law after another, much like contestants in their moot debates would have done. Portia (Balthasar) confirms the identity of each of the participants, asking 'Which is the merchant here, and which the Jew?' (4.1.170), before beginning her cross-examination. She begins by seeking affirmation, 'Is your name Shylock?' (l.172), before asking him to confirm the nature of the case, 'You stand within his danger, do you not?' (l.176) and prompting Antonio to acknowledge he willingly entered into the contract, 'Do you confess the bond?' (l.177). Portia continues to argue her case through an extended series of forensic questions, asking whether Antonio is 'not able to discharge the money?' (l.204), enquiring with stomach-churning coolness, 'Are there balance here to weigh | The flesh?' (ll.251–52) and calmly requesting 'Have by some surgeon, Shylock, on your charge, | To stop his wounds, lest he do bleed to death' (ll. 253–54). She offers Antonio chance to make a final plea, before ordering Shylock to proceed to take his pound of flesh.

Such a moment offers a particularly telling instance of what Lorna Hutson terms Shakespeare's 'forensic rhetoric – the rhetoric of proof, probability, conjecture, and circumstance', which 'asks audiences to infer or imagine what cannot be staged' (247). Hutson argues that Shakespeare learns from the rhetoric of the law courts and moot debates at the Inns the means to make his audiences' imaginations act in a particular way, offering a hypothetical world of dramatic possibility that would not otherwise be stageable (or perhaps even thinkable). Such a reading offers useful insight here into how Shakespeare is able to conjure the horrific spectacle of carving into Antonio's flesh. It is only possible for Portia to utter the words 'take thou thy pound of flesh' (4.1.304) within the context of a law court, in which the phrase is predicated on a series of prior conditions that serve to protect both Antonio and Shakespeare's audience from the terrifying prospect the play toys with.

Shakespeare thus draws upon the practices of the law courts to dramatic effect, while at the same time highlighting the inherently theatrical way in which they operate – the obvious correspondences between an audience and a jury, for instance, and the way that both legal trials and plays depend upon carefully structured dialogue leading to a dramatic denouement. Subha Mukherji's recent study of *Law and Representation in Early Modern Drama* begins by quoting Jean-Paul Sartre speaking in an interview with Kenneth Tynan in 1961: 'The law *is* theatre,' he says, and – at the same time – 'The stage is a courtroom in which the case is tried.' Mukherji points out that Shakespeare and his contemporaries, including Kyd, Marlowe and Webster, often 'open up the action of their plays, explicitly or implicitly, to the judgement, even "sentence", of the theatre audience' (1). Lynda Boose has described the 'comic contract' drawn up between early modern dramatists and their audiences; one party expects attention, the other entertainment. Ben Jonson even writes a satirical version of the imagined contract between players and their audience in the induction to *Bartholomew Fair* (1614). In an age in which the young men of the Inns of Court made up a significant proportion of playgoers at the Theatre and later the Globe, Portia's clever legal arguments are targeted at those watching the play as much as those upon the stage. This is a piece of theatre aimed at reminding its audience of the inherent theatricality of the law itself, as well as exploiting the resources that the law can offer the players.

Different kinds of law in conflict in *The Merchant of Venice*

There is one final aspect of life at the Inns of Court in Shakespeare's London that we wish to focus upon now in the last section of this chapter, as we seek to further understand the courtroom scene that provides *The Merchant of Venice*'s dramatic climax. Early modern London contained differing types of court. The common law courts, which insisted upon the binding nature of precedent and adherence to the letter of the law, operated according to quite different principles to

those of the courts of Chancery, which took a more equitable
approach to the judicial process. In the remaining part of this
chapter we will examine how the trial scene represents the
conflict between these different legal codes in effect in early
modern London. The Inns of Court themselves provided a focal
point for the clash between these widely varying systems of
justice; in Shakespeare's time there were subordinate Inns of
Chancery still attached to them, which espoused very different
legal principles to their own (Shakespeare's Justice Shallow in
Henry IV, Part 2 is a former member of one of them, Clement's
Inn, attesting the dramatist's familiarity with these institutions).
The picture is further complicated by the particular location of
the Inns, some of them – including both Inner and Middle
Temple – falling under the administrative boundaries of the City
of London itself, while others – Lincoln's and Gray's Inns – were
part of the county of Middlesex. 'Jurisdiction in this area,'
Bradin Cormack points out, 'is best thought of as a palimpsest
of alternative liberties' (269). The neighbourhood of the Inns
was thus intersected by an elaborate set of judicial and
administrative networks, each of which embodied their own
legal principles and justice systems. 'Crossing a street
or passing through a gate might bring a law student from
under county-of-city jurisdiction into Middlesex jurisdiction,'
Cormack continues, 'or into an Inn (as both school and
home) whose academic and professional status privileged it in
ways similar to London's private jurisdictions more generally'
(269). The complexity of this picture is crucial to explaining
the clash of legal values that Shakespeare stages in *The
Merchant of Venice*, in which the courtroom scene explores the
relative merits of the systems of Chancery and common law
that coexisted (not always peaceably) in early modern London.

Portia's initial attempt at resolving the impasse between
Shylock, Antonio and Bassanio is to make an impassioned plea
for mercy in the face of the moneylender's continuing insistence
on demanding what he considers to be justice. Still in disguise
as the lawyer Balthasar, Portia delivers one of Shakespeare's
most famous speeches in praise of this virtue:

The quality of mercy is not strained:
It droppeth as the gentle rain from heaven
Upon the place beneath. It is twice blest:
It blesseth him that gives, and him that takes.
'Tis mightiest in the mightiest; it becomes
The thronèd monarch better than his crown.
His sceptre shows the force of temporal power,
The attribute to awe and majesty,
Wherein doth sit the dread and fear of kings.
But mercy is above this sceptred sway;
It is enthroned in the hearts of kings,
It is an attribute to God himself,
And earthly power doth then show likest God's
When mercy seasons justice. Therefore, Jew,
Though justice be thy plea, consider this:
That in the course of justice none of us
Should see salvation. We do pray for mercy,
And that same prayer doth teach us all to render
The deeds of mercy. I have spoke thus much
To mitigate the justice of thy plea,
Which if thou follow, this strict court of Venice
Must needs give sentence 'gainst the merchant there.

(4.1.180–201)

Echoing throughout her speech are the terms 'justice' and 'mercy', as Portia urges Shylock to transcend the literal interpretation of the law that he has thus far held to, in order to take a more equitable approach to resolving his 'plea'. Equity was the principle that governed the practices of the courts of Chancery, depending on the individual judgement of the presiding judiciary rather than being bound by the precedents of case law, as under a common law system (the main type of law operating in England in Shakespeare's day). Part of the brilliance of Portia's speech is in her attempt to align such clemency with both divine kindness (comparing it to 'gentle rain' from heaven) and – at the same time – the robust power of the 'thronèd monarch' ('mightiest in the mightiest,' she says). As such, the rhetoric of Portia's speech itself embodies the principle of flexibility that lies at the heart of equitable interpretations of the law. In urging upon the 'Jew', Shylock, a Christian model of mercy as a means to 'salvation', Portia likewise attempts to suggest that a degree of exchange between differing value systems might be possible, in which he is able to adopt behaviours then commonly attributed to this other faith. Such permeability is characteristic of the courts of Chancery, where an individual judge had greater freedom to apply the law in those specific aspects that he saw fit, and which – it should be noted – coexisted alongside the common law courts for centuries.

This reading of the speech is somewhat at odds with the way in which it is usually interpreted; an entire tradition of criticism takes Portia's words as opposing justice and mercy to one another as if the terms are mutually exclusive. Taking their cue from her repeated identifications of 'justice' with the Jewish faith ('Therefore, Jew, | Though justice be thy plea') and Portia's emphasis upon God's 'mercy' (a concept central to sixteenth-century understandings of Christianity), numerous critics have argued that Shakespeare here provides the culmination of tensions between Jewish and Christian values that they believe underpin the play. It has long been a critical commonplace to read *The Merchant of Venice* as an embodiment of an opposition between an Old Testament or Mosaic sense of divine justice that insists upon a literal exacting of the bond at its heart and a supposedly New Testament doctrine of Christian mercy that allows room for a more metaphorical interpretation of its driving bargain. This tradition reads the opposition between Shylock and Antonio in the play as symbolizing 'the confrontation of Judaism and Christianity as theological systems – the Old Law and the New', as Barbara Lewalski writes; 'the emphasis of the Old Law upon perfect legal righteousness is opposed to the tenet of the New Law that righteousness is impossible to fallen man and must be replaced by faith' (331–32). Such an interpretation of the play depends upon an understanding of Judaism and Christianity as embodying very different moral and legal codes. The Mosaic law central to the Jewish faith derives from the Old Testament (and the idea of the vengeful God we encounter there may go some way to explaining Shylock's desire for revenge), a religion that values justice above all else, as it has been interpreted. Christianity, at least in the form of Protestantism practiced in Shakespeare's London, places a contrasting emphasis upon the workings of mercy, a belief system based on the idea that we are all damned by original sin, and it is up to God to decide if we will be saved. The Reformation had prompted new debates about the place of mercy in the practice of law that continued to rage in Shakespeare's London.

There is then a danger that in opposing Judaic justice and Christian mercy this binary model oversimplifies the moral universe of Shakespeare's play as it reflects the city in which he lived. Terry Eagleton sees 'a sophisticated piece of Christian anti-Semitism' in critical work that makes such a distinction (165–66). Certainly post-Holocaust discussion about *The Merchant of Venice* has been dominated by the play's frequently troubling depiction of the Jewish Shylock, whom Antonio calls a 'misbeliever, cut-throat dog', amongst other things (1.3.107). There is also something particularly shocking about Portia's direct address, 'Jew,' here in a courtroom speech that is about mercy; the word is isolated by punctuation, and Portia seems to almost spit it out. Anti-Jewish feeling seems to have been an unfortunate fact of life in Shakespeare's London. England's Jewish population had been officially expelled from the country by Edward I in the thirteenth century. While some Jews remained in England they were not officially recognized as citizens, and as such were often subject to the seizing of their money and property. Many Jews preferred to convert rather than be expelled from the country, and from the date of King Edward's proclamation until the eighteenth century there was a well-known London institution called the *Domus conversorum*, the House of Converts, located on Chancery Lane (which in turn takes its name from the nearby Inns of

Chancery). Those who were willing to give up their faith – as Shylock gives up his in the final act of the play – were given shelter there.

A further complication for those who would read *The Merchant of Venice* as straightforwardly opposing a supposedly benevolent Christian mercy and unnecessarily inflexible Judaic justice comes from the fact that it is Portia who insists upon an interpretation of the law even more literal than that of Shylock. In a bitterly ironic denouement Portia successfully argues that Shylock can only claim his bond if he is able to do so without shedding any of Antonio's blood:

> Tarry a little, there is something else.
> This bond doth give thee here no jot of blood:
> The words expressly are 'a pound of flesh'.
> Take then thy bond: take thou thy pound of flesh.
> But in the cutting it, if thou dost shed
> One drop of Christian blood, thy lands and goods
> Are by the laws of Venice confiscate
> Unto the state of Venice.

(4.1.301–308)

Portia succeeds in coming up with a legal qualification that makes it impossible for Shylock to assert his bond. Quoting the terms of his carefully worded contract back at him, reiterating what 'The words expressly are', Portia makes clear that just as Shylock has used the law to serve his own purposes so he will be fully subject to 'the laws of Venice' should he transgress them himself. Shylock's famed 'literalism' (many have observed his apparent distrust of metaphor in the play) is overshadowed by that of those who would use it against him, and *The Merchant of Venice* enters the morally murky boundary-lands between the differing value sets that its critics so often attempt to keep apart.

Where Portia's appeal to the principle of equity – asking Shylock to show mercy – has failed, literal adherence to the law here succeeds. Such a result is hinted at in the courtroom scene well before it becomes manifest. 'I crave the law,' Shylock starkly responds to her eloquent rhetoric, 'The penalty and forfeit of my bond' (4.1.202–3). Sensing that her pleas to the moneylender have fallen on deaf ears Portia adopts a different tactic, borrowed from a different legal system. If her case is rejected in Chancery, she will appeal to the common law, invoking the value of precedent in order to lay the foundations for her new arguments. Refusing Bassanio's attempts to buy his way out of the terms of the original contract by offering 'twice the sum' owed (4.1.206), Portia reminds the court that:

> there is no power in Venice
> Can alter a decree established.
> 'Twill be recorded for a precedent,
> And many an error by the same example
> Will rush into the state. It cannot be.

(4.1.214–18)

By reinforcing the unmovable nature of legal 'precedent' here, Portia prepares the court for her insistence on the exact terms of the contract, by which she will ultimately free Bassanio from his debt. She is keen to point out here that ignoring the history of pre-existing case law not only does a disservice to the past but also is highly risky for the future: 'many an error' will 'rush into the state' as a result. This is because the strict adherence to precedent in the common law system means that it will be used to cater for events that cannot possibly be anticipated at the moment it is set down; the lawyers of the future will apply it to circumstances as unimaginable as Portia here finds the idea of operating outside of this legal system altogether: 'It cannot be.'

Just as Portia attempts to utilize the resources of both Chancery and common law, finding that where an appeal to equity fails the principles of precedent prove inescapable, so she argues in fact that mercy and justice are not fundamentally opposed notions. As she says in key lines of her speech, 'earthly power doth then show likest God's | When mercy seasons justice.' Portia makes it quite clear that these are entirely different value systems – one would not, could not, should not, mistake one for the other – but that they are not incompatible. This is the outcome of the famous trial scene with which *The Merchant of Venice* reaches its climax; such are the findings of Shakespeare's audience as we are placed in judgement over his play and his characters. Rather than thinking in oppositional terms the play encourages us to consider the permeable nature of the boundary between the differing value systems of its characters, much as a young lawyer training at the Inns was forced to educate himself in the many differing legal practices of Shakespeare's London. Like those Inns, the play serves as a space in which intellectual and moral values clash, are debated and finally resolved. In this aspect it has much in common with the subject of our next chapter, *Hamlet*, in which drawing out the relationship between the play and St Paul's cathedral offers us an important new way of situating this much discussed play.

5

Religion in Shakespeare's London:

Hamlet (1600–1) and St Paul's

Introduction

To reach St Paul's Cathedral from the Inns of Court, Shakespeare only needed to continue walking east along Fleet Street. On his way he would pass the church of St Dunstan's in the West, where John Donne would serve as vicar from 1624–31. He would cross over the Fleet River (no longer visible to modern visitors), pass the Old Bailey, and then the precinct of the Blackfriars (which we will consider in more detail in Chapter 8) where in 1609 Shakespeare and his fellow King's Men would open their indoor playhouse. Throughout his journey, his view was no doubt dominated by his destination. Approximately 586 feet long or about the length of 13 double decker buses, St Paul's Cathedral towered over the rest of the London skyline. As he climbed the gentle slope of Fleet hill (also known as Ludgate hill) the square tower of the Cathedral would seem to rise up towards the heavens. Finally, passing through Ludgate and into the ancient Roman boundaries of the City proper, the Cathedral would fill his sight as if it had become the city itself.

In the early sixteenth and seventeenth centuries, Shakespeare and his fellow Londoners travelled to St Paul's for many reasons. Christians had visited the Cathedral to practice their faith for nearly seven hundred years. Its crypts and chapels housed the tombs and memorials of many English nobles – a reminder that death came to even the illustrious and powerful. As the writer of some of the most memorable mediations on life and death of the early modern period (including Jacques' seven ages of man speech that we explored in our introduction, as well as Hamlet's soliloquies, which we'll examine here) it is not difficult to imagine Shakespeare wandering amongst the headstones and statues of the dead in St Paul's, contemplating this life and the next.

St Paul's was a social centre where individuals exchanged news and conducted private business. Amongst the chapels and monuments, prayers and more commercial petitions were offered up – often in equal measure. The Cathedral's churchyard was also a hub of activity. Here Shakespeare may have stood alongside other visitors to the yard listening to official sermons, news, and even the occasional public penance. The hubbub Londoners encountered in the yard was further fuelled by the growing popularity of a new source for public information in Shakespeare's lifetime: the early modern book trade. Walking amongst the printing houses, bookshops and stalls which lined St Paul's churchyard, Shakespeare would see bibles, prayer books and printed copies of sermons sold alongside less morally upright texts such as satires, poetry and plays – including in 1603 *Hamlet*. Inside and out, St Paul's was a bustling, and at times chaotic, mix of the sacred and the secular.

Hamlet is a play in which religious images and ideas are similarly positioned alongside the more worldly concerns of its protagonists. As we will see, this dichotomy in St Paul's and in the play reveals points of disconnection between outer appearances and internal reality, creating moments of striking contradiction that ask audiences and readers to consider the ways we claim to know ourselves and others. The play follows the internal and external conflicts of Prince Hamlet who is charged by the ghost of his dead Father to avenge his death by murdering its perpetrator: the current King and Hamlet's uncle, Claudius. Hamlet immediately vows to revenge his father's 'foul and most unnatural murder' (1.5.25), and takes on an 'antic disposition' (1.5.170) to hide his intentions from King and court. From its opening visitation by the ghost of Hamlet's father who is condemned to an afterlife in 'sulphurous and tormenting flames' (1.5.3), to Horatio's closing prayer for Hamlet that 'flights of angels sing thee to thy rest' (5.2.344), Shakespeare's tragedy is instilled throughout with the sights, sounds and spaces of early modern religious life. Yet the universe of *Hamlet* is equally that of the thwarted prayers and spiritual uncertainty that comes with living in a secular society. As we will show in this chapter, a particular source of this discord in the play is the lasting impact of England's religious conversion from Roman Catholicism to English Protestantism known as the Reformation. In the span of several decades and four monarchs (Henry VIII, Edward VI, Mary I and Elizabeth I), England underwent successive, sweeping changes to the national religious identity, the after-effects of which were still being felt in Shakespeare's city as they are in his play.

By the time Shakespeare was writing *Hamlet* (between 1600 and 1601), the Protestant church had been the national religion for nearly half a century. However, the defaced statues and missing altar pieces, mingled the sound of prayers in spoken in English instead of Latin that now echoed in the vaulted ceilings of St Paul's Cathedral, reminded Londoners of the drastic, often contradictory changes of spiritual identity they had undergone in recent memory. In this chapter we will explore the religious landscape of *Hamlet* by examining its connections with important sights in and around St Paul's Cathedral during Shakespeare's time. First, we will examine the interplay of sacred and secular in the spaces and characters of *Hamlet* through the prism of the diverse activities conducted in the Cathedral itself. The second part of this chapter will consider the presentation of Christian ceremony and ideology in *Hamlet* via the idea of iconoclasm – a Post-Reformation programme that sanctioned the removal or destruction of religious images and objects from churches including St Paul's. Finally, we will venture out of the Cathedral and into the churchyard and the heart of London's early modern book trade, where we will consider the ways in which religious attitudes to print and learning may have influenced how *Hamlet* was read by its first readers. In each of these sections we will consider the influence of the Reformation on the individual and society in Shakespeare's London in order to better understand how this complex religious landscape shapes one of Shakespeare's greatest tragedies.

Paul's Walk and the interplay of sacred and secular

St Paul's has been the religious centre of London since Roman times. However, as we learned in our introduction, Shakespeare would not have recognized the iconic domed cathedral that is a feature of the city's skyline today. Now generally referred to as 'Old St Paul's' the cathedral Shakespeare saw as he walked up Ludgate (or indeed from almost anywhere in the city), had a tall square tower. The entirety of Old St Paul's would be severely damaged by the Great Fire in 1666, and two years later was demolished to make way for Christopher Wren's new domed design, well-known to modern visitors to London. Like its successor, the interior of Old St Paul's was comprised of a series of cascading stone arches that formed a wide central aisle and two smaller side aisles running the length of the Cathedral. Walking under these arches, Shakespeare would have seen a variety of religious and non-religious activities occurring side by side; a pew that contained pilgrims one moment might be the meeting place for gossips the next. In this section, we will consider how the interaction of sacred and secular activities in St Paul's and in *Hamlet* reflects the complexities and contradictions of early modern religious identity in Shakespeare's London.

One of the most surprising uses of St Paul's in Shakespeare's day – and one he may have taken part in himself – was the use of the Cathedral's central aisle as a shortcut. Rather than go around the extensive perimeter of the church and its adjoining buildings, Londoners would use the wide middle aisle, known to Shakespeare and his contemporaries as 'Paul's Walk', as a direct route from Ludgate to Cheapside. Visitors and even livestock regularly used this unusual pathway, entering through the main door at the western end, heading straight up the aisle towards the high altar and then taking a sharp left to exit out the north door into the churchyard. Other business conducted at the Walk ranged from the official hiring of scribes, who could be paid to create or copy important documents, to private deals, disreputable swindles and the placing of bets. The alternative purposes of Paul's Walk are captured in *The Second Part of King Henry IV* when Falstaff claims to have 'bought' Bardolph, his frequent companion and accomplice, at St Paul's (1.2.51). The walk would continue to capture the imaginations of playwrights throughout the early seventeenth century; in James Shirley's play, *The Wittie Faire One* (1633), the dim-witted Sir Nicholas Treedle hires himself a tutor there. John Earle's pamphlet *Micro-cosmographie* (1628) also captures the effect of this boisterous activity, describing the Walk as 'a heap of stones and men, with a vast confusion of languages', continuing, 'the noise in it is like that of bees, a strange humming or buzz-mixed of walking, tongues and feet: it is a kind of still roar or loud whisper' (I3ᵛ).

The 'buzz' that Earle describes may recall the endless bustle and chatter of another group of visitors to the middle aisle of the Cathedral. Paul's Walk was also a social destination for groups of upper-class gentlemen known unofficially as 'Paul's Walkers'. These men met in the middle aisle to exchange news and gossip in a very visible and public way. Ben Jonson captured this social display in his comedy *Every Man Out of His Humour* (1600), in which numerous characters meet at Paul's Walk, claiming to conduct 'business' there; in fact they are equally interested in being seen by the right people (3.1).

Contemporary negative attitudes towards the Walkers are perhaps best expressed by Jonson's character Malicente, for whom the Walk shows men at their most ridiculous: 'O, what copy of fool would this place minister to one endued with patience to observe it' (3.1.258–9). We can imagine Shakespeare following Jonson's advice and intently watching the contradiction of the boisterous, buzzing Walkers amongst the solemn dignity of the Cathedral. In *Hamlet*, the emphasis on socializing and gaining status that informs the character and behaviour of Hamlet's two school friends Rosencrantz and Guildenstern would not be out of place amongst the Walkers of St Paul's. Summoned to Elsinore by the King to help discover the source of Hamlet's melancholy, their first lines to him are of the sort of superficial small-talk one would imagine was regularly spoken amongst the posturing gentlemen of the Walk:

HAMLET   Good lads, how do you both?
ROSENCRANTZ   As the indifferent children of the earth.
GUILDENSTERN Happy, in that we are not ever happy.
                 On Fortune's cap we are not the very button.

                                              (2.2.220–224)

Although he describes them as his 'excellent good friends' (2.2.219) and 'lads', Hamlet counters their flowery verse filled with superficial images of idleness ('indifferent children of the earth') and materialism (desiring to be buttons on Fortune's cap) with prose, asserting the fact that he will not take part in their frivolity. Rosencrantz and Guildenstern also share the Walkers' interest in gaining social status by interacting with the right people, in their case, the King and Queen. While they claim to be in Elsinore to 'visit' (2.2.237) Hamlet, their primary occupation is trying to extract information from him to report back to the King. Aware of their ulterior motive, Hamlet compares them to a sponge 'that soaks up the King's countenance, his rewards, his authorities' (4.2.14–15). Portrayed as sycophants who did 'make love' (437 n. 57) to their disreputable employment, Hamlet's criticism of Rosencrantz and Guildenstern echoes negative attitudes towards the Walkers in Shakespeare's London. In his 'Paules Steeples Complaint' (*The Dead Terme*, 1608) Thomas Dekker bemoans the Walkers as propagators of 'knavish villainy' (D4ʳ–D4ᵛ). Rosencrantz and Guildenstern do not thrive but meet a rather inglorious death by execution that is ordered in a letter Hamlet has forged to the King of England. In light of the general disapproval of the Walkers during Shakespeare's lifetime, Hamlet's insistence that 'Their defeat/ Does by their own insinuation grow' (5.2.57–8) suggests that the two essentially get what they deserve. In this way the fates of Rosencrantz and Guildenstern may also be seen as condemning the same kind of aspiring courtiers and busybodies Shakespeare encountered on Paul's Walk.

A destination for walkers and worshippers, St Paul's thus embodied a diverse and controversial combination of secular and spiritual interests. The ways in which *Hamlet* incorporates the realities of early modern religious spaces into its action denote a similarly versatile and complex play space. An example of this theatrical conjuring of religious space that might have resonated with visitors to Old St Paul's takes place when Hamlet describes in a rather unusual way the location of Polonius' body in act four, scene three:

KING   Where is Polonius?

HAMLET   In heaven. Send thither to see. If your messenger
          find him not there, seek him i'th'other place
          yourself. But if indeed you find him not within
          this month you shall nose him as you go up the
          stairs into the lobby.

                                                (4.3.31–6)

Hamlet's dark reference to the smell of Polonius' decaying body – 'you shall nose him' – alludes to a common feature of early modern churches: the tombs and memorials of deceased parishioners which lined the aisles and were buried under the floors. Hamlet's comment that the King will 'nose' Polonius (a pun that plays upon the King's desire to 'know' where Polonius is and the fact that his 'nose' will eventually smell him) makes light of a natural and rather unpleasant result of this practice: the prevalent smell of decomposing bodies. Many of England's great historical figures were interred in the chapels and vaults of St Paul's including John Talbot, one of the great battlefield heroes depicted by Shakespeare in *King Henry VI, Part One*, Sir Francis Walsingham, Queen Elizabeth's secretary and 'spymaster', and Sir Philip Sidney, author of *The Defence of Poesy* and the sonnet sequence *Astrophil and Stella*, amongst other things. As Stephen Greenblatt reminds us, 'Even the liberal use of incense, flowers, and sprigs of rosemary could not altogether have masked the smell of decay that medieval and early modern burial practices almost inevitably introduced into the still air of churches' ((2001), 18). Hamlet's reference to the smell of Polonius' decaying body thus alludes to what must have been a familiar feature of churches in Shakespeare's time. With its monuments to ancient kings and tombs containing generations of Londoners, St Paul's was surely no exception; the ever-present odour would have made it difficult for visitors to the Cathedral to deny the fact that they were standing amongst the dead. Hamlet's reference to 'nosing' the departed in this way is a rather off-colour *momento mori*, a sign of the close proximity of life and death that would not have been missed by the Walker's at St Paul's or playgoers watching *Hamlet* at the Globe, who were more attuned to the use of religious symbolism than most modern audiences. In this way, Shakespeare brings the sights (and smells) of the sacred and secular environment of Paul's Walk to *Hamlet's* Elsinore.

St Paul's was also – and most obviously – a place for worship. In 1588 Queen Elizabeth I attended St Paul's for a service celebrating the defeat of the Spanish Armada. Arriving in London at the end of the 1580s, Shakespeare may have witnessed the Queen entering the Cathedral to thank God for protecting England from Spain and the threat of the Spanish Inquisition. Shakespeare draws upon the performative aspects of religious practice to infuse *Hamlet* with moments of solemnity and reverence of the kind he would have encountered at St Paul's. Central to the success of this element of the play is Shakespeare's understanding and utilization of the connections between prayer and the dramatic soliloquy. The iconic image of Hamlet alone on stage recreates the personal reflection often associated with prayer and mediation in Christian worship.

Perhaps the most literal instance of the soliloquy constructing a sacred space by adapting the sentiment and physical posture of prayer happens in act three, scene three where Claudius, finding himself alone on stage after watching his murder of King Hamlet re-enacted before the whole court by the players, confesses aloud to the murder. His opening lines suggest a spiritual context: 'O, my offence is rank: it smells to heaven; | It hath the primal eldest curse upon't-' (3.3.36–7). Claudius compares his murder of the old King to the Bible story of Cain's murder of his brother Abel in the Book of Genesis (4.11–12), 'the primal eldest curse'. Recalling this tale from the Old Testament, Shakespeare situates Claudius' conscience in a Christian understanding of right and wrong. Trying on different petitions by entreating 'Forgive me my foul murder' and asking 'May one be pardoned and retain th'offence?' (3.3.52, 56), Claudius calls to mind the act of confession, which in some versions of the Christian faith takes the form a prayer recited aloud. As his train of thought reaches its climax, Claudius' speech concludes with a final, pivotal direction to 'Bow, stubborn knees, and heart with strings of steel | Be soft as sinews of the new-born babe' (3.3.70–1). Most actors adopt here the physical posture of prayer. Without specifying that Claudius has removed himself to a chapel, the language and staging of his soliloquy produce the solemnity of a private place of prayer, setting the stage for the dramatic moment when Hamlet discovers him and sees a chance to take his revenge: 'Now might I do it. But now 'a is a-praying' (3.3.73).

Hamlet, we discover, is unwilling to kill Claudius while he is at prayer for fear the murdererous King will be forgiven of his crime. However, Hamlet's decision is quickly called into question; the effect of Claudius' prayer dissolves when it is revealed that things are not as they seem: 'My words fly up, my thoughts remain below. | Words without thoughts never to heaven go' (3.3.97–8). In admitting his failure to pray, Claudius undermines the perceptions of Hamlet and the audience with the unnerving realization that they mis-read Claudius' repentance. Not only is this revelation a pivotal moment in the plot (Hamlet has potentially missed the perfect opportunity to take his revenge), it also reveals a confusion of sacred and secular. Claudius appeared to be praying so Hamlet assumed that he was; he accepted the outer image as a reflection of his inner state.

The frequent discrepancy between interior reality and exterior appearances in an individual is a preoccupation of Shakespeare's play, featuring most prominently perhaps in Hamlet's conscious decision to put on his 'antic disposition' (1.5.170). During the Reformation and its aftermath, the inconsistency of a person's internal and outward spiritual states was a source of unease for Catholics and Protestants alike. While one could – like Claudius or Hamlet here – adopt the postures and go through the outward motions of conforming to established religious doctrine, the question remained: how could anyone really know what was in another's heart? This question has also plagued critical discussions of Shakespeare's own religious preferences. As we will see throughout this chapter, *Hamlet* contains elements of both the Catholic and Protestant faiths. While no existing evidence suggests that Shakespeare was anything other than an obedient member of the established national church, we simply do not know whether his personal faith matched the one he presented to the public. This ability to separate (whether out of necessity or personal inclination) outer and inner, public and private faith may explain how early modern individuals like the Walkers in St Paul's were able to move between sacred and secular actions and ideas even within a major religious space like St Paul's Cathedral. In this way, Shakespeare's portrayal of the contradictions of sacred and secular in *Hamlet* offers a mirror for audiences to observe and examine the potential complexities of everyday religious life in early modern London.

Faith interrupted: Images, rites and religious change

On the night of 17 November 1547, a group of men entered Old St Paul's with an assortment of ropes and tools. In order to avoid unnecessary attention from locals, they waited until after dark to carry out their task. The *Chronicle of the Grey Friars of London* records how that night 'was pulled down the Rood in Paul's with Mary and John, with all the images in the church' (55). This entry documents a dynamic expression of the Protestant Reformation in early modern London – the systematic removal and destruction of what had been significant objects of Catholic worship at St Paul's: the large 'Rood' or cross that hung above the altar and statues of the Virgin Mary and St John. Two years later, the *Chronicle* records an additional incident in which a cloister and chapel in the Churchyard were 'pulled down' and the materials repurposed 'to build the protector's place' – the home of Edward Seymour, Duke of Somerset and Lord Protector of England during the minority of Edward VI that today is still known as Somerset House (58). The above entries are not records of unauthorized religious extremism but in fact represent acts sanctioned by the Protestant government in England, first under Henry VIII, then more aggressively under his son Edward VI, and which continued into the reign of Elizabeth I.

The destruction of religious icons, known as 'iconoclasm', was driven in part by the Protestant belief that such objects violated two of God's basic commandments: 'you shall have no other Gods before me', and 'you shall not make for yourself an idol, whether in the form of anything that is in heaven above, or that is on the earth' (Exodus 20:4). To pray before false icons, they believed, invested these objects with a religious power that properly belonged to God alone. For this reason, early modern Protestants condemned such images as trappings of Roman Catholicism's unnecessarily elaborate style of worship. In act one, scene four Hamlet displays a similar distaste for the ostentatious traditions embraced by Claudius and his court to celebrate his coronation, describing the custom as 'more honoured in the breach than in the observance' (1.4.16). From his childhood in Stratford-upon-Avon, Shakespeare would have been familiar with the effects of iconoclasm. The religious wall paintings of the town's guildhall chapel fell victim to a wave of iconoclastic fervour and were whitewashed over, remaining only partially visible to this day. Shakespeare's father John, a high-ranking member of the town's local government during Shakespeare's childhood possibly oversaw the job himself. By the time *Hamlet* was being performed at the Globe it had been several decades since this fervent national programme of iconoclasm was initiated, but empty shrines, defaced statues and whitewashed walls like the ones in the Stratford guildhall stood as reminders of the uncomfortable, often destructive process of the Reformation. In this section, we will examine the ways in which ceremonies in *Hamlet* also recall this lingering discomfort with Post-Reformation religious identity.

The paring down of performative worship that motivated the programme of iconoclasm also carried over to other tenets of Catholic ideology that Protestants condemned as petty superstitions. One such change was the rejection of the Catholic idea of purgatory. While modern Catholicism defines purgatory as a state of spiritual purification, medieval Catholics understood it to be a place, separate from heaven and hell, where souls would be cleansed of worldly sins before entering heaven. The fire and torment awaiting souls in purgatory was a concern for Catholics and frequently captured in the art and literature of the time. *Purgatorio*, the second book of Dante

Alighieri's epic poem, *The Divine Comedy* (first published 1555, but written between 1308 and 1321), is devoted to the torments of purgatory, which he portrays as specifically designed to reflect each individual vice. Saint Thomas Aquinas warned that the least pain in purgatory 'surpasses the greatest pain that one can endure in this world' (Greenblatt (2001), 21). As a spirit 'confined to fast in fires | Till the foul crimes done in my days of nature | Are burnt and purged away', the ghost of King Hamlet is frequently seen as a soul in purgatory (1.5.11–13). In the context of Shakespeare's experiences of seeing the defaced altar of St Paul's and the whitewashed chapel of the Stratford guildhall, the ghost also becomes a remnant of the old faith.

However, if King Hamlet's ghost was meant to serve simply as a reminder of the Catholic doctrine of purgatory, then it might be expected that he would be most concerned with cleansing himself of his sins. On the contrary, he quickly rejects Hamlet's sympathy for his suffering with a dismissive 'Pity me not' (1.5.5). The ghost, we soon discover, has another agenda entirely: 'If thou didst ever thy dear father love', he commands, 'Revenge his foul and most unnatural murder' (1.5.23, 25). The ghost's true interest, it seems, is not in ending his suffering in the afterlife but avenging himself in this one. Old King Hamlet's ghost therefore poses an intriguing contradiction. He may remind audiences of an important aspect of Catholic ideology, but his failure to 'act' like a proper purgatory ghost undermines the authority of this doctrine by essentially giving it a rival in the form of worldly revenge. In this way, the ghost personifies the competing interests of the walkers and worshippers of St Paul's, whose own negotiations of 'old' and 'new' attitudes towards religion could, as we have seen, also result in duplicity and contradiction.

The Protestant programme of simplifying worship carried out as part of the Reformation also prompted changes to religious ceremonies or 'rites'. Roman Catholicism endorsed seven such rites, also known as sacraments, through which God's grace was conveyed to the people present: baptism, confirmation, confession, the Lord's Supper (or Eucharist), marriage, ordination, and Extreme Unction (or Last Rites). By contrast, the Protestant church followed Luther and Calvin's beliefs that only rituals actually performed by Jesus in the Gospels counted as sacraments. As a result, the seven sacraments were reduced to two in Shakespeare's England, baptism and the Eucharist, with the rest shortened to simple prayers. The replacement of full rites with less elaborate prayers in the early modern church is reflected in a series of shortened or abridged ceremonies that take place in *Hamlet*. For example, the haste with which the 'funeral baked meats | Did coldly furnish forth the marriage tables' for the union of Gertrude and Claudius implies that King Hamlet's funeral is a noticeably shortened event (1.2.179–80). Polonius' burial is similarly depicted as much abbreviated. Laertes laments that his father's 'obscure funeral' contained 'No trophy, sword nor hatchment o'er his bones, | No noble rite, nor formal ostentation' (4.5.205, 206–7). His particular use of the words 'rite' and 'formal ostentation' here call to mind the simplifying of church services that was part of the Protestant Reformation. Moreover, Laertes' argument that the missing 'ostentation' will 'Cry to be heard as 'twere from heaven to earth' suggests that the missing 'noble rite' is required by God (4.5.208, 207). In this way, Laertes' plea challenges King Claudius' decision to simplify Polonius' funeral, an intriguing and potentially dangerous inference for Shakespeare to make in a country where Elizabeth I, as head of the church, was responsible for enforcing England's own programme of religious reform including the modification of ceremonies for burying the dead.

The distress caused by what Beatrice Groves eloquently describes as 'maimed' rites is again expressed in Laertes' repeated cries of 'What ceremony else?' at the burial of his sister Ophelia (Groves, 3; 5.1.212, 214). Whether fully conscious of her actions or not, Ophelia has committed one of the most extreme sins imaginable in the Christian faith by taking her own life. In Shakespeare's lifetime, this would prevent her from receiving the proper Christian funeral that would help convey her soul to heaven. Despite this, Ophelia is granted a minimal ceremony in the play. Yet Laertes' frustration at his sister's maimed rites continues, reaching a crescendo with his cursing of a priest: 'I tell thee, churlish priest, | A ministering angel shall my sister be | When thou liest howling' (5.1.229–31). Laertes' desire for a more elaborate ritual suggests the distress of those longing to reinstate the fuller rites of Catholic worship. However, his assertion that despite her earthly sin Ophelia will be 'a ministering angel' also evokes the Protestant belief that true spirituality and a place in heaven is not determined by what Catholicism describes as 'good works' but rather by an inherent grace granted by God known as 'predestination'. Followers of the Protestant reformer John Calvin believed that before the beginning of time God chose who would ascend to heaven after death and who would not. These people (the 'elect') would achieve heavenly salvation regardless of their actions during their life on earth. (The fact that members of the elect did not know they were saved until after they died was an understandable source of anxiety for the faithful.) By suggesting that in spite of her sin, Ophelia will in fact be an angel after death Laertes shows he believes that she is predestined for heaven. However, in simultaneously desiring ceremony and embracing the doctrine of grace by faith alone, Laertes embodies a contradiction, combining elements of both Protestant and Catholic practices much like the ghost of Hamlet's father. Like the remnants of iconoclasm in St Paul's, Laertes offers a tragic image of the incongruous interplay of Catholic and Protestant religious values in early modern religious practices.

Reading *Hamlet* (and Hamlet) in St Paul's Churchyard

If Shakespeare continued his progress up Paul's Walk and out of the north door of the Cathedral he would immediately find himself in the final area of St Paul's we will be discussing – the Churchyard. Beyond the stone monuments and high vaulted

ceilings of the Cathedral Shakespeare would enter a small
open square bustling with noise and activity. At the far end of
the yard he would see the large octagonal podium known as
Paul's Cross. Here sermons, news and other events (including
the execution of four of the Gunpowder Plot conspirators in
January 1606) were conducted in public view. If Shakespeare
stood before Paul's Cross and turned around 360 degrees,
he would see that the yard (also known as the 'Cross yard')
was surrounded by multi-storied buildings, much like those
on the north side of the Strand described in Chapter 3.
These properties, frequently containing both businesses and
tradesmen's homes, formed a ring around the yard with many
smaller structures on the south side built against the walls of
the Cathedral itself. It was these buildings that housed the
printing presses and bookstalls of London's emerging book
trade, and Shakespeare would have recognized their identifying
signs: the Green Dragon, the White Horse, the Gun, the Holy
Ghost, the Greyhound and the Parrot, to name just a few.

Modern textual scholars are intrigued by the relationship
between Shakespeare and the editions of his plays produced
by these early London publishers and printers (known as
'stationers'). Many, like David Scott Kastan, believe that
Shakespeare was a playwright who wrote for the stage and
had little interest in seeing his plays in print. Others, such as
Lukas Erne, contend that Shakespeare saw himself as a literary
dramatist who wrote his plays with the knowledge that they
would one day be read. Whether or not he was interested in
seeing his plays sold in St Paul's, the yard must have been an
inspiring place for Shakespeare and his fellow playwrights.
Here it would seem as if the whole world had been brought to
their doorstep, made readily accessible by the invention of
moveable type and the printing press. Wandering amongst the
various shops and stalls in the churchyard Shakespeare found
books on almost every conceivable subject including history
(such as Holinshed's *Chronicles* – a prime source for history
plays like *Richard II*, as we have seen), poetry (including Ovid's
Metamorphosis, which we discovered in Chapter 1 was a

source for classical allusions in *Titus Andronicus*), science (like the *Insectorum Theatrum* or *Theatre of Insects* which we will discuss alongside *The Tempest* in Chapter 8), and – most prominently – religion. By the end of 1603 Shakespeare's *Hamlet* would also be numbered among the books in St Paul's Churchyard and in this final section we will consider how *Hamlet's* move from the stage to the printed page offered additional opportunities for readers to consider Shakespeare's play within the religious discourses of St Paul's and early modern London.

With its capacity to quickly reproduce information for mass dissemination, Protestants immediately saw the printing press as an important tool for promoting the fundamental ideas of the Reformation. In John Foxe's *Book of Martyrs* (1563, 1570), (which we know from our study of *Titus Andronicus* that Shakespeare was certainly familiar with) printing is depicted as one of God's own weapons: 'the Lord began to work for His Church not with sword and target to subdue His exalted adversary, but with printing, writing, and reading' (1583, Book 6, 731). As we have seen, Protestants simplified prayers and rites with an eye to creating a direct spiritual relationship between man and God. The intimacy of reading and the individual contemplation it encouraged supported the Protestant pursuit of what Elizabeth Eisenstein has called a 'priesthood of all believers' (171). This idea – that individuals seek understanding of God and their relationship with him through their own contemplation of religious texts – is evident in the prayers uttered by the faithful at Protestant services: 'Blessed Lord, who hast caused all holy Scriptures to be written for our learning; grant that we may in such wise hear them, read, mark, learn, and inwardly digest them' (Baker (2007), 24; Cummings, 272). These lines from *The Book of Common Prayer* reminded parishioners that religious texts were not read simply to be revered; they must be closely studied ('Read, mark, learn') so they could be 'inwardly digested'. This style of reading is reminiscent of the interpretative processes that Hamlet and Horatio embark upon when they 'observe', 'note' and then interpret Claudius' response to the *Murder of Gonzago* (3.2.76, 80).

Visitors to St Paul's Churchyard had what must have felt like endless options for personalized religious study. They could purchase a copy of the latest sermon (the best-selling genre of Shakespeare's time) to reread and scrutinize, as well as Bibles, prayer books, and other printed guides to the spiritual life. A number of books are featured in *Hamlet*, although Shakespeare offers few details regarding their contents. Before Ophelia's encounter with Hamlet in act three, scene one (known for Hamlet's command that Ophelia 'Get thee to a nunnery' (3.1.120)) Polonius hastily hands her an untitled book to use as a prop that 'may colour' her encounter with Hamlet as a chance meeting, rather than a discussion being secretly watched by Polonius and the King (3.1.44). Similarly, when Hamlet is pressed by Polonius to reveal what he is reading in act two, scene two we get no more information than that the book contains 'Words, words, words' (2.2.189). However, *Hamlet* is infused with the culture of critical examination and self-discovery associated with Protestant programmes of reading described above. King Hamlet's first words to his son are a command to 'Mark me', in much the way Reformed Christians were urged to mark their texts, noting points of particular doctrinal importance or spiritual value (1.5.2). Moreover, Shakespeare incorporates the language of knowledge acquisition already seen in *The Book of Common Prayer* into the speech of his protagonist:

Yea, from the table of my memory
I'll wipe away all trivial fond records,
                    [. . .]
And thy commandment all alone shall live
Within the book and volume of my brain.

                              (1.5.98–9, 102–3)

In an important article on early modern note-taking and memory systems Peter Stallybrass, Roger Chartier and others connect the 'table' of Hamlet's memory with a particular kind of early modern notebook which was popular in the seventeenth century and was probably amongst the books for sale in St Paul's Churchyard during Shakespeare's time in London. These 'writing tables' typically included a printed almanac and featured a number of specially-treated erasable pages where notes could be written and then erased so the paper could be re-used. A writer would use a metal-point stylus to etch their ideas into the special surface. Through the image of the writing 'table', Shakespeare suggests that Hamlet inscribes or imprints his father's murder into his memory, an internalizing that echoes the inward digestion suggested by *The Book of Common Prayer*. However, Hamlet's ultimate intention for the memory, to incite him to revenge and murder, is hardly one the writers of *The Book of Common Prayer* had in mind. Shakespeare once again evokes an element of sacred practice only to challenge it, confronting religious doctrine with the complications of a secular world.

Alongside the many religious texts for sale in the St Paul's Churchyard, a fairly new item appeared around the same time Shakespeare arrived in London. These were the printed copies of plays recently performed in playhouses like the Globe. Plays were sold in books called quartos, the equivalent to a small modern-day paperback. Between 1594 and 1623 thirteen of Shakespeare's own plays were originally sold this way in St Paul's Churchyard with many of them appearing in second and even third editions shortly after. Today one can still stand in St Paul's churchyard and, with a little imagination, see where in 1594 *Titus Andronicus* was sold 'at the little north door of Paul's at the sign of the Gun', and where in 1623 Edward Blount sold *Mr. William Shakespeare's Comedies, Histories and Tragedies*, the first printed collection of Shakespeare's plays also known as the First Folio, at the sign of the Black Bull. When *Hamlet* appeared for the first time in print in the shop of the bookseller Nicholas Ling, Hamlet's reflective soliloquies suddenly could not only be heard by theatre audiences they could also be 'read, mark(ed), and learn(ed)' by readers. 'To be or not to be' was no longer just a dramatic moment but a philosophical question permanently fixed on a page waiting for an answer. In a culture where the written word was seen as a tool for not only discovering and developing individual identity but also for getting closer to God, the 'textual performance' of *Hamlet* in print became another opportunity for early modern Londoners to read, mark, and learn.

Nicholas Ling, co-publisher and seller of the first editions of *Hamlet*, had a particular idea of how *Hamlet* would appeal to readers in print. In his shop Ling sold (and also edited) another popular early modern form of publication known as commonplace books or miscellanies (Melnikoff, 98). Commonplace books were small pamphlets in which collections of quotes and proverbs were organized by category to facilitate thematic study and easy memorization. As with many publications of the time, commonplace books frequently featured religious ideas and often included categories addressing spiritual concepts such as God, Hell, sin, and virtue. During Shakespeare's lifetime some stationers had begun to mark common sayings – or *sententiae* – in books of poetry and drama by placing eye-catching marks such as inverted commas beside the quotations – the early modern equivalent of highlighting. Zachary Lesser and Peter Stallybrass believe stationers included these marks in their printed texts to suggest passages that readers might want to collect and transcribe into their own commonplace books for future reference and study. The appearance of such marks in Ling's 1603 edition of *Hamlet* suggests that the stationer believed his readers would be interested in the printed play not only as a record of performance but as a text to be studied more closely for its themes and ideas; a feature that led Lesser and Stallybrass to describe Ling's edition as 'Shakespeare's first literary drama' (417).

A businessman interested in selling books, Ling used commonplace markers to highlight portions of *Hamlet* that would especially appeal to the customers who frequented his shop. For example, he marked numerous lines from Polonius' well-known speech in act one, scene three, where he offers

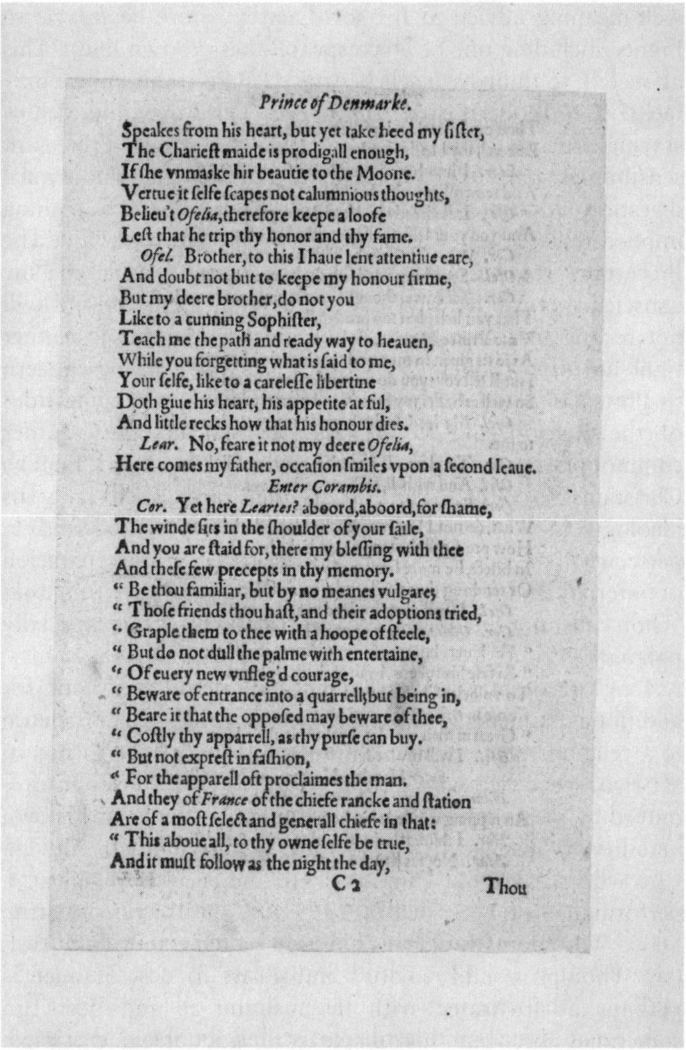

Prince of Denmarke.

Speakes from his heart, but yet take heed my sister,
The Chariest maide is prodigall enough,
If she vnmaske hir beautie to the Moone.
Vertue it selfe scapes not calumnious thoughts,
Belieu't *Ofelia,*therefore keepe a loose
Lest that he trip thy honor and thy fame.
    Ofel. Brother, to this I haue lent attentiue eare,
And doubt not but to keepe my honour firme,
But my deere brother, do not you
Like to a cunning Sophister,
Teach me the path and ready way to heauen,
While you forgetting what is said to me,
Your selfe, like to a carelesse libertine
Doth giue his heart, his appetite at ful,
And little recks how that his honour dies.
    Lear. No, feare it not my deere *Ofelia,*
Here comes my father, occasion smiles vpon a second leaue.
                    Enter Corambis.
    Cor. Yet here *Leartes?* aboord, aboord, for shame,
The winde sits in the shoulder of your saile,
And you are staid for, there my blessing with thee
And these few precepts in thy memory.
" Be thou familiar, but by no meanes vulgare;
" Those friends thou hast, and their adoptions tried,
" Graple them to thee with a hoope of steele,
" But do not dull the palme with entertaine,
" Of euery new vnfleg'd courage,
" Beware of entrance into a quarrell; but being in,
" Beare it that the opposed may beware of thee,
" Costly thy apparrell, as thy purse can buy.
" But not exprest in fashion,
" For the apparell oft proclaimes the man.
And they of *France* of the chiefe rancke and station
Are of a most select and generall chiefe in that:
" This aboue all, to thy owne selfe be true,
And it must follow as the night the day,
                    C 2   Thou

FIGURE 6 *William Shakespeare,* Hamlet *(1601), with Ling's commonplace markers (C2r) (by kind permission of The Huntington Library, San Marino, California. Rare Book number 69304. Shakespeare, William. Hamlet. 1603.)*

well-meaning advice to his son Laertes before he travels to France including one of Shakespeare's best known lines: 'This above all, to thine own self be true' (1.3.77). This choice may feel trite to modern ears from overuse. However, the idea of staying true to one's conscience was central to Protestant sensibilities, particularly in light of the fact that the inward digestion advocated by Protestant approaches to reading implied that the self was infused with the word of God. The Protestant reformer Martin Luther himself declared 'my conscience is captive to the Word of God. I cannot and will not recant anything, for to go against conscience is neither right nor safe' (Baker, 29). Conscience was a prime concern to Protestants and Catholics alike during the changing tides of the Reformation in England. Behind Polonius' rather commonplace advice lies the struggle felt by many English Christians to remain faithful to their prescribed religious ideology. In a society in which this labour could end in persecution or, as we have already discussed, in the separation of internal and external identities, Polonius' assertion that 'Thou canst not then be false to any man' (1.3.79) is especially poignant.

Ling's recommended lines might entice readers to look for additional moments in *Hamlet* that explore ideas of conscience in a religious context. For example, they may have turned to act two, scene two where, amazed by how the Player King is moved by meaningless stage action, Hamlet thinks of his own inability to revenge his father and wonders aloud 'Am I a Coward?' (2.2.506). Famously an audience member at a performance of Peter Hall's 1965 RSC production starring David Warner answered this question with a resounding 'Yes!' (see Thompson and Taylor's introduction, 24). Hamlet is perhaps as frustrated with his inaction as audiences can sometimes be, but his displeasure goes beyond simple procrastination. He particularly admires how the Player 'Could force his soul so to his own conceit' (2.2.488); Hamlet himself longs to be able to align his 'soul' (conscience), with his vengeful or 'bloody' thoughts (4.4.65). In desiring to 'force his soul' Hamlet reveals that he would not be satisfied to merely perform the act of revenge; as with the 'book and volume of his brain' image discussed earlier, he wishes to go further, internalizing the intention so it becomes a part of his person. Hamlet expresses a similar dissatisfaction in his third, and most famous, soliloquy: 'To be, or not to be' (3.1.55). Here again his conscience, aware of the 'slings and arrows of outrageous fortune' (3.l.57) as well as the 'dread of something after death' (3.l.77), chooses to endure the known sufferings of this world rather than usher in the unknown of the next. As in the case of 'Am I a Coward?', Hamlet's conclusion that 'conscience does make cowards' (3.l.82) is as much about the failure to act (in this case, commit suicide) as it is about the fact that he cannot reconcile his conscience to his desired actions. In this way, Hamlet reinforces Polonius' original advice of being 'true' to one's self by repeatedly attempting to reconcile his own internal and external personae. As we have seen throughout this chapter, the contradiction of internal and external is not limited to the individual concerns of the Prince of Denmark – it is echoed in the conflicting desires of both Laertes and Claudius, as well as the juxtapositions of sacred and secular in St Paul's.

Similarly Hamlet's 'To be, or not to be' soliloquy pits the internal against the external, exploring the very essence of faith itself: the commitment of the personal will or conscience to an idea with no external guarantee or proof. In his soliloquy, Hamlet offers no images of suffering in the afterlife comparable to the ones given by the ghost of Hamlet's father. Instead, all his examples of misery or distress in this soliloquy relate to earthly life: 'The slings and arrows of outrageous fortune', 'whips and scorns of time' and 'Th'oppressor's wrong, the proud man's contumely, | The pangs of despised love' are all identifiable forms of a 'weary life' that Hamlet is prepared to suffer (3.1.57, 69, 70–1, 76). What are most terrifying to Hamlet – and prevent him from acting – are the unknowns of 'what dreams may come' and the 'undiscovered country' (3.1.65, 78). This uncertainty about what lies beyond death 'puzzles the will', inhibiting Hamlet's ability to act (3.1.79). Paralysed by the unknown, it becomes apparent that what he needs, more than simply to act or not ('To be, or not to be'), is to take a leap of faith – to commit, believe and hold steady based on available evidence and in spite of the possible consequences of a torturous afterlife. Faithful men and women on both sides of the English Reformation who read Shakespeare's play would certainly identify with Hamlet's struggle in this soliloquy and in the play overall – for many his dilemma would encapsulate the central struggle of all personal worship and, as we have seen throughout this chapter, was of particular importance in the unsettled religious landscape of early modern London.

While Hamlet's discoveries only add to his frustrations, an early reader of the first edition of *Hamlet*, guided to those moments in the text that amplify the theme of conscience by Ling's commonplace markers, may have seen Hamlet's personal failures as victories of the moral conscience and an attempt to live a good Christian life. Hamlet finally has his revenge during the fencing competition in act five, scene two, taking advantage of the chaos caused by the sudden poisoning of his mother the Queen (from a cup Claudius meant for Hamlet) to wound the King with a poisoned blade. Nevertheless, the hope that his actions will ultimately be understood in a positive light is echoed in his final request that his friend Horatio live on to 'report me and my cause aright' (5.2.323). We cannot know for certain how readers engaged with *Hamlet* in these first readings. However, the commonplace markers in Ling's publication and the integration of both Protestant and Catholic ideology throughout the play meant that the 1603 printed text of *Hamlet* had much in common with the diverse social and religious environment of St Paul's, and much to offer the reader who discovered the play on the bookstalls there. As we have seen, the spaces, images, ceremonies, and language of *Hamlet* reveal a play infused with the intense and complex religious debates of Post-Reformation London. *Hamlet* is not a play about religion, but it is a play in which religion appears alongside the events that constitute a life, including death, family, love and the search for understanding. After *Hamlet* Shakespeare would go on to write other tragedies, including *King Lear*, the subject of our next chapter. However, none of his subsequent plays would parallel *Hamlet's* use of contrasting images of sacred and secular to explore the impact of religion in the life of the individual. In this way, *Hamlet* gives us a privileged glimpse of the intricate relationship between religion and life in Shakespeare's London.

6

Medicine in Shakespeare's London:

King Lear (1605–6) and Bedlam

Introduction

If St Paul's Churchyard, with its bustling bookstalls, lively debate and learned public sermons, represented the beating heart of intellectual and spiritual life in Shakespeare's London, the next stop on our journey takes in a very different kind of location, characterized by a very different kind of babble and activity. Just a little north and west of St Paul's lies another notable landmark in Shakespeare's city: Bethlehem hospital, commonly called Bedlam, which was originally situated at Bishopsgate. Like most medical institutions the hospital began life as a monastery, converted to an asylum for the sick and especially the mentally ill upon the dissolution brought about as a result of Henry VIII's religious reforms (described in the previous chapter). As we will see, Bedlam was far removed from today's image of what a hospital should be like, and much of what went on there would not now be considered the practice of medicine. But the small yet high-profile institution served as a focal point for Shakespeare and his contemporaries in their thinking about sickness and health, notions of what they might call normal and abnormal behaviours and the interconnected possibilities of care and cure. As such it will form the key location for our study of *King Lear*, one of Shakespeare's next major tragedies.

Extraordinarily, he would write *Hamlet, Othello, King Lear* and *Macbeth* all within one seven-year period around the turn of the seventeenth century, along with many other plays as well. *King Lear* is unique among this group in being a play predominantly concerned with the process of ageing, of what it means to grow old, and how relationships between generations alter across time. 'Know that we have divided | In three our kingdom,' Lear announces at the beginning of the play, 'and 'tis our fast intent | To shake all cares and business from our age, | Conferring them on younger strengths,' (1.1.36–39). With its tale of a weary king casting off his crown and dividing his kingdom between his daughters it is a play unusually preoccupied by the fragility of physical and mental health. Gloucester's bodily agonies – he is brutally blinded at the bidding of Lear's daughter Goneril who commands Cornwall to 'Pluck out his eyes!' (3.7.5) – are paralleled by Lear's cerebral suffering as his majesty dissolves into madness. The dramatic crux of the play finds him stripped of his crown, position of power and even most of his clothes, alone on the heath with only his fool and a Bedlam beggar calling himself Poor Tom for company. 'Here I stand your slave,' he rages at the howling wind and lashing rain, 'A poor, infirm, weak and despised old man' (3.2.19–20). Lear's metaphorical journey to Bedlam is the trajectory charted by this play. We will reconstruct it in this chapter, as we seek to understand how Shakespeare and his contemporaries thought about medicine, what Bedlam represented to early modern Londoners, and how these things informed the writing of *King Lear*.

The idea that what is supposed to cure you might in fact kill you haunts *King Lear*. The trials its central characters Lear and Gloucester undergo in the hope of achieving better mental and moral health push their frail bodies to the point of collapse.

Shakespeare plays upon the notion that medical treatment can be a dangerous proposition at a local level as well; in the depths of his despondency Lear himself construes poison as a kind of medicine, his only hope of cure ('If you have poison for me, I will drink it,' 4.7.72). Likewise, when Regan declares herself 'Sick, O, sick!' in the final scene of the play her sister Goneril (who is responsible for having her poisoned) remarks in an aside, 'If not, I'll ne'er trust medicine' (5.3.97). This moment exemplifies not only the popular understanding of the time, in which the line between poison and remedy was finely and uncertainly drawn, but also a broader tendency throughout the play to turn to the language of medicine at moments of particular dramatic tension. Vocabulary associated with sickness and health plays an unusually significant role in *King Lear*, and Goneril's knowing remark here registers the vexed understanding of early modern medical practice that Shakespeare and his contemporary Londoners shared. As we shall see, medicine was a wide-ranging and disparate collection of practices in the period (much of which was far removed from what we today would consider conducive to good health). As a result, the play's medical language also varies considerably, and Shakespeare draws upon a series of very different medical registers in the allusions he makes throughout his tragedy.

Some of Shakespeare's knowledge of medicine appears to derive from his acquaintance with John Hall, a Stratford-based physician who would in 1607 marry the playwright's daughter Susanna, and whom the playwright knew from 1600 onwards. The son of a Bedfordshire doctor, Hall received his BA and MA from Cambridge and studied at Montpellier, although there is no evidence he held formal medical qualifications (as was true of many practicing physicians of his day). Hall's practice in Stratford was extremely successful though, as is evidenced by the detailed case histories he recorded in his notebooks, some of which would be published after his death as *Select Observations on English Bodies* (1657). As the title of this volume suggests, Hall's medical style was one defined by the close monitoring of each individual patient's condition, adjusting his planned treatments in careful response to what he observed. As such Hall was at the forefront of a movement to shift early modern medical practice away from the purely theoretical and towards a model based on scrutiny of the specifics of each case, interpreted according to the experience of the doctor; we will study the place of observation and experience in *King Lear* as this chapter progresses.

Hall's practical, observational style of doctoring put him in conflict with those early modern medics whose practice continued to derive from the teachings of Galen. The ancient Greek physician propounded the theory that the body is governed by four humours (blood, phlegm, black bile and yellow bile), and that all illnesses owe to an imbalance in these substances in the body, often as a result of environmental conditions. Hall's own approach had more in common with the infamous Paracelsus (whose flamboyant and inflammatory character was ironically reflected in one of his family names, Bombastus). A Swiss-German fifteenth-century physician, Paracelsus' influence was just beginning to be felt in early-seventeenth century London – a delay in the transmission of his ideas that attests to just how controversial they were. He was the first doctor to advocate for the value of experience to medical practice, the detailed observation of each individual patient and condition, and the testing of new drugs and treatments in small and careful dosages. Paracelsus was also famed for carrying out (mostly) accurate human dissections, an activity forbidden to Galen by the religious and cultural beliefs of his own time. Hall's approach to treating his patients, who ranged from the poor to the nobility, was thus at the forefront of the movement initiated by Paracelsus that was just gaining momentum in Shakespeare's lifetime, although the playwright himself tends to espouse a more straightforwardly Galenic approach to his descriptions of the human body and its condition. While recent critics have therefore cautioned against reading too much into Shakespeare's relationship with Hall, others (particularly those who themselves have medical training) have suggested that the unusually acute clinical descriptions of both physical and mental illness in the plays may owe something to their conversations.

Medicine in Shakespeare's London

This chapter will look at a single case history from the many examples of sick and disturbed patients who Shakespeare places upon his stage, examining the medical language of *King Lear*, the nature of Lear's own personal malady and the ways in which critics have over time attempted to 'diagnose' what so horribly afflicts the play and its characters. Most important, however, we will place the play within the London in which it was written, taking Bedlam as a focus for this study, and charting the influence of this particular location upon the play through both an examination of direct references to it in the text of Shakespeare's tragedy and also by exploring certain key ideas associated with the hospital that inform *Lear's* composition.

As we have just learnt, no single approach can be fully said to characterize early seventeenth-century understandings of health, disease and the human body. The conflict between Galen and more recent medical thinkers such as Paracelsus was not the only clash of values taking place in Shakespeare's city over attitudes to health and illness, however. Early modern London was filled with a range of different medical practitioners who each took very different approaches to attempting to heal the sick. The College of Physicians, founded in the early sixteenth century, had attempted to establish a hierarchy amongst healers in which the university-educated classical learning of physicians was privileged. Nonetheless, surgeons, apothecaries, midwives, quack-doctors, and wise women continued to be the first point of contact for the majority of the unwell in Shakespeare's day. As the plague returned again and again, decimating London's population at an alarming rate, so the number and range of approaches to illness multiplied. The diversity of diagnoses, treatment methods, medicines, and other healing techniques proliferated with equal rapidity. R.A. Foakes' introduction to the Arden *King Lear* presents the play as one that contains a multitude of different possible interpretations within its text, as different characters each offer a differing understanding of the events that make up its central action (8–10). Similarly, the experience of the sick in Shakespeare's city cannot be isolated as a singular phenomenon, but rather should be thought of as a universe of vastly varying possibilities, with a similarly varied range of outcomes.

It is instructive to consider some particularly well-known patients treated in Shakespeare's London in order to understand the medical world in which he writes *King Lear*, and which so strongly exerts its presence upon the play. The notorious case of Mary Glover has recently been highlighted by Kaara Peterson as having particular relevance for Shakespeare's tragedy. Glover was a young woman from a relatively prosperous and 'godly' family, who began to display disturbed behaviours, including fits. Some thought this affliction was the result of witchcraft practiced against her in retaliation after she had an altercation with one Elizabeth Jackson, who subsequently stood trial for having bewitched Glover in 1602. London's leading physicians were brought in to examine Glover including Edward Jorden, who subsequently gave an account of her case in his *A Briefe Discourse of a Disease Called the Mother* (1603). There Jorden suggests that Glover was afflicted by a condition known as *hysterica passio*, in which the womb was believed to move around the body causing a range of distressing symptoms to (female) patients including pain around the heart and breathlessness (C1^r–C1^v). Such early modern medical explanations were ultimately ignored, however, when Jackson was found guilty of having practiced witchcraft upon Glover, invalidating any secular diagnosis of her condition. The episode shows the clash in Shakespeare's London between multiple different understandings of the human body and those forces that could cause it to suffer illness, juxtaposing physiological learning (albeit of a kind founded upon the since discredited Galenic model of humoural theory) with folk medicine and popular beliefs about bewitchment.

One further aspect of Glover's case is worth noting here; it seems to have become something of a sensation in Shakespeare's city, generating unusual publicity and attention amongst early modern London's leading citizens. Historians have described the way in which Glover's fits became a public spectacle, with Londoners flocking to the family home to view her condition, some believing it to be the work of Satan, others wanting to witness a medical phenomenon, and still more convinced that Glover was a fake. The theatrical, some would say performative, nature of Glover's fits provides an important context for our understanding of what will happen to King Lear, and indeed for the behaviour of Edgar in the play. Subject to a plot designed to oust him from his father's affections by his (illegitimate) brother Edmund, Edgar takes on the identity of Poor Tom of Bedlam, feigning lunacy. Declaring his intention to adopt this disguise, Edgar calls it 'the basest and most poorest shape I That ever penury in contempt of man I Brought near to beast', before proceeding to clothe himself in the ragged and filthy garb of the hospital's inhabitants (2.2.178–80). His speech here foregrounds the same aspect of performativity that some discerned in Mary Glover's apparent madness.

Another notable case in early modern London with which Shakespeare was familiar is that of the Portuguese doctor Roderigo Lopez (c.1517–1594). Resident in the city from 1559 and shortly thereafter appointed to the College of Physicians, the Jewish Lopez served as doctor to the Earl of Leicester and later the Queen and her household. Having attracted the enmity of his former patient, the Earl of Essex, Lopez was accused by him of conspiring to poison Elizabeth I, resulting in a charge of high treason upon which he would be hung, drawn and quartered at Tyburn. The repercussions of the Lopez case were felt across the city and continued for some time, helping to engender a widespread fear of untrustworthy physicians that was perpetuated by writers such as Francis Bacon, who warns of the need to choose one's doctor with care. Drawing upon the work of Montaigne, Bacon suggests that medics may even go so far as to make their patients ill in order to ensure continuing business. The Lopez case had a particular impact upon the world of the stage. His execution in 1594 coincided with the composition of Shakespeare's *The Merchant of Venice*, with its highly derogatory portrayal of the Jewish Shylock. A revival of Christopher Marlowe's play, *The Jew of Malta* – in which the Jewish merchant Barabas unscrupulously seeks revenge after being stripped of his assets by his enemies – was also staged this same year. The performance of Marlowe's play was seemingly designed to evoke in unflattering terms Lopez's own Judaism (he had continued to practice the faith in secret after his father's forced public conversion to Christianity in 1547). Again, we see that many of our modern perceptions of the place of doctors in society are challenged by the understanding of the physician's role held by Shakespeare and his contemporaries. Rather than being construed as a source of comfort, healing and even cure, doctors were often viewed with suspicion and, on occasion, fear. As a result, early modern Londoners frequently preferred the services of healers and family members who lacked formal education or training to officially accredited physicians. It is this world in which Shakespeare wrote *King Lear*, and it is this complex and disparate view of medicine that his play reflects.

Medicine in *King Lear*

The opening scene of the play employs Galenic terms to question the nature of blood ties, and the relationship between such physical familial bonds and those of affection. Lear asks his three daughters to tell how much they love him; Goneril's response is that he is 'Dearer than eyesight' to her, mattering more than 'health', and that she loves him to the point of breathlessness (1.1.56, 60). Cordelia's supposed betrayal when she refuses to speak of her feelings for her father in such hyperbolic terms is also figured in physiological language. Lear denounces her for betraying her own body by rejecting her closest relations, declaring 'Here I disclaim all my paternal care, | Propinquity and property of blood,' banishing her 'as a stranger to my heart and me' (1.1.114–15, 116). Her 'offense', in Lear's eyes, is 'unnatural' and 'monsters' the blood ties that she should feel as bonds of love, a rhetoric of deformation that will continue throughout the play (1.1.220–21). If Cordelia's alleged crime is imagined as a corruption of her blood, one key element in the Galenic body, then Lear's own mis-steps are likewise portrayed in medical terms. When Lear banishes the loyal Kent, who attempts to stand up for Cordelia, he responds, 'kill thy physician, and thy fee bestow | Upon the foul disease' (1.1.164–65). Not only does the King fail to take the prescribed measures to cure his condition, Kent suggests, but in rejecting the advice of those with his best interests at heart he feeds his disease further. Goneril describes her father's erroneous judgement as a sign of his 'long-engrafted condition', and the 'unruly waywardness that infirm and choleric years bring with them' (1.1.298, 299–300). An excess of choler, the bodily fluid particularly associated with anger, is also diagnosed in the King of France when he leaves with Cordelia indignant at her father's treatment of them: 'France in choler parted,' we learn (1.2.23); later in the play he will again be termed 'hot-blooded France', (2.2.401). Cornwall's increasing ire likewise causes him to be called 'fiery' and 'hot' (2.2.293), symptoms of a surplus of choler in Galenic understanding.

Throughout *King Lear*, Cordelia is closely linked to the heart, an organ with which she is identified through the etymology of her own name ('Cor-' is from the Greek for 'heart'). It is the mismatch between Lear's expectations for how his beloved youngest daughter should behave towards him and her own sense of what is morally right that ultimately shatters the King's own heart. From quite early in the play he imagines her actions to have weakened this vital organ; she 'drew from my heart all love | And added to the gall,' Lear says, suggesting that she has brought about in him a humoural imbalance that will make him ill (1.4.261–62). Other characters within the universe of the play also perceive him as being afflicted in the heart; even an anonymous knight met by Kent in his exile describes the King as having 'heart-struck injuries' (3.1.17). If the deepest of these cuts is made by Cordelia's failure to speak of her love for her father in the opening scene, further blows are struck by the increasing hostility that Goneril and Regan display towards Lear, reneging on their promises to accommodate him and his large retinue and each making clear in turn that he and his court are not welcome in their homes. Lear's response is to wonder if his other daughters are also sick at heart, a suggestion that displays a certain logic given their close connection by blood. In a reference to the increasingly public and detailed dissection of human cadavers that was beginning to take place in seventeenth-century London he orders: 'Then let them anatomize Regan; see what breeds about her heart', asking, 'Is there any cause in nature that make these hard hearts?' (3.6.73–74). The notion that wicked behaviour can bring about a hardening of the heart, or that hardness of the heart reflects immorality more generally, is Biblical in origin. Here the King believes that Regan's outwardly unkind behaviour will be mirrored in her bodily organs. The play thus reflects another central tenet of Galenic medicine, which posited a direct connection between the health of the body and that of the soul.

King Lear can in many ways be read as a play about the injuries inflicted upon the hearts of its major characters; W.E. Slights has recently characterized the role of the heart in the play 'as the battlefield where competing aspects of the self engage' (168). The culmination of the tragedy necessarily results in the rupturing of these vital organs. The play's harrowing final scene is dominated by the language of the heart; fittingly Cordelia – the character most closely identified with this body part – is at the visual and emotional centre of its bleak tableau. Edgar here serves as a messenger, recounting the narrative action of the play's subplot. He describes his father's torments having been blinded by Regan and her servant, his own nursing of Gloucester, and the eventual failure of these efforts to return the old man to health. In another iteration of the play's recurring inversions of the relationship between sickness and health, Edgar expresses his own pain at being forced to speak of such suffering by wishing that the organ that should sustain his life would instead bring it to an end: 'O, that my heart would burst!' (5.3.181). As we learn more of Gloucester's descent into pain and terror, it becomes clear that in willing this to happen Edgar wishes to replicate the fate of his father, whose own heart has been unable to sustain the brutality inflicted upon it: 'his flawed heart, | Alack, too weak the conflict to support, | 'Twixt two extremes of passion, joy and grief, | Burst smilingly' (5.3.195–98). Edgar's last phrase here suggests a welcoming of death; there is 'joy' here amidst the 'grief'. As in Galenic medicine it is the 'extremes of passion' that have brought about Gloucester's tragic end, an excess of emotion that is to blame for his death. Edgar's speech is important for another reason too – it foreshadows Lear's own death in the final moments of the play, just as the subplot featuring Gloucester and his errant sons (not present in any of Shakespeare's sources) has likewise mirrored that of Lear and his daughters.

The immediate cause of Lear's own death is the wound inflicted upon his battered heart by the death of his favourite daughter, Cordelia, in a scene renowned for plumbing the darkest depths of tragedy. Lear's horror at her death would have been shared by Shakespeare's first audience, who would have expected a rather happier ending, given their knowledge of his source materials, in which both the King and his daughter survive. His reaction swiftly turns to denial, as he frantically searches for signs that she still lives. In his distraught state Lear implements two of the classic tests used by early modern doctors to ascertain whether patients had stopped breathing or not. 'Lend me a looking-glass;' he asks first, 'If that her breath will mist or stain the stone, | Why then she lives' (5.3.259–61). A moment later – in a gesture made much of by many stage

Lears – he appears to seize upon a feather, holding it close to her face; 'This feather stirs, she lives', he declares with a mixture of desperation and delusion (5.3.263). It is unclear, we might note, whether Lear actually has a mirror or a feather with which to perform these tests; the rapid shift between them suggests both may merely be figments of his fervent imagination. We find precedent for both of these diagnostic tests in the printed medical literature of Shakespeare's day, widely available on the bookstalls of St Paul's. Indeed, scholar Kaara Peterson traces the detail of checking both mirrors and feathers for signs of respiration to a series of classical medical texts, including works by Pliny, Fontaine and Aetius, as well as Galen himself. Citing the case of one 'Good-wife Archer of Stratford,' reported in John Hall's medical casebooks, Peterson has written of the enormous popularity of what she terms 'revivification narratives' in early modern London, 'tales of miraculous resuscitations of female patients believed dead but merely suffering from grievous hysterical ailments' (4). Lear's frantic employment of the second test, using a feather, after the first has failed to show signs of life, 'suggests a similar insecurity with the initial trial that these medical writers register about their experiences with early modern undead,' she argues (86). Lear's tragedy lies in the disparity between his own willed uncertainty about his daughter's state, his panicked employment of well-known medical techniques in an attempt to search out signs of life, and the absolute conviction that she is dead: 'I know when one is dead and when one lives; | She's dead as earth' (5.3.258–59), he says upon first entering with her body in his arms (Shakespeare's most devastating stage direction). The dramatist uses the device of these familiar medical tests in order to play these impulses off against each other, and to toy with the hopes of his audience. Lear's findings are, amongst other things, a bleak indictment of such clinical practices and their failure to find the longed-for evidence that his daughter lives: 'Why should a dog, a horse, a rat have life | And thou no breath at all?' (5.3.305–6), he howls. She is beyond the care of doctors, nurses and Lear himself.

King Lear's complaint

As we have seen, Lear's ultimately futile hope that he can resuscitate Cordelia owes something to early modern medical thinking about a much-discussed figure in Shakespeare's London: the female hysteric, whose displaced womb causes her a range of distressing symptoms, including swooning so convincing that she appears to be dead. Shakespeare seems to have been well aware of the proliferation of works describing this condition; Hermione's fate in *The Winter's Tale* (1610–11) may likewise derive from descriptions of the faints and subsequent revivals of hysterical women (she is turned into a statue for much of the play, before returning to life in the closing scenes). Interestingly though, it is not Cordelia who displays the symptoms of hysteria throughout the play, however much we wish she too might come back to life. Rather Lear himself seems to identify with – and display signs of – the condition. This is a source of considerable consternation amongst critics of the drama, who are puzzled by the fact that the link between the disease and the uterus in early modern medical understanding make it a uniquely female condition in the period.

What exactly is wrong with King Lear? What kind of illness does he suffer from? Is his complaint mental or physical? And when does it begin to manifest itself? While generations of readers and watchers of the play have been quick to diagnose some form of dementia in his behaviour we need to be very careful about such retrospective, and anachronistic, assertions. F.D. Hoeniger, who has made a detailed study of *Medicine and Shakespeare in the English Renaissance*, has compared Lear's symptoms to those described in early modern medical treatises, finding the closest analogues in Timothy Bright's *A Treatise on Melancholie* (1586) (also a key source for Hamlet's condition, it seems) and its better-known successor, Robert Burton's *The Anatomy of Melancholy* (1621). He believes that Lear's complaint would have been considered by early modern doctors to be an acute case of 'hypochondriac melancholy developing into mania', pointing out that Paracelsus considered such illnesses to be closely linked to unsettled weather conditions, notably thunderstorms, of the kind we see in the play (330). Burton describes this affliction as follows: 'There is a leaping all over their bodies, sudden trembling, a palpitation of the heart, and that grief in the mouth of the stomach, which makes a patient think his heart itself aches,' engendering a feeling of 'suffocation.' Burton continues, 'from these crudities windy vapours ascend to the brain, which trouble the imagination,' and 'enforce it to many absurd thoughts' (Vol. 1, 382–83). Other critics have suggested a range of alternative explanations for the King's suffering, including the idea that the division between his natural body and the body politic (the King's Two Bodies, as described in our second chapter) might be to blame for the fragmentation of his sense of self and overall mental health.

In fact Lear himself tells us what he believes to be the matter. On seeing his loyal nobleman Kent in the stocks quite early in the play he declares 'O, how this mother swells up toward my heart! | *Hysterica passio*, down, thou climbing sorrow' (2.2.246–47). Lear's reference to the 'mother' here evokes common medical parlance of the time, in which this term was used to refer to the condition more properly known in clinical reference texts as '*Hysterica passio*', the condition Mary Glover suffered from, as we encountered earlier in this chapter. Lear correctly glosses it in the following line, deriving the word from the Greek root '*hysterikos*', meaning 'from the womb'. In his popular treatise, *A Brief Discourse of a Disease called the Suffocation of the Mother*, Edward Jorden describes how 'This disease is called by diverse names amongst our Authors. Passio, Hysterica, Suffocatio, Praefocatio, and Strangulatus uteri, Caducus matricis, etc.,' which he translates as 'In English the Mother or the Suffocation of the Mother, because most commonly it takes them with choking in the throat: and it is an affect of the Mother or womb' (C1^r–C1^v). The conundrum of how and why Lear might think himself afflicted with what was, by definition, a female illness, has much preoccupied those critics of the play who wish to diagnose his malady. It remains a moot point whether he really does believe himself possessed of a womb in his rapidly deteriorating grasp upon reality, or rather is speaking metaphorically here. Scholars including Janet Adelman have pointed to the fact that one known case of male *hysterica passio* was documented in the literature of the period (300–301, n.27). Crucially, this appears in a text that has long since been established as a major source for *King Lear*, Samuel Harsnett's *A Declaration of Egregious Popish Impostures* (1603), from which much of Edgar's speech in his guise as Tom o'Bedlam is borrowed. In this polemical text attacking Catholic priests who continued the outlawed practice of exorcism, Harsnett (chaplain to the Bishop of London) tells the story of one Richard Mainy, who diagnosed himself as a sufferer of *hysterica passio*. Harsnett reprints Mainy's testimony describing his condition and symptoms as an appendix to the *Declaration*, and it became another notorious medical phenomenon in Shakespeare's London. As in the case of Lear, there is some doubt as to whether Mainy remains fully convinced he has a uterus, or whether he merely compares his illness to that arising from a malignancy in this organ. Furthermore, Peterson has suggested that Harsnett displays his own scepticism towards Mainy's account and that Shakespeare attributes a similar delusion to Lear in the expectation that his first audience would recognize the allusion as one to a known malingerer and fraud, therefore taking his mistaken self-diagnosis as yet another sign of the King's folly (61).

Bedlam in *King Lear*

The questions of the veracity of diagnoses of mental illness – brought into focus in Shakespeare's London by the infamous Mainy case – are also present in the play in another form, too. Having rejected Cordelia and been cast out by his other two daughters, Lear finds himself without shelter, protection or any of the trappings of power to which he has been accustomed. At this most humbling of moments he encounters the character of 'Poor Tom' (3.4.50), actually Gloucester's legitimate son and heir Edgar, whose bastard brother Edmund has attempted to discredit him, forcing him to flee and take on the disguise of a madman. In a transformational speech Edgar turns himself into this unhappy alter ego, an apparent resident of Bedlam, where we situate this chapter:

> My face I'll grime with filth,
> Blanket my loins, elf all my hair in knots
> And with presented nakedness outface
> The winds and persecutions of the sky.
> The country gives me proof and precedent
> Of Bedlam beggars, who, with roaring voices,
> Strike in their numbed and mortified bare arms
> Pins, wooden pricks, nails, sprigs of rosemary;
> And with this horrible object, from low farms,
> Poor pelting villages, sheepcotes and mills,
> Sometime with lunatic bans, sometime with prayers,
> Enforce their charity. Poor Turlygod, poor Tom,
> That's something yet: Edgar I nothing am.

(2.2.180–92)

In the course of this extraordinary soliloquy Edgar casts off his own identity, worth 'nothing' to him now, and instead takes on that of 'Poor Turlygod, poor Tom', a filthy, half-naked wretch. Both Edgar and Shakespeare himself take inspiration for this disguise from the 'Bedlam beggars' that were notorious in early modern London. The passage evokes the kind of display that was regularly witnessed by visitors to this hospital for the mentally ill during the period, with its inhabitants' blanketed 'loins', knotted hair, 'roaring voices', 'bare arms' and disturbed acts of self-mutilation (one way of thinking about Edgar's own transformation perhaps). The stark despair of this description allows Shakespeare to sharpen our wonder that even this woeful figure is 'something yet', when compared to the untenable position Edgar has been placed in by his brother.

Bedlam, or Bethlehem, Hospital (to give it its proper name) was in Shakespeare's day a relatively small institution of some 30 or so patients, each of whom possessed a willing sponsor prepared to underwrite the financial costs of their stay, including food and clothing. All its inmates had a form of mental illness considered to be treatable (the institution did not admit incurable lunatics owing to lack of space). Despite this mandate, treatment was of a minimal nature; very little by way of what we might today consider medical or therapeutic activity took place there, and only the bare necessities of care were provided. Until the later seventeenth century, when the Hospital moved to larger, purpose-built and widely admired premises at Moorgate, designed by Robert Hooke, the patients were housed in a cramped former priory. It was difficult to keep the male and female patients apart (with predictable results) and visitors were often appalled by the squalor. It is possible that Shakespeare was amongst a group of players who attended the nearby court at Bethlehem's sister institution, Bridewell, a prison that mainly housed men and women arrested for supposedly immoral behaviour or sexual crimes, and which was administered by the same governors as Bedlam from 1557 onwards. On 5 November 1602 the actor Christopher Beeston, one of the Lord Chamberlain's Men, appeared there, accused of having raped a woman. Accompanied by several members of the company he was brought before the Bridewell court to answer the charges of 'one Margaret White a prisoner of this house'. She alleged that he had 'committed with her the abominable sin of adultery in most filthy and brutish manner', forcing himself upon her in an attack that was said to have taken place locally 'in an alley without Bishopsgate on midsummer eve last' (Salkeld, 381). Critic Duncan Salkeld, who gives an account of the episode in a recent article, thinks it 'inconceivable that Shakespeare did not know of either the allegation of the Bridewell hearing', and goes so far as to suggest that the playwright was himself present amongst the group of players who jeered in the court and who offered vocal defence of their fellow actor (382). If this is the case we can tangibly place him within the world of Bedlam and its environs that we are describing here, and to which *King Lear* is indebted.

If Shakespeare had indeed attended this hearing at Bridewell shortly before composing *King Lear* he would have seen the comings and goings of the many visitors who came to the institution and the neighbouring Bedlam Hospital to witness the spectacle provided by notorious inmates such as Margaret White, who was accused of 'incontinent living' (Salkeld, 381). Visitors were an important part of the daily operations of the hospitals. In an era before government-funded healthcare or the commoditization of illness as an industry (which would follow with the establishment of private asylums in the eighteenth century), Bedlam relied entirely on charitable donations to fund its activities. Thus this London institution needed to be sure of eliciting sympathy for its patients and its mission from possible donors. Bedlam has long been thought of as a kind of tourist attraction in Shakespeare's city, and there is certainly some evidence that visitors to London sought out its particular display of abjection as a form of entertainment, to be gazed upon with a mixture of disgust, amusement, and relief at one's own comparatively blessed state. That Shakespeare reverses this pattern, having Edgar desire the lamentable fate of the Bedlam beggar as being preferable to his own condition, is intended as a measure of his deep despondency.

We might think usefully then about the relationship between Bedlam and the theatres of early modern London, and the ways in which Shakespeare plays upon this in *King Lear*. Some more recent critics have suggested that the number – and voyeuristic nature – of visitors to Bedlam during the sixteenth and early-seventeenth centuries has been exaggerated. Ken Jackson powerfully challenges the critical commonplace that the hospital was perceived as a place of amusement akin to the bear-baiting pit or even the theatre in Shakespeare's city.

Rather it seems that – exactly like going to the theatre, in fact – a visit to view the inmates of London's first hospital for the mentally ill was a more complicated undertaking, carefully managed by the governors of Bedlam in order to elicit a range of emotional responses. The picture is further complicated by the fact that, in the absence of other documentary evidence of what happened there, much of what we know of the place derives from early modern drama, which returns repeatedly to scenes set in, or referring to, the asylum. John Webster, John Fletcher, Thomas Middleton and Thomas Dekker all write plays featuring groups of lunatics behaving in ways reminiscent of those seen at Bedlam, while Dekker and Middleton's *The Honest Whore (Part One)* (1604) and Dekker's collaboration with Webster, *Northward Ho!* (1607) specifically include scenes set in Bedlam itself.

If the early modern theatre is interested in staging Bedlam, then the hospital is likewise eager to produce a display likely to ensure the maximum level of charitable generosity from its visitors. Just as Edgar here believes his disguise as Poor Tom may earn sympathy denied to him as Gloucester's son, so the Governors of the institution were similarly hoping to prevail upon spectators, to 'Enforce their charity', to borrow Shakespeare's words (in what seems almost an oxymoron; charity must be freely given in order to be truly charitable, one might argue). *King Lear* evokes the figure of the Bedlam beggar precisely in order to make the same plea for empathy amongst its audience members. The play's dramatic climax, as Lear is battered by storms upon the heath and 'this tempest in my mind' (3.4.12), is the moment when the King first begins to show feeling for his fellow man, prompted by his pity for Poor Tom. Having found himself placed in the position of those 'Poor naked wretches,' that 'bide the pelting of this pitiless storm,' with 'houseless heads and unfed sides,' and 'looped and windowed raggedness,' Lear immediately encounters one such lost soul, as if his wandering mind has conjured a spirit (3.4.28–31). He can only infer that Poor Tom must have suffered the same ordeal he himself has endured, asking 'Didst thou give all to thy two daughters? And art thou come to this?' (3.4.48–49). The appearance of Edgar disguised as a Bedlam beggar has enforced Lear's own charity, causing him to place himself in the shoes of another person, to imagine the suffering of another human being, for the first time in the play (and perhaps in his life). Charity – inspired by empathy – thus lies at the heart of Shakespeare's tragedy as it lies at the heart of the experience of visitors to Bedlam. Margreta De Grazia has pointed out that the title page of the first quarto edition of *King Lear* (1608) states that it was '*played before the Kings Majestie at Whitehall upon S. Stephens night*', 26 December, when the poor were entitled to hospitality (32). A day of enforced charity, in fact, when London's 'Poor naked wretches' had the right to the sympathy and sustenance that are denied to a king in the performance space at Whitehall.

This reversal of roles again brings us back to the idea of performativity in the play, and the sense that sanity and kingship, as much as mental illness and the guise of a Bedlam beggar, are all things that can be put on and just as easily cast off. Scholar Derek Peat has pointed out that while many of Shakespeare's dramatic contemporaries (such as those listed above) feature scenes of mental illness and even directly evoke Bedlam in their plays, he alone is preoccupied by the question of feigned or performed madness in his great tragedies, *Lear, Hamlet* and *Macbeth* (112). We might note that the figure of the Bedlam beggar in early modern London evoked not just actual inhabitants of the Bethleham Hospital but also those destitute men and women vagrants on the city's streets who pretended to be mentally ill inmates of the institution. Thomas Harman, author of *A Caveat for Common Cursitors* (1567) includes an image of a similar act of appropriation (D2ᵛ). There is some suggestion that Edgar's performance of madness reflects this recognized phenomenon; also known as an 'Abraham man', such figures 'feign themselves to have been mad, and have been kept either in Bethlehem, or in some other prison a good time,' writes Harman (D1ᵛ). Thus for Shakespearean critic William C. Carroll, Edgar's disguise

FIGURE 7 *From Thomas Harman's* A Caveat for Cursitors, &c. *(1567) (The Bodleian Libraries, The University of Oxford, 2698 d. 73, p.32)*

would have elicited suspicion amongst the play's early London audiences, as well as sympathy; for Elizabethans the figure of Poor Tom was 'a stereotype of the con-man' who merely pretends to be mad, and whose 'mug-shot' appeared regularly in 'the dozens of books, pamphlets, and royal decrees on the rogues and vagabonds of the kingdom,' he observes (431). Such figures were often described in terms very similar to the language used to depict actors in the period, emphasizing their use of costumes, rhetoric, gesture and make-believe. Edgar's choice of the Bedlam Beggar as his miserable alter ego thus provides Shakespeare with the opportunity to acknowledge commonly held misgivings about the nature of the theatre, a position particularly vehemently maintained by Puritans in early modern London. By presenting Poor Tom as the figure who eventually engenders pity and thus humanity in the king, Shakespeare subtly suggests that a form of salvation can be discovered within the theatre's 'wooden O'.

King Lear is a play particularly troubled by the idea that things may not be what they seem. The daughter who cannot speak of her love turns out to love the most, while those who initially perform devotion go on to display great cruelty. Much of the Fool's otherwise nonsensical dialogue speaks great wisdom about the dangers of hypocrisy. Edmund and Edgar are misjudged by those around them, and in fact are the moral opposites of how they first appear. A seemingly mad man (Poor Tom) leads the play's characters to a safer, more logical place. A blind man (Gloucester) comes to have true vision, albeit too late to save him. And a King loses all the trappings of his office, himself coming to resemble those 'Poor naked wretches' for whom he finally feels pity. In perhaps the play's most moving line of all, Lear quietly recognizes, 'I fear I am not in my perfect mind' (4.7.63). Lear's traumatic insight that he might not truly be himself displays a fear of going mad that could only be fully felt by the sane (a feeling that might have been very familiar to the actors who put on the identities of others on Shakespeare's stage). As he stares over the precipice he finds himself in a position shared by the many mentally ill inhabitants of early modern London, conscious that his own identity is being erased, subsumed by a greater affinity to humankind itself.

King Lear seems to suggest that it is only through great loss and suffering that we can find in ourselves true empathy for our fellow human beings. As such it has long been read as containing a moral message that deals in universals. It is often spoken of as the greatest of all tragic drama, by which admirers of Shakespeare's play seem to imply that its meaning has resonance for everybody who encounters it on the page or the stage. Yet, we have also seen, the play is written out of a very precise cultural moment in a particular place. This chapter has traced the relationship between *King Lear* and the medical world of Shakespeare's London, particularly the presence of the Bedlam Hospital in the play. The early seventeenth-century visitor to Bedlam, who sees its inhabitants stripped of their identities by both their conditions and the treatment afforded them under early modern medical practices, and who feels a sympathy that stems from a recognition of something shared that prompts them to an act of charity, mimics the journey of *King Lear*'s audiences, and of the play's great tragic protagonist himself.

7

Economics in Shakespeare's London:

Timon of Athens (1607) and the King's Bench Prison, Southwark

Introduction

In 1618, Geffray Minshull wrote a pamphlet describing an especially miserable location in Shakespeare's London. He calls this site 'a grave to bury men alive', a 'Microcosmus, a little world of woe', 'a place that has more diseases predominant in it, than the Pest-house in Plague-time' (B2^r) and the 'Bankrupt's banqueting-house, where he sits feasting with sweet meats borrowed from other men's tables' (B2^v). Minshull is describing the King's Bench Prison in Southwark where he had been imprisoned for debt the previous year. Like many Londoners, Minshull – a law student at Gray's Inn – found himself in financial difficulty and suffered under the harsh legislation that governed relationships between creditors and debtors in early modern England's developing economy. The King's Bench Prison was one of many penitentiary buildings that existed in Southwark, an area of London south of the river Thames that, as we know, also housed the Globe and several other playhouses. In this chapter we shall see how in *Timon of Athens* these Southwark neighbours – playhouse and debtors' prison – collide in Shakespeare's imagination to produce an emotionally compelling account of one man's financial woes that encouraged early modern Londoners to question the principles underpinning their changing economy.

Timon is a tragedy Shakespeare wrote in collaboration with fellow playwright Thomas Middleton in 1607. It tells a story that may well have resonated with Southwark prisoners like Minshull. Timon is a wealthy Athenian lord with lots of friends, whom he entertains with lavish banquets and gives to generously; he is also the patron of three artists, a poet, a painter and a jeweller. Only one of Timon's associates, the philosopher Apemantus, refuses his gifts and instead cynically exposes the superficial and mercantile nature of the protagonist's 'flatterers' (1.2.80). Apemantus' decision is proved right in the second half of the play when Timon's excessive lifestyle and misguided generosity have left him in debt. When he seeks financial help from his so-called friends they refuse him. Cursing them and the city, Timon heads into the wilderness, vowing to hate 'all humanity' (3.7.104). Meanwhile, soldier Alcibiades banished by the Athenian Senate (for defending a junior officer accused of murder), vows revenge against the city and likewise goes into exile. When Timon discovers gold in the forest and chances upon Alcibiades he offers to fund the soldier's assault on Athens. Timon exits for the last time in act five, scene two, saying he 'hath done his reign' (5.2.108). Unusually for a Shakespearean protagonist, he dies offstage; it is unclear whether he commits suicide or dies from what he calls his 'long sickness | Of health and living' (5.2.71–72). The play ends in tragedy as Alcibiades marches on the city and announces 'Dead | Is noble Timon' (5.5.77–78).

In portraying Timon's economic excesses and downfall, Shakespeare and Middleton infuse their play with the language of commerce used in the streets, shops, courts and indeed prisons of early modern London, with words like 'bond', 'credit' and 'debtor' recurring frequently throughout the play. Moreover, as we have found repeatedly throughout this book, a fictional locale (Athens) becomes a site to think through some of the most pressing issues facing Londoners in the period. In order to contextualize this play, we will explore the harsh reality of London's economy and the role that Southwark's theatres and prisons played in critiquing this cut and thrust financial world. In the first part of the chapter we will consider how the city's economy changed in the early modern period, and the ways that those developments are examined in *Timon of Athens*. The second part will address the very specific economics of the early modern playhouse, discovering how the world of credit and debt that Shakespeare and Middleton depict in the play was especially relevant to those working in London's theatre industry. In the final parts of the chapter we will explore Southwark, particularly the Globe and the King's Bench Prison, and see the way in which these locations influence the dramatists' portrayal of Timon's financial woes. Throughout the chapter we will consider how London's changing economy, as reflected in its prisons and playhouses, came to shape Shakespeare's collaborative tragedy.

Credit and debt in Shakespeare's London

In sixteenth-and seventeenth-century London debt became an increasingly pressing social issue, because of an emerging culture of credit and moneylending that came about as a result of rapid economic growth. Before this time financial relations had generally been limited and well-structured, consisting largely of small communities of individuals who exchanged services, products and gifts; such systems were headed by a wealthy landowner or patron who exercised overall financial control, and demanded deference and loyalty. In *Timon of Athens* Shakespeare and Middleton focus on this significant change in the manner of financial and social interaction brought about by economic growth. In a situation familiar to many Londoners, and especially those incarcerated at the King's Bench Prison, an Athenian Senator demands Timon repay a debt owed to him, instructing his servant 'Get on your cloak and haste you to Lord Timon | Importune him for my moneys' (2.1.15–16). The Senator needs the money because he in turn owes it to other people ('My uses cry to me'), and waiting for Timon to reimburse him has detrimentally affected his financial reputation: 'my reliances on his fracted dates | Have smit my credit' (2.1.20, 22–23). This web of financial entanglements is the opposite of a small, well-structured community-based system – instead, his interactions are complex and entirely depersonalized. Rather than a specific named creditor, a single individual, it is his 'uses' that cry to him, a series of debts ('uses' of money) that he owes to several people, probably strangers to him beyond this financial arrangement. The Senator claims to 'love and honour' Timon (2.1.22), but friendship is secondary to the anonymous, financial associations that govern his actions.

As economic historian Craig Muldrew points out, the early modern period saw a rapid growth in trading, markets and consumption, and the supply of gold and silver could not keep up with demand. With limited amounts of real currency in circulation, economic transactions increasingly relied on a culture of informal and socially based credit relations. Many financial interactions took place without the use of money; instead, verbal promises of credit or debt and written bonds were exchanged (as happens in *The Merchant of Venice*). This system was fuelled by economic expansion but also enabled further growth as large-scale financial transactions – such as the setting up of businesses, the purchasing of large quantities of goods and international trade – could take place more easily, not through the transfer of cumbersome amounts of currency but instead through credit and bonds. Like the Senator in *Timon of Athens* (who has multiple 'uses' or financial obligations), more and more early modern Londoners – including shopkeepers, craftsmen with businesses, merchants and consumers – were increasingly involved in interconnected exchanges of credit and debt. They were no longer financially involved with a limited number of neighbours, friends and members of their local community, as in the past, but rather linked to an ever-growing number of unknown, distant and even foreign individuals, with vastly different cultural attitudes to money.

In Shakespeare and Middleton's play, we see Timon lost in the same transition between two different systems of economic and social interaction that early modern London was still negotiating, failing to grasp the shift from a social economy, based on loyalty, to one that is depersonalized and commercial. In his first appearance, Timon enters mid-conversation, discussing a friend's financial problems:

TIMON   Imprisoned is he, say you?
MESSENGER   Ay, my good lord, five talents is his debt,
                His means most short, his creditors most strait.
                Your honourable letter he desires
                To those have shut him up, which failing,
                Periods his comfort.
TIMON   Noble Ventidius, well!
                I am not of that feather to shake off
                My friend when he most needs me. I do know him
                A gentleman that well deserves a help,
                Which he shall have. I'll pay the debt and free him.

                                                    (1.1.97–106)

In this initial exchange we encounter the economic language of transaction spoken in the shops and markets – as well as the debtors' prisons – of early modern London, which, as we shall see, proves important to Timon's tragedy. Ventidius owes 'five talents' (a unit of money based on the weight of gold or silver) to those who have lent him money. As he cannot pay his debt, his 'creditors' have exercised their right to imprison him; Ventidius is in the same position as those inmates of the King's Bench Prison who are detained by their creditors until their debts are paid. Luckily, he finds a way to secure his freedom though a 'letter' from his wealthy friend Timon that promises to pay his creditors. While the financial nature of this exchange is made explicit here, Timon views the episode in an entirely different way. For him, his actions are motivated by a sense of friendship and honour, rather than the mechanisms of credit and debt. 'Noble Ventidius' is a 'friend', a 'gentleman' who 'needs' Timon. His response emphasizes social and emotional ties, drawing attention to Ventidius' status and their personal connections. Moreover, Timon attributes Ventidius' decision to ask him for help to his personal reputation, rather than his economic standing: 'I am not of that feather to shake off | My friend', he states. Timon's payment of his friend's debt is bound up with his self-identity, serving to demonstrate that he is of a different 'feather' (character) to other, presumably less generous or honourable, members of the community. As we will discover, the tragedy of the play is the fact that Timon is out of step with his contemporaries, specifically the new exacting economic reality that they have embraced. He still thinks in terms of an economy that links wealth with friendship, patronage and honour.

Middleton and Shakespeare expand upon this point a few lines later. An Old Athenian comes to Timon to complain that Lucilius, one of Timon's servants, has been courting his daughter. This situation is unsatisfactory to him as he believes that Lucilius is too poor to marry his wealthy daughter:

> One only daughter have I, no kin else
> On whom I may confer what I have got.
> The maid is fair, o'th' youngest for a bride,
> And I have bred her at my dearest cost.

(1.1.124–27)

In his choice of vocabulary, the Old Athenian reveals the economic interests underpinning his position. He is concerned with where his fortune ('what I have got') is bestowed and notes the money ('cost') he has already spent on bringing his daughter up. The word 'bred' is also significant here. It is usually animals such as cattle who are owned and reared, or 'bred', for profit, a verb that reveals the way this father considers his daughter as a profitable financial asset, like livestock. These lines remind us that early modern marriage was another kind of economic transaction. Yet Timon fails to recognize the fiscal concerns underlying the Old Athenian's statement. With considerable naivety, he notes that Lucilius is 'honest' (1.1.131) and asks whether the young couple love one another. Timon is interested in Lucilius' moral rather than his monetary worth, seeing marriage as a question of emotion rather than economics. Assured of the couple's affection he offers to match the Old Athenian's estate and give Lucilius a 'fortune' (1.1.147) of his own.

Such an act, Timon notes, represents 'a bond in men' that embodies the more humane economy he prefers to inhabit (1.1.148). Timon's unknowing alienation from the economic ethos of his society is especially apparent in his use of the word 'bond' here. As we saw in Chapter 4, in the economy of early modern London the word 'bond' was a contract between creditor and debtor. Bonds were the financial arrangement that fuelled London's prosperity while also trapping many into crushing debts. Indeed, Timon later finds himself in debt because his creditors demand that his 'bonds' are paid back (2.1.34). However, Timon uses this financial term in its earlier, non-financial, sense in his dialogue with the Old Athenian. In these early moments of the play Timon makes clear that for him, a 'bond' is the emotional and social connection between individuals that keeps societies together. The tragic drama will chart Timon's gradual, and extremely painful, realization that it is rather economic bonds of the sort that increasingly governed social constructs in Shakespeare's London that link his society, not those of friendship that he (misguidedly) places his faith in here. Shakespeare and Middleton thus permit Timon to voice nostalgia for an older economic system and may therefore implicitly critique the emerging economy that jeopardises the value of human loyalty their protagonist espouses at the start of the play.

At the same time, this narrative is complicated by Timon's foolhardy financial dealings, which contribute to his own downfall and thus affect the extent to which we can sympathize with this character. The protagonist's naivety persists even when he finds himself in debt and, perhaps for some members of the audience, becomes more akin to wilful self-delusion. For instance, he tells his servant Flavius not to worry about his financial problems:

> If I would broach the vessels of my love
> And try the argument of hearts by borrowing,
> Men and men's fortunes could I frankly use
> As I can bid thee speak.

> (2.2.177–80)

In emotionally heightened language, Timon argues that he can easily appeal to the 'hearts' of his friends in order to obtain money ('men's fortunes'). Unlike any other character in the play, Timon discusses financial interactions in elaborate and emblematic terms. He uses a shipping metaphor as he imagines approaching his friends here: in sailing terms, 'broach' describes a vessel or ship, veering into the wind. Timon believes he could as easily change the course of his friendships by asking for money, because they are full of affection ('vessels of love'). This metaphor is not only a somewhat obscure and sentimental way of discussing a loan, but also rather unusually associates the language of shipping with friendship and love. As a prosperous trade central to London's economy, shipping was at the forefront of the city's rapid fiscal development and integral to the emerging system of credit and debt we have already described. Timon again shows he is at odds with his society by conceiving of this flourishing early modern industry in personal and emotional terms. In contrast, those around him firmly separate money and trade from love and friendship. Lucullus, for example, refuses to help Timon, noting 'this is no time to lend money, especially upon bare friendship without security' (3.1.41–43). Whereas bonds between men are central to Timon's personal economy, in which financial and social interactions are seen as absolute opposites, to Lucullus friendship is 'bare' without financial guarantees and the two sets of values are inextricably linked. In this way Middleton and Shakespeare force Timon (and with him their audiences) to confront the questions and contradictions arising from London's changing economy and its impact on self-identity, friendship and society. Next we consider why such issues were especially pertinent to both playwrights and the industry in which they worked, and how they manifest themselves in the staging of the play.

Theatre economics

For those who worked in the early modern theatre, like Shakespeare and Middleton, debt and subsequent imprisonment were a surprisingly regular occurrence. Amanda Bailey has shown that borrowing money (and the risks associated with such an undertaking) was integral to the way in which actors, playwrights and theatre managers ran both their personal finances and theatrical businesses. Members of the theatre community often had to take out loans in order to fund expensive projects; most obviously the construction of playhouses, such as the Globe, but also necessary expenditures such as props and costumes. The account book of Philip Henslowe (who, we learnt in our introduction, owned the Rose theatre) gives us some insight into playhouse economics in Shakespeare's London. His inventory of costumes and props demonstrates the significant investments theatre companies made to achieve an impressive stage aesthetic. Henslowe details rich clothing such as 'damask', 'silk', 'cloth of gold' and 'velvet', and in some cases pays as much £20 for a single item; this is an extraordinary amount of money if we consider that Henslowe paid playwrights on average £3 for writing a play for the Rose. With such outgoings, it is easy to see how financial difficulties were an occupational hazard in an industry where income was by no means regular. Theatrical success depended on sustaining public popularity and audience numbers in an ever-competitive market in which several playhouses now competed for revenues. But it also depended on avoiding disasters: playhouses were sometimes destroyed by fire (the Globe and the Fortune both burnt down), damaged by rioting audience members (the Red Bull suffered this fate), closed by authorities for performances deemed seditious (as the Blackfriars playhouse was in 1608) or shut down entirely to avoid the spread of plague (this happened to all playhouses in London quite regularly).

Playing was financially precarious to say the least and it is little wonder that in this climate playwrights and actors Ben Jonson, George Chapman, Henry Chettle, Robert Daborne, Thomas Dekker, William Haughton, John Lyly, John Marston, Philip Massinger and Cyril Tourneur found themselves incarcerated for debt on more than one occasion; Middleton himself was held in custody for being unable to repay £5 he owed in 1608 and his father had spent time in debtors' prison too. As far as we know Shakespeare was never imprisoned for debt, although his father John did have serious financial problems in the late 1570s and was forced to mortgage property in order to raise funds. In addition, as we learned in Chapter 4, Shakespeare had experienced financial difficulties with the Lord Chamberlain's Men over their disastrous legal bond with Francis Langley of the Swan; he must have been familiar with the economic vicissitudes of his industry. It is Thomas Dekker, however, who provides perhaps the most extreme example of a theatrical career marred by debt. Despite his success with plays such as *The Shoemaker's Holiday* (1599) and *The Honest Whore* ([c.1605–6] a collaboration with Middleton), Dekker found himself imprisoned at the King's Bench for a debt of £40 in 1612. He would spend the next seven years in jail, during which time his wife died and his playwriting career was effectively frozen. In Dekker's own words this period was a 'long sleep, which for almost seven years together, seized all my senses,' he writes, 'burying me to the World, in the lowest grave of Oblivion' (*Dekker His Dream* [1620], A4ʳ). As this text demonstrates, however, he did turn to writing about his personal experience, seeking to capitalize on his troubles. His output during these years, to which we will return, gives us an insight into the emotional impact of debt imprisonment upon early modern Londoners. Dekker was not the only writer to generate income from personal hardship in this way. Plays about debt and debtors' prisons (such as *Every Man Out of His Humour* [1599], *Eastward Ho!* [1605] and *The Roaring Girl* [c.1607–10]) became very popular during the seventeenth century and, as recent research by Ruth Ahnert suggests, prison literature became its own very well-read genre during this time.

When Shakespeare and Middleton explore economic changes, debt and its impact in *Timon of Athens* they thus address issues relevant to their industry, as well as London at large, and contribute to a growing body of plays dealing with this subject. For Shakespeare, Middleton may well have been an obvious choice of writing partner for co-creating a play that examined London's changing economy. Aside from his first-hand experience of debt, Middleton's previous plays are also particularly concerned with the economic realities of urban life. Not long before starting *Timon*, he had written *A Trick to Catch the Old One* (1605) a play about two rival London merchants and their financial scamming. In *Michaelmas Term* (1605/5) Middleton also centres his plot on corrupt financial practices in early modern London. Middleton, therefore, had already begun to articulate the difficulties arising from the city's increasingly credit-based economy. Furthermore, the younger playwright also had experience of writing for Shakespeare's company at the Globe: in 1605 the King's Men performed his *A Yorkshire Tragedy* (c.1605–6) and a year later, *The Revenger's Tragedy* (1606).

In the new play Middleton co-wrote with Shakespeare for the King's Men in 1607, Timon's fortune is invoked by a rich visual and acoustic aesthetic that draws on and exhibits the King's Men's impressive inventory of costume and props. The play opens with a Poet, Painter and Jeweller discussing their wealthy patron, Timon, and showing off their works (a dedicatory poem, a painting and a jewel), which they hope he will purchase. There is a particular irony to the whole scene, of course, as Middleton and Shakespeare were both poets who wrote for wealthy patrons. Benefiting from their association with James I's theatre company, the playwrights also received patronage from the City of London (Middleton regularly wrote pageants for the Lord Mayor) and the Earl of Southampton (to whom Shakespeare dedicated his early narrative poems, as we saw in Chapter 2). *Timon* constitutes a self-conscious portrait of the cynical and sycophantic relationships patronage might produce in its least attractive forms.

The sensory decadence of *Timon*'s opening continues as the play progresses. Timon's friends enter to the sound of '*Oboes playing loud music*' and encounter a '*great banquet*' (1.2.1); later a trumpet flourish announces the arrival of Cupid, followed by '*a masque of* Ladies' dressed as '*Amazons, with lutes in their hands, dancing and playing*' (1.2.129). Masques, as we have seen, were generally performances for royalty or aristocracy, involving music, dance and elaborate classical references. In order to emulate the wealth usually associated with such performances on the Globe stage actors wore rich and expensive costumes, like those detailed in Henslowe's account books.

After the masque, Timon calls for 'Lights, more lights!' (1.2.235). Candles were another costly item: the number an early modern Londoner could afford to burn to light his house of an evening was a sign of his prosperity, or lack of it. At the King's Men's indoor theatre, the Blackfriars, where they performed from 1609 onwards (and which we examine in the next chapter), Shakespeare's company certainly demonstrated their own affluence; the theatre's impressive candlelight was noted in several contemporary descriptions. Performed at the Globe in 1607, *Timon of Athens* brings the expensive aesthetic of indoor candlelight to the outdoor playhouse in a way that anticipates the players' acquisition of the Blackfriars. The play may well have been written with the knowledge that performing regularly in an indoor theatre would soon be a possibility; it certainly would have suited the space if performed there after the company took up residence at their indoor venue a couple of years later. The first few scenes of the play thus create one of the more conspicuous displays of material culture to be found on the stages of early modern London, of a kind that audiences would soon come to expect once players began to move inside.

As we have established, Middleton and Shakespeare had significant experience of the precarious nature of the theatre industry, and the way in which financial success could be as illusionary and fleeting as performance itself. In a reflection of this insecurity, the rest of *Timon of Athens* offers a striking contrast to its opening act. Here we enter the world of poverty where Timon is consumed and eventually destroyed by his financial problems. In opposition to the visual decadence of act one, the stage now becomes filled with the visual symbols of debt: Timon's loyal servant Flavius enters with 'many bills in hand' (2.2.0); the Senator's servant hands Timon 'a note of certain dues' (2.2.19); Flavius goes begging to Timon's friends with 'an empty box' that needs filling with money (3.1.16) and stepping out of his house Timon is presented with 'bills' from various creditors (3.4.83–87). In the most direct contrast with the opening act, Timon holds another banquet but this time serves dishes of 'lukewarm water' (3.7.88). Tricking his so-called 'friends' into one last feast, he confronts their 'reeking villainy' (3.7.92). Flavius also encourages us to reassess the extravagance seen in act one; complaining about Timon's debts, he points out that 'every room | Hath blazed with lights' (2.2.160–61). The word 'blaze' here, used to describe Timon's excessive use of candlelight, associates these actions with destructive fire, evoking the way in which he has been destroyed by his lavishness.

Dekker tells us that the greater a man's 'possessions are, the apter he is to take up and to be trusted: the more he is trusted, the more he comes in debt', and so a man is 'undone' (*Lanthorne and Candlelight* [1609], F2^r). The debt-ridden playwright suggests that the wealthier a gentleman appears – when judged by his possessions and other trappings of financial success – the more likely it his spending is funded by loans, and thereby the more prone he is to sink further into debt. Many such gentlemen were incarcerated at the King's Bench Prison because their extravagant lifestyle had caught up with them. Timon is a portrait of the excessive consumerist who ends up in financial difficulty of the kind described by Dekker and readily witnessed in Shakespeare's city.

Southwark: Outside the City walls

In 1599 Thomas Platter, whom we met in our introduction, took a journey 'over the water' to the 'strewn-roof house' and saw a play (Platter, 365). Like many who visited Southwark's Globe, this Swiss tourist had to cross the river Thames by boat or by walking across London Bridge. If he glanced over his shoulder while making the crossing he would have seen London's very well-developed north bank spread out behind him, including all the locations we have thus far encountered in this book: Tyburn, Westminster, the Strand, the Inns of Court, St Paul's and Bedlam Hospital. The City of London also stood north of the river – the walled legal and civic entity ruled by the Lord Mayor and his council. Looking to the south, things looked very different. Here, as we also noted in our introduction, there was more green land and fewer buildings than in the north. As Platter got closer to the south bank of the river, he would have seen the Globe, Bear Gardens, George Inn and Holland's Leaguer brothel (famed for its Dutch prostitutes). The governors of the City tried as hard as possible to push these kinds of illicit and frivolous activities well outside its walls, and so it is on London's outskirts, in neighbourhoods such as Southwark, that we find playing, along with prostitution, drinking, gambling and animal baiting. Many critics have identified early modern Southwark as an especially seedy locale; Steven Mullaney argues that such areas outside the City wall were underworlds where laws and regulations were uncertain if not suspended.

In *Timon of Athens*, Shakespeare and Middleton imaginatively explore the implications of Southwark's position outside the City walls. Debt-ridden Timon directs his anger at the corrupt metropolis in which amoral values have been allowed to thrive: 'Burn house, sink Athens, henceforth hated be | Of Timon man and all humanity!' (3.7.103–4). He imagines his city as a corrupt house, but also a sinking ship; and vows to hate all humanity, grandiosely speaking of himself in the third person. With these lines Timon's transformation from generous socialite to misanthropic outsider begins; yet it is only when he has physically left the city (in act four, scene one) that Timon expounds upon his hatred of Athens and achieves the detachment from its society that his new cynical persona demands. In the play's most famous speech, Timon rants against the city wall that surrounds Athens, deriding and disowning those who conduct their business within: 'O thou wall | That girdles in those wolves' (4.1.1–2). Perhaps like those early modern Londoners who left the City and entered Southwark seeking a particular kind of illicit entertainment, Timon's mind turns to corrupted sexuality once outside the walls. His anger against Athenian society is increasingly combined with images of sexual promiscuity, lascivious behaviour and venereal disease; Timon hopes that 'Matrons, turn incontinent' (4.1.3), or become sexually debauched; he orders maids 'to thy master's bed', imagining their 'mistress is o'th' brothel' (4.1.12–13); and wishes 'lust and liberty | Creep in the minds and marrows' of the city's 'youth' (4.1.25–26). Timon's language and imagery here suggest he has entered a seedy underworld, at odds with the normative values of Athenian society, much as the south bank was figured as embracing an alternative morality (or even dispensing with it altogether) in Shakespeare's London.

   Timon's position also reflects upon that of the Globe theatre
itself, in which audiences likewise found themselves outside
their own city wall. Gazing back at the well-developed north
bank of London, Southwark offered a critical distance and a
space for reflection, as well as being a place for entertainment.
The Globe audience might not share Timon's anger – or his
predicament – but we may well discern in this scene a playful
blurring between fictional and playhouse locales. Existing
outside of their respective city walls, both the setting of the
play's latter scenes and the location of Shakespeare's theatre
allows them to function as a place from which the society they
look back on can be scrutinized. As such, *Timon of Athens* has
much in common with several other Shakespeare plays –
including *A Midsummer Night's Dream, As You Like It, King
Lear, Cymbeline* and *The Winter's Tale* – in which characters
escape a civilized but often disturbed city, or court, to find
emotional distance and contemplation outside, in woods or
other natural settings.

   There were then unsavoury aspects of many parts of
Southwark, and Timon's sexually corrupted language perhaps
reflects this particular characteristic of the area. But, as we have
seen throughout this book, Shakespeare's London – like the city
today – was an ambiguous and complex place. A single location
had multiple and frequently contradictory identities – the
Strand was the home of the rich and fashionable, as well as
servants and apprentices; St Paul's was both a sacred and
secular focal point; Bedlam was a hospital as well as a place of
entertainment. Southwark was similarly multifaceted. It was
governed by a disorganized mixture of different authorities, as
historians such as Valerie Pearl and David Johnson have
explained. Although well outside the walls and separated by the
river Thames a part of Southwark fell under the jurisdiction of
the City of London and was known as the 'twenty-sixth ward
of Bridge Without'. In 1550, the City had taken over much of
the land around modern-day Borough High Street. The Globe
existed in a different, but adjacent, area known as the Clink,
which was controlled by the Bishop of Winchester, while other

parts of Southwark were ruled by another governing body, the Justices of Surrey, whose somewhat lax governance may be one of the reasons why illicit activities such as prostitution flourished there. In this part of Shakespeare's London, therefore, the interests of these differing civic bodies – the City of London, the Bishop of Winchester and the Justices of Surrey – coexisted, competed with and undoubtedly contradicted one another. While authority and control was consequently somewhat confused here it would be a mistake to assume that the area was ungoverned and ungovernable, as has often been maintained. Even outside the walls of the City it was impossible to entirely escape the social and political structures governing Shakespeare's London, as Timon discovers in relation to his own city.

Despite his rejection of Athens' values and its citizens, Timon finds himself drawn back into its environs when, searching for food, he instead finds gold:

> Earth, yield me roots
>
> [*Digs in the earth*]
>
> Who seeks for better of thee, sauce his palate
> With thy most operant poison. – What is here?
> Gold? Yellow, glittering, precious gold?
>
> (4.3.23–26)

Although he is outside the city walls, Timon's discovery of the gold suggests the inescapable power of the economic system that he has tried to leave behind. The fact that even Athens' wilderness yields gold rather than roots, plants or other natural sustenance suggests the city's unhealthy obsession with money. Middleton and Shakespeare are playing here with the Biblical phrase 'Money is the root of all evil' (1 Timothy 6:10): searching for plant 'roots' to eat, Timon instead finds gold, the symbolic root of his tragedy, as well as that of many others, he hints. In lines that may imply a critique of the excessive power gold holds within an emerging capitalist society, Timon laments its capacity to turn 'Black white, foul fair, wrong right | Base noble, old young, coward valiant' (4.1.29–30). By listing these pairs of opposing abstract adjectives and nouns, Timon very starkly evokes the bewildering influence that money has in his world, and in Shakespeare's London.

Timon's rediscovered wealth means that those he left in Athens soon seek him out. A Senator comes to offer Timon an apology: 'The senators with one consent of love | Entreat thee back to Athens' (5.2.25–26). In language deliberately designed to appeal to Timon as he was before his troubles, the message from the senate entreats Timon to return with 'love' and offers him 'special dignities' (5.2.27), titles conferring honour and status, if he does return. Imitating Timon's rhetoric at the beginning of the play, the Senator does not mention debt, credit or money at all, but attempts to manipulate him by evoking those ideals of loyalty, nobility and honour he previously espoused. Yet the events of the play have caused Timon to reject his previous values, hence his negative reply: 'Lend me a fool's heart and a woman's eyes | And I'll beweep these comforts, worthy senators' (5.2.42–43). With a combination of sarcasm and sexism (only a fool would believe such 'comforts'; only a woman would respond to it with tears) Timon exposes the senator's manipulative sentimentalism. But the line has an underlying poignancy too; in a reversal of the character trajectory undergone by King Lear, Timon's misanthropy means he is now without a heart and has closed his eyes to humanity. Above all, this exchange reveals the inescapability of the Senate's authority and insidiousness of its attempts to control him. Like Londoners in Southwark, Timon finds that being outside the city walls means occupying a somewhat ambiguous space that offers only an illusion of true liberty.

Southwark's prisons

In the final part of this chapter we wish to turn to one very specific place in early modern Southwark whose presence pervades Middleton and Shakespeare's play: the King's Bench

Prison. In *The Praise and Virtue of a Jail and Jailers* (1623), poet John Taylor lists 'Jails or Prisons full eighteen' in early seventeenth-century London: the Tower, the Gatehouse, the Fleet, Newgate, Ludgate, Poultry Counter, Wood Street Counter, Bridewell, the White Lion, the King's Bench, Marshalsea, the Southwark Counter, the Clink, St Katherine's, East Smithfield, New Prison, Lord Wentworth's and Finsbury. Taylor notes that of these, 'Five jails are in Southwark placed', namely the Clink, Southwark Prison, the Marshalsea, the King's Bench and the White Lion (B3^v). Here we have another example of Southwark's contrariness: alongside those places of illicit and illegal activity already explored in this chapter were sites of correction, authority and control. The area known as the Clink perhaps best exemplifies Southwark's contradictions, a place in which the Globe, several animal baiting arenas and a number of brothels stood close to the Clink prison. One can visit the site of the prison today, a tourist attraction with a museum, and wander a few minutes along the Thames to find the Globe, gaining one's own sense of the opposing characteristics of Shakespeare's Southwark. The proximity of the dark and claustrophobic entrance of the Clink to the brighter, more expansive location of the Globe on the river hints at the complexities of early modern Southwark.

Southwark's prisons held Londoners incarcerated for a variety of crimes, including theft, assault, slander and vagrancy. It is, however, the so-called debtors' prison, the King's Bench that is of particular relevance to our interpretation of *Timon of Athens*. This penitentiary was situated on the east side of Borough High Street (today the area is known as Angel Place, just near the church of St George the Martyr). Established in the 1380s, the prison took its name from the court that it originally served – the King's Bench was one of England's earliest law courts dealing with both criminal and civil cases. By Shakespeare's lifetime, it had become a prison exclusively for those in debt or declaring bankruptcy. From the fourteenth century, the legal system enabled creditors who were owed money to have their debtors arrested (much as Shylock does to

Antonio in *The Merchant of Venice*). This extreme measure –
or the threat of it – enabled creditors to coerce their debtors
into payment. It also meant that the debtor could not abscond
before the debt was paid; instead they were effectively held
captive until a financial settlement could be reached.

This system flourished because of a quirk of the law that
meant the estate and goods of a debtor were protected against
his creditor, who could only claim the debtor's liberty, in effect
his personhood or body. The body of the debtor, rather than
their goods, thus stood as substitute for the debt owed. As a
consequence, the prison writings of both Dekker and Minshull
often imagine the creditor or jailer as a cannibal, physically
feeding off the debtor. For Minshull, the creditor is 'bloody-
minded' (B4^r) in claiming the debtor's body; similarly the jailer
'has a devilish stomach for he eats men' (G4^r). Dekker is even
more explicit in his descriptions of the prisoner: 'he is a kind of
dead carcass – creditors, lawyers, and jailers devour it,' he
writes ('A Prisoner', P2^r). For Dekker the creditor is a violent
predator, who 'has a quick scent to smell out his game, and a
good deep mouth to pursue it, yet never opens till he bites, and
bites not till he kills, or at least draws blood, and then he
pinches most doggedly' ('A Creditor', P3^v–P4^r). Middleton and
Shakespeare employ the same metaphor of cannibalism as a
figure for economic interaction in *Timon of Athens*. The
philosopher Apemantus, who alone sees through Timon's false
friends, recognizes that this wealthy man is a sacrificial figure,
figuratively and financially consumed by those around him.
When asked to dinner by Timon he declines the invitation
noting, 'I eat not lords' (1.1.207), a cryptic rejection of the
system of noble patronage. Apemantus wishes to distinguish
himself from those members of Athenian society who depend
upon Timon's financial support, continuing to 'feed | Most
hungrily' on his hospitality (1.1.258–59) and to 'taste Lord
Timon's bounty' (1.1.281). Apemantus does stay to observe
the banquet, however, and his use of cannibalistic imagery
becomes yet more explicit: 'It grieves me to see so many dip
their meat in one man's blood, and all the madness is, he cheers

them up too' (1.2.41–42). In consuming Timon's wealth in this way, these so-called friends are figured as feeding off a willing victim. Timon's servant Flavius also notes the way his master is devoured by those around him. He warns 'Happier is he that has no friend to feed' (1.2.206), and scolds Timon for hosting 'riotous feeders' (2.2.159). Faced with his mounting debts, Timon begins to employ similar cannibalistic imagery when talking about himself. In an unmistakable echo of Shylock's attempts to extract his pound of flesh from Antonio in *The Merchant of Venice*, he tells his creditors 'Cut my heart into sums', 'Tell out my blood', 'Tear me, take me' (3.4.90, 92, 97). Like other early modern debtors, Timon's person and his debt become one; his body becomes a substitute for the money he owes. And so, while Timon is not imprisoned for debt, he is bound by the language and imagery of the debtors' prison.

For those held at the King's Bench, imprisonment for debt was often completely ineffectual as, without liberty, debtors were unable to work and re-pay the money they owed. The cost of imprisonment often resulted in further debt: like all early modern prisoners, including the inhabitants of Bedlam we encountered in our previous chapter, debtors had to pay for their lodgings, food and clothing. Prison officers had no salary but instead earned money by providing services to prisoners, or accepting bribes in return for improved living arrangements. Within the system there was a social hierarchy, with wealthier prisoners paying for accommodation in the Master's Ward, those with less money buying a bed in the Two-Penny Ward and the poorest and most unfortunate imprisoned in the ominously nicknamed 'Hole'. Sometimes odd situations arose whereby it was cheaper for a debtor to pay to live in relatively comfortable prison accommodation than it was to pay off his debts, be released and face the economic realities of life outside prison. On the other end of the economic scale, prisoners who could not afford basic accommodation and sustenance fees had to surrender their cloaks and other items of clothing. Writing on early modern London's prisons, Jean Howard notes that this loss of clothing (as the prisoner found themselves moving down the accommodation hierarchy) became a frequent trope in writing by prisoners. Moreover in plays about debtors' prison it was often the case that the character in debt would appear in shabby clothes, having lost the expensive outfits that they initially wore. In *Timon of Athens*, Middleton and Shakespeare emulate this textual and performance trope. As we have seen, when Timon exits the city and rants against its wall he rejects every aspect of its society in a long diatribe. Part of this speech includes the vow, 'Nothing I'll bear from thee | But nakedness, thou detestable town' (4.1.32–33). Editors and actors of the play have generally agreed that during this extended tirade Timon strips off his clothes, the most obvious symbols of his prior financial and social status, choosing to live naked in the woods. This image – of the actor's exposed body onstage – provides a stark and poignant contrast to the opulence of the banquet seen in the first half of the play, as well as offering another point of comparison to the nearly naked Tom o'Bedlam in *King Lear*, one of many similarities between the two tragedies that have led some scholars to suggest that the plays may have a closer relationship than usually thought, or even that the collaborative *Timon* could be an earlier prototype for Shakespeare's tragedy.

While he writes compassionately and movingly of such destitution, Shakespeare himself enjoyed an unusually lucrative dramatic career. In 1597 he bought New Place, a large and relatively expensive property in Stratford-upon-Avon, just one of several financial investments he made during his lifetime. Indeed in 1613, just three years before his death, he purchased a house in the Blackfriars near his company's indoor theatre (a place we will visit in our next chapter). In London's developing economy Shakespeare himself therefore represented a somewhat unexpected success story and it is perhaps unlikely that he would write a play that would entirely condemn the system that had brought him such gains. Yet in *Timon of Athens* the playwright imagines the opposite of his own healthy financial situation, perhaps recalling the experiences of his collaborator, Middleton, as well as his own father's financial troubles (John Shakespeare fell into debt in the 1570s, Peter Holland recounts in his entry on the playwright for the *Oxford Dictionary of National Biography*). Together both dramatists examine the most extreme and unhappy consequences of early modern London's credit and debt culture. Timon's story echoes that of many who found themselves imprisoned in the King's Bench Prison – destitute, disillusioned and devoured by the society that surrounds them. The sympathy early modern Londoners felt for Timon, tempered by frustration at his self-delusion, may thus have been designed to encourage audiences to critically evaluate London's past and present economy. With its increasing reliance on bonds rather than the exchange of currency, growing consumerism and international trade, the finances of Shakespeare's city represent the beginnings of the capitalist system in which we now live. The popularity of the National Theatre's 2012 production of *Timon of Athens*, with Simon Russell Beale in the title role, may owe some of its popularity to the fact that in an age of 'credit crunch', 'debt management' and 'bond markets', modern Londoners, especially those who work in the city's financial district, find the play particularly resonant.

8

Experimentation in Shakespeare's London:

The Tempest (1610–11) and Lime Street

Introduction

The publication of *The Theatre of Insects* – appearing under the Latin title *Insectorum sive minimorum animalium theatrum* in 1634 – allowed early modern readers to explore the natural environment that surrounded them in England in microscopic and hitherto unprecedented detail, while simultaneously introducing exotic creatures from elsewhere in the world. With chapters on bees, wasps, flies, hornets, silkworms, woodlice, scorpions and butterflies, amongst other species, the book is an important early publication in the field of natural science. For example, there are several detailed drawings of butterflies, shown with wings open and closed, the elaborate patterns on their wings etched out in black and white; surrounding the sketches are detailed descriptions in Latin describing each species and their unique differences. This impressive collaborative book includes the work of Thomas Moffet (1553–1604), who provided much of the accompanying text and is credited as its author on the title page, alongside the illustrations of Thomas Penny (*c.*1530–1589).

Moffet and Penny were residents of Lime Street, the centre of
scientific experimentation and research in early modern London
and the penultimate location in our journey across Shakespeare's
city.

Lime Street was situated in the east of the city, running from
Fenchurch Street in the south to Leadenhall Street in the north.
A visitor to the street today would find the home of the
insurance company Lloyd's of London: architect Richard
Rogers' skyscraper inspired by the Pompidou Centre in France.
In Shakespeare's time, Lime Street contained equally notable
buildings; John Stow describes its 'divers fair houses for
merchants and others' (142). In these houses lived pioneers
such as Moffet, Penny and others including scholar James
Cole (1563–1625), botanist Mathias de L'Obel (1538–1616)
and historian Emmanuel van Meteren (1535–1612). These
men strove to describe, analyse and understand the natural
world both in England and further afield. Their influential
work on animals, plants, insects and minerals meant that from
this small street in a corner of London they contributed to, and
helped to shape, the key scientific debates of their time.

Much like these Lime Street residents Shakespeare also
addresses changing understandings of the natural world in *The
Tempest*. Written in 1611, *The Tempest* tells the story of
Prospero, the rightful Duke of Milan, who has been ousted by
his brother Antonio and lives on an island with his daughter
Miranda and his servants, Ariel and Caliban. Using his powers
of enchantment, or 'Art', he orchestrates a storm and the
shipwreck of a vessel containing Antonio, Alonso the King of
Naples, his son Ferdinand and his court. The play sees Prospero
engineer a series of magical encounters and happenings on the
island involving those shipwreck survivors, culminating in the
restoration of his own dukedom and a marriage between
Miranda and Ferdinand. After a detailed exploration of early
modern Lime Street, this chapter will consider how
Shakespeare's play draws on differing types of scientific
knowledge circulating around his city. We will then focus on
Prospero's magic in more detail, suggesting the ways in which

Shakespeare's character would not seem out of place amongst Lime Street's residents. Throughout the chapter, but especially in the final section, we will see how Shakespeare treats this play, one of his last, as a laboratory in which to stage his own theatrical experiment, utilizing the resources of the indoor Blackfriars theatre, newly acquired by the King's Men and now at his disposal.

Lime Street

In *The Jewel House: Elizabethan London and the Scientific Revolution* Deborah E. Harkness offers a study of the Lime Street community that demonstrates the ways that their work laid the foundations for the scientific revolution of the following centuries. Harkness outlines this enclave as a fairly sparsely populated, quiet area of London, but one with international reach – a communication hub and intellectual base for those interested in the natural world. We can imagine its spacious gardens, where plant specimens were grown, examined and stored, and the houses where experiments and discussions took place. Perhaps there might be an excited buzz as members of the community returned from fieldwork abroad; the group travelled extensively around England and Europe, gathering observations of, and specimens from, the natural world. Or a letter might arrive from abroad, enclosing exciting new natural objects that the recipient could show off. Harkness describes James Cole taking delivery of a spider specimen, a sketch of a rhinoceros horn and some sunflower seeds from his uncle in Antwerp, for instance (30–31).

Stepping inside one of the fine houses noted by Stow a visitor to Lime Street in Shakespeare's day would see books on a range of different subjects, odd-looking scientific instruments, specimens of plants and animals in various containers, drawings and notes. The interior of Lime Street's houses may have looked like what we would today think of as a laboratory – a building constructed especially for scientific experiments, often part of an established educational or commercial site, such as a university or a factory. But in early modern London, science had not been institutionalized; the idea of a purpose-built space for experiments did not exist until the end of the seventeenth century. Instead experimental science took place in existing spaces ranging from shops to university residences and rooms at court. Most of all it occurred in the homes of those who had the time, space and finances to pursue their interests in the natural world. Ordinary houses and gardens like those of Lime Street were the sites where what we now know as modern science developed.

As well as such evidence of experimentation, an early modern visitor might notice in a Lime Street home a cabinet filled with unusual looking objects and artefacts. Cabinets of curiosities were collections of odd, unusual and wondrous relics and objects stored either in an entire room or a specially made wooden cabinet, depending on the size of the collection. Lime Street residents valued them as objects of intense interest: in 1599 Mathias de L'Obel took tourist Thomas Platter (whom we have met already in this book) to visit Sir Walter Cope's cabinet of curiosities in Kensington, for example. Platter describes seeing an African charm made of teeth, a felt cloak from Arabia, shoes from many strange lands, an Indian stone axe, the twisted horn of a bull seal, the bauble and bells of Henry VIII's fool, a unicorn's tail, an artful Chinese box, an Indian charm made of monkey teeth, a sea mouse, and an Indian canoe, amongst other things (Mullaney, 60). Such cabinets of curiosities tell us that there was an appetite for the exotic as well as the plain odd in Shakespeare's London – and a desire to experience spaces that imaginatively transported those who entered them to far-off lands, much as the playhouses of the city did through performance.

We do not know if Shakespeare visited Lime Street, but he was undoubtedly aware of the ideas of London's burgeoning scientific community as their practices spread. As a regular in the bookshops of St Paul's, Shakespeare would have seen increasing numbers of publications that sought to explore and explain the natural world. *The Theatre of Insects* joined other works of natural history in offering detailed images and descriptions of animals, plants and the human body. Publishers also printed texts on emerging scientific disciplines such as mathematics, geometry, alchemy and astronomy. A brief survey of a few representative titles demonstrates the range of interests finding a voice, and a market, during Shakespeare's lifetime: John Gerard's *The Herbal or General History of Plants* (1597); Lime Street resident Mathias de L'Obel's *Plantarum ser stirpium icons* (1581); Conrad Gesner's *The Practice of the New and Old Physicke* (1599); Roger Bacon's *The Mirror of Alchemy* (1597); and George Henisch's *The Principles of Geometry, Astronomy and Geography* (1591) could all be purchased in early modern London. It is readily apparent that new ideas about the world, its inhabitants and their characteristics were circulating in and around Shakespeare's city, often via Lime Street, which served as a hub for the exchange of such information. And, as we have seen throughout this book, the theatre was a place where Shakespeare examined and tested ideas emerging from his city. This space was his laboratory and it is unsurprising that he should take the growing understanding about the natural world then emerging in his own city and place it under his dramatic microscope. In the following pages we shall see that in *The Tempest* Shakespeare is interested in precisely the questions that similarly preoccupied Lime Street's residents: what is the 'New World' and how can it be described? What are the alchemical processes and what do they achieve? Finally, what counts as an 'experiment' and what can we learn from it?

Brave New World

Early on in *The Tempest* Caliban describes himself as the true native inhabitant of the island upon which Prospero and Miranda have been shipwrecked, and upon which the events of *The Tempest* take place:

This island's mine by Sycorax, my mother,
Which thou tak'st from me. When thou cam'st first
Thou strok'st me and made much of me; wouldst give me
Water with berries in't, and teach me how
To name the bigger light and how the less
That burn by day and night. And then I loved thee
And showed thee all the qualities o' th' isle:
The fresh springs, brine pits, barren place and fertile.
Cursed be I that did so! All the charms
Of Sycorax – toads, beetles, bats – light on you,
For I am all the subjects that you have,
Which first was mine own king; and here you sty me
In this hard rock, whiles you do keep from me
The rest o'th' island.

(1.2.332–344)

Critics have frequently contextualized this interaction between Prospero and Caliban in relation to the exploration and scientific investigation of the New World taking place at the time Shakespeare wrote the play. In the late 1590s and early 1600s European colonists from Spain, Portugal, France, Holland and England explored parts of the Americas. Accounts of their travels were devoured by eager readers in Europe, who were intrigued by the exotic and various peoples, animals and plants from the New World, as well as the encounter between colonizer and the indigenous 'other'. The experience of colonization is apparent in Shakespeare's text – in repeated use of the words 'mine' and 'island' Caliban attempts to assert his claims over his native homeland. But Prospero, like his real-life European counterparts, has colonized the island using a variety of manipulative strategies. He has overcome Caliban through affection ('thou strok'est me'), sustenance ('give me | Water with berries in it') and education ('teach me').

Drawings of the New World, particularly those by colonialist and painter John White (1577–1593), have become famous early modern representations of the encounters between

Westerns and the Native American population, showing the colonialists' fascination with the ways of life they encountered on their expeditions. Unsurprisingly White was in contact with the Lime Street community, contributing sketches and specimens from his travels to their collaborative botanic endeavours; indeed, some of his work formed part of *Insectorum Theatrum*. Like his Lime Street contemporaries, Shakespeare was also interested in travel narratives. *The Tempest* draws on William Strachey's 'True Reportory of the Wracke, and Redemption of Sir Thomas Gates', concerning a 1609 shipwreck on the coast of Bermuda. Although not published until 1625, details (such as those we discuss below) suggest Shakespeare may have read Strachey in manuscript form. Shakespeare could also have been familiar with titles published in London around the time he wrote his play, such as Sylvester Jourdain's *A Discovery of the Barmudas* (1610), Richard Rich's *News from Virginia* (1610) and John Smith's *A True Relation of Such Occurences and Accidents of Noate as Hath Hapned in Virginia* (1608).

In staging the relationship between Caliban and Prospero, it has long been recognized that Shakespeare imagines the possible exchanges that took place when early colonialists encountered the native inhabitants of the new lands they visited. Caliban introduces the natural wonders of the island – 'fresh springs, brine pits, barren place and fertile' – in return for Prospero teaching him to name the sun and moon and, of course, how to speak; 'You taught me language,' he will say, rather accusingly (1.2.364). As in many of the texts describing the encounter between English imperialists and the New World natives they set out to conquer, both sides are transformed by their interaction; Prospero and Caliban educate one another. However, the power dynamic that marks colonial endeavours is also apparent: Caliban has been forced to relinquish his native claim as 'king' of the island that he previously owned, becoming Prospero's 'subject'.

Interpretations of *The Tempest* over the course of the twentieth century have been affected by changing attitudes to Western colonial power, and postcolonial critics interested in the cultural legacy of the imperial history of the United States and Britain have been intrigued by this interaction between Shakespeare's characters. In some readings, Prospero is an arrogant colonizer forcibly claiming an island that rightly belongs to Caliban or indeed Ariel, who come to symbolize the victimization of indigenous peoples. Seminal critical work in this area includes social scientist Octave Mannoni's *Psychologie de la Colonization,* an examination of French colonization of Madagascar, which was provocatively translated with the title *Prospero and Caliban* in 1956. Playwrights and novelists have been inspired to explore *The Tempest* explicitly from the perspective of the 'colonized' Caliban and Ariel: Aimé Césaire's re-telling of Shakespeare's play, *Une Tempête* (1969), depicts Prospero as a specifically white master, Caliban as a black slave and Ariel of mixed European and African ancestry. More recently, Tad William's novel, *Caliban's Hour* (1994), set ten years after the events of the play, presents an in-depth, sympathetic view of Prospero's former slave, who travels to Milan in order to confront his previous master. Casting choices, setting and costume in productions of *The Tempest* have often been influenced by shifting views of contemporary colonial projects such as relations between the United States and Latin America, Britain's role in the Caribbean and, more recently, the West's role in Iraq, Afghanistan and Palestine.

Returning the play to its seventeenth-century context, we can see Shakespeare examining the ways in which individuals respond to encounters with the exotic, and the impact that the heightened interest in the New World (and other foreign locations) was having on contemporary culture. Like those first travellers whose accounts were circulating around Lime Street and other parts of London, the characters in *The Tempest* attempt to understand what they see before them in a strange new land. Faced with Prospero's magical 'banquet', Sebastian comments:

A living drollery! Now I will believe
That there are unicorns; that in Arabia

There is one tree, the phoenix' throne, one phoenix
At this hour reigning there.

                                                    (3.3.21–24)

Sebastian describes the banquet as a 'drollery', a comic puppet
show, enacted by 'living' beings – somewhere between the
fictional and the real. He also refers to the wondrous but
dubious claims of those who have travelled extensively; such
narratives, much like those that circulated around Shakespeare's
London, seem to involve things firmly belonging to the realms
of fiction and fantasy, such as 'unicorns' and the 'phoenix' bird.
Indeed the mention of 'unicorns' returns us quite directly to
London – as we noted earlier, a 'unicorn's tale' was one of the
items Thomas Platter found in Sir William Cope's Kensington
cabinet of curiosities. And an image and description of the
unicorn is found in Edward Topsell's *The History of Four-
Footed Beasts*, a serious zoological catalogue published in
London in 1607. A few lines later Antonio articulates commonly
held suspicions toward travel narratives when he notes
'Travellers ne'er did lie,| Though fools at home condemn 'em'
(3.3.26–27). Indeed early modern travel writers, such as
Thomas Coryat (*Coryat's Crudities*, 1611) and Thomas Harriot
(*A Brief and True Report of the New Found Land of Virginia*,
1588), demonstrate a palpable anxiety about whether their
accounts are too fantastical to be believed. In encountering a
new and strange environment, the noblemen that Prospero has
brought to the island already imagine how their reports of
what they have seen might be interpreted back home. Gonzalo
admits as much when he wonders: 'If in Naples | I should report
this now, would they believe me?' (3.3.27–28).

Earlier in *The Tempest* Trinculo likewise considers how
'strange fish' Caliban might be viewed in England (a place the
royal jester has visited). He thinks about the money he could
make exhibiting Caliban as an exotic specimen, and recalls the
practice of paying 'to see a dead Indian' (2.2.32); after Martin
Frobisher's journey to North America in 1576 native Americans

were brought back to England and displayed to a paying public in just this way. This practice continued throughout Shakespeare's lifetime. In an article entitled 'Trinculo's Indian' Alden T. Vaughan recounts how in 1611, the year Shakespeare's play was first performed, a Native American called Epenhow was brought to England and displayed in London. When Stephano discovers Trinculo and Caliban entwined, hiding from the storm, he also considers the economic and cultural value of this oddity. He hopes to recover this 'monster of the isle', to 'keep him tame, and get to Naples with him', going on to observe that 'he's a present for any emperor' (2.2.64, 67–69). Shakespeare's depiction of such acquisitive attitudes to Prospero's island reflects the fact that the curiosity regarding animals, plants and people from other lands fostered by the Lime Street community had become a firm fixture in the cultural (and indeed economic) world of early modern London.

These two scenes in the play are moments when Shakespeare explicitly alludes to the travel narratives so popular amongst the Lime Street community and their fellow Londoners. However, the play is also full of other descriptions of the island that can be seen as heightened and lyrical emulations of such accounts and may even reflect studies of natural history Shakespeare may have encountered on the bookstalls of St Paul's. As we noted earlier, one of the probable sources for the play was Strachey's 'True Reportory' (1609), a text that describes in vivid detail the storm that caused a Bermuda shipwreck. Strachey describes how the 'sea swelled above the clouds and gave battell unto Heaven'. As Gwilym Jones has pointed out, a similar conceit is used by Miranda in describing Prospero's storm: 'The sky, it seems, would pour down stinking pitch | But that the sea, mounting to th' welkin's cheek, | Dashes the fire out' (1.2.3–5). As in Strachey's account, the storm's force causes the sea to mount up to meet the 'welkin's cheek', climbing into the sky. Likewise when Gonzalo arrives on the island he surveys it like any savvy colonizer might, noting that the grass is 'lush and lusty' (2.1.55) and imaging the type of 'plantation' (2.1.144) he would create. Gonzalo's speech is an extended verbal borrowing from a contemporary piece of travel literature readily available to Shakespeare and his fellow Londoners: Montaigne's essay 'Of the Caniballes', which describes the culture of Brazilian Indians, was published in translation in 1603. The essay depicts a nation 'that hath no kind of traffic, no knowledge of Letters', and 'no use of service, of riches, or of poverty; no contracts, no successions', in fact 'no occupation but idle'. Shakespeare's imagining of Gonzalo's commonwealth offers an almost verbatim version of this text: 'no kind of traffic | Would I admit,' he says (2.1.149–50). Like Montaigne, he goes on to suggest, 'Letters should not be known; riches, poverty | And use of service, none;' he will allow no 'contract, succession', while the islanders shall have 'No occupation, all men idle' (2.1.151–52, 53, 55). Again Shakespeare's writing absorbs and transfigures the wide-ranging printed texts circulating around early modern London, displaying the wonders reported therein for his playhouse audiences to marvel at. We might in this respect read the exotic imagery of *The Tempest* as Shakespeare converting the playhouse itself into an imaginative cabinet of curiosities, a space that immerses the audience in a remote and alien universe and, when the play is over, returns them to the streets of London with a fresh perspective on a more familiar world.

Prospero's experiments

Shakespeare might thus be seen as a practical intellectual, gathering knowledge from the many different resources around him to create his stage worlds. In many ways, the playwright would not seem out of place amongst the inhabitants of Lime Street, who sought to master their environment through learning, asserting their proprietorship by curating its marvels and displaying them to their fellow Londoners. Prospero, whom many have read as an onstage alter-ego for the dramatist himself, is likewise a scholar who studies the world around him in order to reshape it as he desires, using the knowledge he gleans from his books to make wondrous things happen. We learn very early

on in the play that he is 'reputed' for his study and knowledge
of the 'liberal arts' (1.2.72–73). When he was Duke of Milan
Prospero admits that he neglected 'worldly ends, all dedicated |
To the closeness and the bettering of my mind' (1.2.89–90); his
library was full of volumes that, he confesses, 'I prize above
my dukedom' (1.2.168). For Prospero, it is through the study of
the emerging scientific disciplines such as arithmetic, geometry
and astronomy, which were gaining popular readerships in
Shakespeare's London that he has learnt to experiment with and
control the environment that surrounds him. Certainly Caliban
attributes Prospero's power to his studies when he reminds
Stephano and Trinculo to seize Prospero's books, 'for without
them | He's but a sot' (3.2.92–93). For Caliban, Prospero's
power lies in his books, and as such contrasts directly with his
own natural, experiential knowledge of the island, its 'fresh
springs, brine pits, barren place and fertile' (1.2.339) and of
course its 'Sounds and sweet airs' (3.2.136).

We can trace the pseudo-scientific knowledge Prospero
draws on throughout the play to particular books published –
and intellectual interests emerging – in the early modern
metropolis. Prospero informs Miranda that his enemies have
been brought to the island, and he has found that his 'zenith
doth depend upon | A most auspicious star' (1.2.181–82). The
lines reveal that Prospero has been practicing astrology,
watching the stars in order to read his fortune ('zenith') and
discover the best moment to bring his brother and King Alonso
to the island. Similar astrological readings took place in
Shakespeare's London, in which Queen Elizabeth I herself had
a special advisor on such matters, astrologist John Dee (1527–
1609). Just as Prospero consults his horoscope in order to
discover the most appropriate time to put into effect his plans
to reclaim his dukedom, so Dee advised Elizabeth on auspicious
dates for important events; allegedly he chose the queen's
coronation date according to the alignment of the stars.

The play evokes another kind of knowledge that was
fashionable in Shakespeare's London: alchemy, the putative
form of science according to which it was thought base metals

could be turned into gold. George Ripley's *The Compound of Alchemy* (1591) offers readers a guide to the 'ancient hidden Art of Alchemie,' along with 'other Excellent Experiments'. This type of book offered early modern Londoners a step-by-step guide as they sought to practice their own experiments at home. There was an ongoing interest in alchemy in the capital at this time; just a year before *The Tempest* was premiered Shakespeare's theatre company performed Ben Jonson's enormously popular play *The Alchemist* (1610). Jonson's comedy sees three London criminals using the art of alchemy to con the foolish and greedy out of their money; it was regularly performed by the King's Men and seen at court at least twice. In *The Tempest* Shakespeare picks up the alchemical theme and language first brought to the London stage by Jonson just a year before. However, instead of taking a comic approach to such pseudo-scientific practices, Shakespeare instead uses the language of alchemy more seriously, as a metaphor for the emotional changes that Prospero brings about in those around him. Like metals transformed by the alchemical process, characters in Shakespeare's play move from one moral or emotional state to another at his instigation. For example, Antonio and Alonso are forced to face their guilt over ousting Prospero from his Milanese dukedom; Miranda and Ferdinand fall in love and get married; Caliban and Ariel are enslaved and finally freed. John Mebane has pointed out that even the play's title derives from alchemical terminology, in which a 'tempest' describes the act of boiling substances in order remove impurities and transform base metal into gold.

Critic Peggy Munoz Simonds persuasively argues that *The Tempest* is in fact a 'theatrical exercise in alchemical transmutation' (541). Indeed, the language of alchemy pervades the play, just as it would have been heard frequently in early modern Lime Street. When Alonso is confronted by Ariel, and by his culpability in Prospero's demise, he vows to join Ferdinand (whom he believes to be dead) in a watery grave: 'I'll seek him deeper than e'er plummet sounded' (3.3.101). In this dark moment of emotional transformation, Alonso evokes the practices of alchemical experimentation; a 'plummet' is a mechanism used to determine vertical distances and is made of lead, a key component of alchemy. At several points in the play the 'freshness' of the garments of those shipwrecked on the island is noted (by Ariel 1.2.118 and by Gonzalo 2.1.65; 70; 97–99). For Simonds these references allude to the alchemical process of extensively washing metals before attempts at transmutation and therefore symbolize the way in which characters' flaws are exposed and cleansed by the end of the play, as Ferdinand's grief for his father leads ultimately to their reconciliation, while Trinculo, Stephano and Caliban's murderous plot is eventually uncovered. It is perhaps little wonder, therefore, that as Prospero's experiment reaches its conclusion at the end of *The Tempest* his alchemical vocabulary also intensifies:

> Now does my project gather to a head.
> My charms crack not; my spirits obey; and time
> Goes upright with his carriage.

> (5.1.1–3)

As the Arden editors of the play note, the word 'project' was used to describe an alchemist's experiment in which powder is cast upon a metal infusion to effect its transmutation into gold or silver. Gathering 'to a head' similarly suggests the process whereby metals are heated to boiling point, and 'crack' here suggests the breaking of the laboratory flasks if heated too high during alchemical experiments. Throughout *The Tempest*, but especially in these lines, Shakespeare thus evokes the world of the Lime Street laboratory, bringing together the world of early modern London and that of Prospero's island in his own piece of theatrical alchemy.

Alchemical experimentation is thus embedded in *The Tempest*'s language but also embodied by one particular character. Like the metals that early modern alchemists wished to transform, Ariel can transmute into different states, shifting from one form to another. Ariel's mercurial nature provides some of the most beautiful imagery of the play, as well as offering the possibility of stunning stage effects; his harpy and water nymph costumes are often a visual highlight of any production. His very first lines demonstrate the scope of his powers: Ariel comes to do Prospero's bidding, 'to fly | To swim, to dive into the fire, to ride | On the curled clouds' as his master wishes (1.2.190–92). Shakespeare here associates the character of Ariel with multiple elements – water, fire and air – and makes clear that he is able to switch between these different states with ease. Just as the alchemist seeks to transmute metals and minerals into gold, so Prospero orders the transformation of Ariel from water nymph to harpy.

Encompassing astrology and alchemy, we have seen the far-ranging and powerful nature of Prospero's art. At the end of the play – in one of Shakespeare's most famous speeches – Prospero describes the kind of experiments he has practised:

> I have bedimmed
> The noontide sun, called forth the mutinous winds,
> And 'twixt the green sea and the azured vault
> Set roaring war; to the dread-rattling thunder
> Have I given fire and rifted Jove's stout oak
> With his own bolt: the strong-based promontory
> Have I made shake, and by the spurs plucked up
> The pine and cedar; graves at my command
> Have waked their sleepers, ope'd and let 'em forth
> By my so potent art. But this rough magic
> I here abjure.

(5.1.41–51)

Prospero draws attention to his control over both the earth (the sun, wind and sea) and the elements (water, air and fire), using a series of verbs to emphasize the dynamism of his actions; he has 'bedimmed', 'set roaring', 'given fire', 'made shake' and 'plucked up' different aspects of his surroundings. Most disturbing here is the suggestion that he has practised necromancy – raising the dead ('sleepers') from their graves – an act of interference in the afterworld that early modern Londoners would consider to be black magic. Thus Prospero's speech alerts us to the diverse and ambiguous range of activities grouped together around the idea of 'science' in Shakespeare's city, embodying some of the multiple, often contradictory, approaches to documenting and controlling the natural world circulating at this time. The juxtaposition of 'potent art' and 'rough magic' within the same verse line perhaps best exemplifies such tensions. Throughout the play, Prospero has referred to his practices as both 'art' and 'magic'; here he does so again but in the same breath, leaving us asking what is the difference between the two terms? Why is one 'potent' and the other 'rough'? Shakespeare's play provides us with no answers to such conundrums, reflecting the uncertain state of scientific disciplines in his city. In early modern London science itself was in transition and branches of study that we now see very much as pure superstition – astrology, alchemy and necromancy – still had some authority. Like those living on Lime Street, Prospero finds himself on the cusp of the scientific revolution, engaged in old practices while pre-empting aspects of what we now understand as modern science, employing both 'potent art' and 'rough magic' alike in the service of his ends.

Knowledge and experience in *The Tempest*

In *The Tempest* Shakespeare engages with the changing philosophies about the nature of knowledge and scientific research that we have hinted at above. During his lifetime there was an increasing emphasis on the idea of experience as an important way of gaining knowledge, making the conducting of experiments an important task for the scientist. In contrast, earlier modes of research had downplayed the value of making, doing and testing in favour of scholastic and cerebral learning. As critic Elizabeth Spiller has argued, Shakespeare examines these two different forms of knowledge in *The Tempest*, ultimately concluding that experience is central to human understanding; a similar point is made in *King Lear*, as discussed in Chapter 6. In *The Tempest* we see this explored most fully in the character of Miranda. Tutored by her father since their arrival on the island she has received an education of 'more profit | Than other princes' (1.2.172–73) – in other words she is more educated than even male royal heirs. But having known only Prospero, Caliban and the island, she is highly naïve; she has theoretical scholarship but no practical experiential knowledge. Unsurprisingly when Miranda encounters Alonso and his noblemen at the end of the play they represent a 'brave new world' for her (5.1.183).

Other characters in *The Tempest* also encounter a division between cerebral knowledge and felt experience, between theory and practice. Alonso has long been theoretically aware of the fact he wronged Prospero by supporting Antonio's overthrow of his brother. But it is not until he experiences Prospero's magic for himself that this transgression is truly felt and acknowledged:

> O, it is monstrous, monstrous!
> Methought the billows spoke and told me of it;
> The winds did sing it to me, and the thunder –
> That deep and dreadful organpipe – pronounced
> The name of Prosper. It did bass my trespass.

> (3.3.95–99)

Tormented by the death of his son, and further tested by a disappearing magic banquet and a frightening Ariel dressed as a harpy, Alonso's guilt (or 'trespass') emerges: Prospero's experiment has worked. Notable here is the way Alonso's language focuses on what he has felt through his senses, particularly through sound (of 'billows', 'winds' and 'thunder'); it is only through tangible experience that Alonso reaches emotional clarity.

While Prospero himself is the instigator of experiments that lead other characters to make emotional discoveries in this way, he too finds himself learning as a result of the events that take place on the island. As we noted, he has lost his dukedom through an over-emphasis on (or perhaps over-indulgence in) scholastic learning; he had been distracted, 'rapt' by his study (1.2.77), thus enabling Antonio to seize power from him. It is only by re-engaging in the world around him, practising his magical arts rather than merely studying his books, that Prospero wins his dukedom back. But more than this, through the experiments of the play, the wronged duke achieves self-knowledge. In a particularly touching moment, Prospero rejects the course of revenge that he formerly wished to pursue against his brother and Alonso. Ariel points out that if his master could see his victims his 'affections | Would become tender' (5.1.18–19), insisting he would himself respond that way, if he were capable of such emotion. The ever-changeable Ariel, who has magically transformed into many shapes, here images himself as human, conjuring a sense of empathy and forgiveness that Prospero conspicuously lacks. In another transformation wrought by the magic of the play's language, Ariel manages to secure a promise from Prospero:

> Though with their high wrongs I am struck to th' quick,
> Yet with my nobler reason 'gainst my fury
> Do I take part. The rarer action is
> In virtue than in vengeance.

> (5.1.25–28)

The great magician himself has not remained impervious to the events on the island; the experience of seeking to exact revenge for his 'high wrongs' has altered what he theoretically believed he wanted. Prospero vows to temper his emotions ('fury') with 'reason'. Like some of those he has experimented on, the ruler of the island thus moves from base thoughts to 'nobler' and 'rarer' action, realizing that 'virtue' – in this sense, mercy and forgiveness – is more valuable than 'vengeance'.

In this shift in emphasis in the value placed upon theory and practice, and the increasing importance of experience over book learning, *The Tempest* reflects developing approaches to knowledge during Shakespeare's lifetime. As we have seen, the play is engaged with the vastly diverse experimental sciences of early modern London, from the travel literature of the New World, to older practices such as alchemy. But why did Shakespeare turn his mind to experimentation at this point in his career and in this particular play? We would like to suggest in the final section of this chapter that the reason lies in the fact that *The Tempest* is written for a new playhouse, which offered novel theatrical possibilities. As such, the play itself might be considered an experiment.

Theatrical experimentation

As we have learned, Shakespeare's company of players had performed at the Globe in Southwark (the subject of our previous chapter) from 1599 onwards. But in 1609 they were offered the chance to perform at the Blackfriars, an indoor theatre situated across the river near the heart of the City of London. And so from this point on, the King's Men (as they were now known) performed at the Globe in the summer months and in the winter retreated indoors to perform at the Blackfriars, a theatre constructed within the existing frame of what had been a medieval monastic building. This indoor theatre was a very different space from the Globe, and not only because it had a roof to protect audience members from the weather.

The Blackfriars was a smaller venue (approximately 900 audience members in contrast to as many as 3,000 at the Globe). The Sam Wanamaker Playhouse (Figure 8) recently opened next to Shakespeare's Globe, gives us some idea of the experience of the Blackfriars playhouse. While not a replica of the Blackfriars, the Sam Wanamaker Playhouse shares many of the features of Shakespeare's indoor playhouse. The Blackfriars' candle-lit hall had seats for everyone; there were no standing 'groundlings' here. Crucially this indoor theatre attracted an audience more affluent than that found at the Globe – minimum admission at

FIGURE 8 *The Sam Wanamaker Playhouse (2014) (by kind permission of Shakespeare's Globe, photograph by Pete Le May)*

the Blackfriars was six pennies, the cost of the best seats in the house at outdoor theatres. And for the first time in the history of English theatre, this audience paid more to sit closer to the stage; an emphasis was placed on seeing the action close-up. But this audience also came to hear impressive music; the acoustics of an indoor theatre were particularly suitable for a range of instruments – including violas, organs, recorders and flutes – that would have been lost in the acoustic space of the open-air Globe. Thus late on in his career Shakespeare had an exciting creative opportunity, a new type of playhouse to inspire him. And it seems that the Blackfriars had a revitalizing effect upon the playwright; the stimulating conditions of performance at this indoor venue would shape his writing in innovative ways. We see the effects of this perhaps most clearly in *The Tempest*. Written roughly two years after the company began their occupation of the Blackfriars, Shakespeare had developed a clear sense of the particular capabilities (and challenges) of this playhouse and had begun to experiment with its potential by the time he wrote the play. In concluding this chapter, we will consider the aural, visual and generic experimentation found in *The Tempest*.

Shakespeare's play certainly utilizes the acoustic environment of the Blackfriars to the full. For a playhouse that suited a wide range of instrumentation, Shakespeare chose to write his most musical play. There is only one 'silent' scene in *The Tempest* (Miranda and Ferdinand's courtship in act three, scene one). In every other scene of the play, Shakespeare's text specifies that music and sound effects are integral to the action. In particular, Ariel's songs shape the drama: for example, Ferdinand follows the spirit singing 'Full Fathom Five' inland, thereby meeting Prospero and Miranda (1.2.397–405). The song's appeal lies partly in the fact it is perfectly in tune with Ferdinand's grief over his supposedly 'drowned father' (1.2.406). Ariel's music similarly leads on Caliban, Trinculo and Stephano, who subsequently fall for the trap Prospero sets for them, and the spirit '*Sings in Gonzalo's ear*' (2.1.300) thereby ensuring that Sebastian and Antonio's traitorous plan to kill the sleeping Alonso is likewise interrupted. More than just a plot device, however, instrumental accompaniments create atmosphere and foster emotion in this play, as when 'solemn and strange music' heralds the ethereal banquet presented for Alonso and his lords in act three, scene three. Another sound effect – the '*noise of hunters*' – underscores Caliban, Trinculo and Stephano's frightening interaction with Prospero's spirits, this time 'in shape of dogs and hounds' (4.1.254).

Yet *The Tempest* is also a play of visual experimentation that responds to the particular aesthetic of the Blackfriars playhouse. Under candlelight its wealthy audience flaunted their best jewellery and clothing; contemporary accounts describe those who 'glittered' at the Blackfriars. In *The Young Gallants Whirligig* (1629), for instance, Francis Lenton would satirize the 'Torchy Friars', in which the 'silken', 'satin' and 'spangled' attire of the well-dressed spectators 'glistered' (C4^v). *The Tempest* showcases an array of detailed and highly decorated costumes, creating an onstage visual display to match a glamorously attired audience and what scholars believe to have been a lavishly decorated playhouse. Spectacular outfits specified by Shakespeare's text include Prospero's '*magic robes*' (5.1.0), the fresh and 'new-dyed' garments (2.1.65) of the shipwrecked nobles and, of course, Ariel's costume when he appears as a '*harpy*', a mythical bird (3.3.52). In act four, scene one, Caliban, Stephano and Trinculo are distracted from their plans to murder Prospero by the '*glistening apparel*' Ariel leaves waiting for them (4.1.193). Shimmering under the theatre's candlelight, such elaborate costumes contributed to the spectacular visual display of *The Tempest* at the Blackfriars.

Shakespeare also rewards those higher-paying members of his audience sitting closest to the stage with stunningly detailed visual effects. Act three, scene three offers an extended spectacle in which the King is presented with a banquet, accompanied by '*strange shapes*' who '*dance about it with gentle actions of salutations*' (3.3.17). This 'living drollery' (3.3.21) amazes the men: 'Such shapes, such gestures and such sound', marvels Alonso (3.3.38). The vagueness of the King's language here suggests that this sensual display surpasses description. Indeed, in modern performance, the banquet is often a high point as costume, set and prop designers attempt to interpret Shakespeare's somewhat ambiguous stage directions and to evoke an equal sense of wonder in modern audiences. This banquet is superseded by another eye-catching effect when Ariel (in his guise as a harpy) '*vanishes*' the banquet away with '*a quaint device*' (3.3.52). Again stage directions offer only a brief hint of what would have been a striking theatrical effect: a banquet disappearing before the eyes of both characters and audience. The elusive nature of the play's stage directions are possibly a result of the fact they were written by Ralph Crane, the King's Men's scrivener. In this administrative role, Crane was in charge of writing out copies of the company's plays for publication; his stage directions in *The Tempest* serve to describe what happened onstage for readers; they do not prescribe what actors and those involved in staging the play should do, as we might expect from a performance script. Nonetheless, a long tradition of theatre directors and interpreters of the play have deduced that the '*quaint device*' mentioned here may well have been a mechanical apparatus; the play's Arden editors note that in modern productions the table-top on which the banquet was placed is usually overturned to reveal a clear surface. It is possible that this was an innovative '*device*' that the King's Men experimented with at the Blackfriars; certainly there are no comparable examples in the rest of Shakespeare's canon. *The Tempest*'s characters are frequently in awe of the visions before them, perhaps reflecting the similarly wondrous response of early audiences at the Blackfriars who saw the magic of Prospero, and that of Shakespeare, at close quarters.

A final experimental element of *The Tempest* lies in the play's genre. In Shakespeare's First Folio (effectively his collected works, published in 1623) the drama is presented as a comedy, but it has continued to confound critical categorization, incorporating moments of tragedy, such as Alonso's grief for the son he believes to be dead. The play also ends on a demonstrably ambiguous note. The celebrations for the marriage of Ferdinand and Miranda and joyous reunion of the shipwrecked Neapolitans are undermined by the doubts with which Shakespeare leaves us about Antonio's rather unconvincing contrition towards Prospero – is this really a happy ending for the two brothers? Significantly, the final few lines of the play address not the young generation and their future but rather the ageing Prospero's demise: 'And thence retire me to my Milan, where | Every third thought shall be my grave' (5.1.311–12).

A particular generic innovation in *The Tempest* is Shakespeare's experimentation with a masque scene in a comedy. As we have discovered, masques were highly choreographed dramatic pieces performed at court with especially composed music and extravagant costumes. Shakespeare stages a masque in act four, scene one of *The Tempest*, when Juno, Ceres and Iris sing and dance in celebration of marriage and fertility in order to bless the union of Ferdinand and Miranda. But in yet another iteration of the play's almost compulsive generic experimentation, this celebratory and magical moment is abruptly disrupted as Prospero remembers 'that foul conspiracy | Of the beast Caliban and his confederates | Against my life' (4.1.139–141). Shakespeare thus juxtaposes the happy associations of Miranda and Ferdinand's union with the murderous plot against Prospero's life. In doing so, he resists the generic conventions of the marriage masque as an all-encompassing moment of celebration, joy and warmth, the inclusion of which here simultaneously challenges the boundaries of the comedic form.

It is apparent therefore that *The Tempest* not only uses the language of early modern experimentation deriving from alchemy, astrology and natural history but also is itself an experiment. In writing the play Shakespeare responded to the demands of his company's recently acquired indoor theatre and, in doing so, carried out his own experiment in stagecraft. As we have seen, he did not have to look far for evidence of rapidly developing proto-scientific ideas in early modern London, with the neighbourhood of Lime Street, a centre for the exchange of such knowledge, just a short distance from the Blackfriars playhouse. The pioneering approaches to exploring, recording and controlling the workings of the natural world that emerged from Lime Street are a constant presence in *The Tempest*, in which we have discerned many references to subjects that fascinated its inhabitants, including discoveries from the New World, alchemy, astrology and the debate about the relative value of learning and experience. Despite its lateness in Shakespeare's career *The Tempest* always feels fresh and innovative, enjoying continued popularity amongst modern theatre-makers and audiences. Shakespeare's colleagues in the world of early modern London theatre seem to have shared this sense of the play's experimental nature. Seven years after his death they chose to place *The Tempest* at the forefront of the First Folio. *The Tempest* has continued to open up a 'brave new world' of scientific and theatrical experimentation to audiences and readers ever since.

Epilogue:

Henry VIII (1613) and the Tower of London

The Blackfriars theatre is believed to be the setting for the first performance of the last of Shakespeare's plays we will be concerned with here, the collaborative historical drama *Henry VIII*, written with John Fletcher in the final years of his stage career (only *The Two Noble Kinsmen*, another jointly-authored play, follows it in chronologies of his works). While no record of a performance at the Blackfriars survives, a number of moments in the play seem to self-consciously allude to this location, prompting some critics to posit that Shakespeare and Fletcher wrote *Henry VIII* specifically for the indoor playhouse (although we know that it was also performed at the early modern Globe). It was in the monastic hall at Blackfriars that Henry VIII had been granted a divorce from Katherine of Aragon eighty-four years before the play was first produced. Shakespeare and Fletcher specify that their re-enactment of this scene also occurs in the Blackfriars hall (2.4), making this space a key location for the play. The character Henry VIII declares the Blackfriars a centre of 'learning' in the city, reflecting its proximity to the Inns of Court (2.2.136). Arden editor Gordon McMullan has pointed out that the Blackfriars' urbane and sophisticated audience, partly made up of London's law students, would have enjoyed the satirical and iconoclastic nature of the drama (McMullan, introduction, 10). The Blackfriars' proximity to the Inns also makes it the perfect place for Henry's scholars to set out their arguments in favour of the divorce; he calls it 'The most convenient place that I can think of' (2.2.135).

Henry VIII thus shares with *The Tempest* its likely first performance venue and with *The Merchant of Venice* its dependence upon a pivotal courtroom scene (directed at an audience of young lawyers who valued wit and learning). It shares elements with the other plays studied in this book as well, and our examination of this problematic history play will provide us with the chance to revisit many of the locations encountered on our journey through Shakespeare's city, concluding with a summary of the ways in which his plays respond to the early modern London in which they were written. More than any other Shakespeare play *Henry VIII* is a drama explicitly set in London (perhaps reflecting the influence of his collaborator, Fletcher), which draws upon particular locations within the city in a more transparent way than we have seen previously. In the latter part of this chapter we will look in particular detail at act five, scene three, which contains a wealth of references to different locations in Shakespeare's city, invoking many of the places studied here, as a means of both summarizing and concluding our readings of the plays written there. But first we will turn to the last of our London locations, one of the most iconic landmarks in the city both then and now: the Tower of London. This will form the focus of our reading of *Henry VIII* as a play underpinned by – but itself also seeking to undermine or usurp – history. We will pay particular attention to the idea of succession, the key trope that underwrites the drama.

First it is useful to consider Shakespeare's personal relationship to the city of London in the last years of his career, not out of a desire to instigate the kind of biographical reading of his plays that this book has sought to avoid, but rather because understanding where Shakespeare was in 1613 can help us to make the case for *Henry VIII* as a London play.

It is also important for our understanding of *Henry VIII* to challenge the commonly held misconception that Shakespeare left London sometime after composing *The Tempest* in 1611, retiring to Stratford to live out his remaining days in a sort of domestic or rural idyll. There is evidence (largely financial records) that Shakespeare committed more resources to Warwickshire in the later part of his life, purchasing a property portfolio in the town at a cost of nearly £900, engaging in legal battles to protect his land there from enclosure, and contributing to a bill put before parliament for the repair of roads around Stratford. However, we have no way of knowing exactly how he divided his time. It is also the case that he continued to invest heavily in London property, buying the Gatehouse at Blackfriars just adjacent to the hall in which Henry VIII's divorce was granted and where his play *Henry VIII* was likely performed in 1613. The fantasy of Shakespeare's retirement to Stratford seems in part to have been perpetuated by a desire amongst critics and audiences to see *The Tempest* – especially Prospero's casting down of his rod and book, and the magical powers they symbolized – as the playwright's farewell to the theatre. This outdated understanding of his career has been amended as a fuller awareness of the collaborative plays he wrote subsequently has gradually emerged. It is now established that *The Tempest* is not Shakespeare's last work, and that he continued to spend considerable amounts of time in London co-authoring plays, visiting his literary friends and managing his property. *Henry VIII* is a play written in the midst of the city in which it is clearly set, strongly immersed in the sights and sounds of Shakespeare's London.

The action of *Henry VIII* spans the trajectory of this book, moving from Whitehall and Westminster through the heart of the City to the easternmost outpost of early modern London, the Tower, which casts its forbidding shadow over the entire drama. Several major characters are sent to the Tower in the course of the play, presaging the ultimate fate of its major female protagonist, Anne Bullen – or Boleyn – whose rise is charted in the play. Anne reaches her apotheosis in the drama's

coronation procession, in which she is led to Westminster
Abbey to be anointed Queen by the Archbishop of Canterbury,
a journey that departs from the Tower in accordance with a
tradition that monarchs should spent the night preceding the
ceremony there. The Tower thus comes to signify the highest
reaches and lowest depths to which the play's characters can
rise or fall. It is an inherently contradictory symbol of glory
and despair in *Henry VIII*, reflecting what recent critics have
identified as the rather paradoxical nature of the Tower in the
early modern imagination. As one of London's most visible
and frequently visited landmarks – in Shakespeare's London as
today – the Tower has a particular hold over the inhabitants of
his city that makes it a particularly fitting place at which to end
our study. Like London itself, always changing and yet always
the same, the Tower represents ideas of continuity and change;
it is the place where lives are ended, some of them royal lives,
and where fresh beginnings are made, as new rulers begin their
reigns. The Tower thus embodies the principle of succession
that so dominated early modern political life. Kings and queens
are made and die there, giving the Tower a uniquely powerful
position in Shakespeare's world and in the universe of *Henry
VIII*. Kristen Deiter has observed the particular association of
the Tower with royalty and especially royal authority,
explaining how it serves as an emblem of both repression and
resistance in the period. Deiter's research focuses on early
modern 'Tower plays'; she counts twenty plays featuring the
site produced in the years 1590–1624 alone, arguing that the
drama of the period helps create, as much as it reflects, popular
perceptions of this 'icon' of London life. While we might expect
to find the Tower portrayed as the ultimate symbol of royal
control, sometimes taken to its extreme in the tyrannical
practices of torture, imprisonment and execution carried out
there, Deiter argues that it is more often figured as 'an emblem
of opposition to the crown and as a bodily and spiritual icon
of non-royal English identity' (24). Noting that Tower Hill was
the location for apprentice riots in 1595 and that the Tower is
frequently depicted as a place in which the monarch's power is

challenged, misplaced or deliberately subverted, Deiter
describes its 'dual representation as a traditional symbol of
English pride and an emblem of conflict' (29). Its location on
the eastern edge of London, abutting the city walls, meant it
stood as an outpost of royal authority that sometimes found
itself at odds with the City Fathers, whose area of jurisdiction
served to separate the Tower from the heart of political power
at Westminster.

This disparity mirrors the nature of the Tower itself, at
once central to early modern London life, a fundamental
stronghold of political power, and at the same time peripheral,
located on the furthest reaches of the metropolis. The buildings
collectively referred to as the 'Tower' were also a somewhat
ramshackle, disjointed collection. The most prominent of
these is the ancient White Tower, where royalty has been
imprisoned, including Richard II. In Shakespeare's *Richard III*
the malignant monarch of the play's title has the young princes
who threaten his claim to the throne murdered there, in
perhaps the most infamous episode in the Tower's literary
history. The White Tower was built upon Roman foundations,
giving rise to the popular early modern belief that Julius Caesar
had constructed the edifice. But the Tower complex also housed
an armoury, the Jewel House (where royal gems were stored;
the Crown Jewels are displayed there to this day), a menagerie
of animals (including the ravens whose call is synonymous
with the bleakness of the Tower itself for many), a proto-
museum (containing a display of former monarchs carved
from wood, costumed and seated upon wooden horses,
known as the Line of Kings) and a site of execution for
privileged members of the nobility. Perhaps most crucially
the Tower combined the functions of both a fortress and a
prison, defending Shakespeare's London against enemies
without and within. In early modern London it held weapons
and housed the Yeoman of the Guard who would keep out
those who were unwelcome, but also kept within its imposing
walls precious treasures needing protection; it trapped
those who had offended the ruling elite within its cold, damp

confines, and it also sheltered princes and princesses, offering its protection to new monarchs as they embarked upon the holy office of kingship. Queen Elizabeth I had direct experience of these two contrasting aspects of the Tower's function, having been imprisoned there during the reign of her half-sister Queen Mary I and then spending time there before her own coronation on 15 January 1559.

The Tower in *Henry VIII*

We see this somewhat paradoxical nature of the Tower at work in *Henry VIII*, in which it is used to keep certain characters within the circles of privilege, power and preference that make up the court and, at the same time, to shut others out. Loss of the King's favour means being sent away from London, as will happen to Katherine (who is sent to Kimbolton in Huntingdonshire, where she languishes in sickness and eventually will die [4.1.34]) and Cardinal Wolsey (exiled to 'Esher House, my lord of Winchester's' [3.2.231], actually one of his own properties that has already been confiscated from him). For those even worse off, alienation from the King meant banishment to the Tower. Yet, as already hinted, it is Anne's journey from the Tower that will see her finally attain the status of Queen, the highest possible office and the ultimate sign of her acceptance at court after years of negotiation that would eventually see the end of Henry's marriage to Katherine and her own installation as royal consort. Shakespeare and Fletcher's extraordinary depiction of the chatter amongst those watching her coronation procession on London's streets captures the astonishing nature of her journey. The gentlemen onlookers register a sense of the sanctity of this occasion: 'When by the Archbishop of Canterbury | She had all the royal makings of a queen,' including 'holy oil, Edward Confessor's crown, | The rod, and bird of peace' (4.1.86–89). At the same time they make a series of bawdy jokes and highly sexualized remarks; the Third Gentleman remarks that he has been

'Among the crowd i'th' Abbey, where a finger | Could not be wedged in more,' a leering allusion to what else might be 'wedged' into Anne. He continues, 'I am stifled | With the mere rankness of their joy' (4.1.57–59). The Third Gentleman's comments here mingle the scent of holy incense with that of the rank body odours of the crowd. Anne, so long disparaged as the King's whore, is now made 'saint-like' (4.1.83), her physical journey from Tower to the Abbey standing in for this much greater shift in moral position and status. Yet the gentlemen's language here makes clear she will not be allowed to forget where she has come from – or where she is ultimately going to.

Throughout the play we are also reminded that the Tower will be Anne's final destination; she will be beheaded there for adultery after the dramatic action has ended. The path from Tower to Westminster and back again represents the cycle from good to bad fortune her character will undergo. Several other figures depicted here also experience the turning of fortune's wheel, vacillations of fate that will see them lose royal favour and end their days in the Tower, in a way that presages what will eventually happen to the new Queen. The play begins with the downfall of the Duke of Buckingham, conspired against by his own surveyor who imputes to him treasonous ambitions towards the crown (1.2.133–35). The surveyor recounts a prophecy that 'The Duke | Shall govern England' (1.2.170), made to Buckingham's chaplain by one Nicholas Hopkins (1.2.147), recalling with the utmost specificity that the conversation in which this was revealed to him took place 'at the Rose, within the parish | Saint Laurence Pountney' (1.2.152–53). The church of St Laurence stood on Candlewick Street in the heart of the City, between the Blackfriars and the Tower; Buckingham's manor house in the parish was known as the 'Rose'. If Buckingham's reported misdemeanour is tied to a precise location within early modern London that would have been well known to Shakespeare and Fletcher's first audience, then his punishment likewise is vividly located within the city: ' 'Tis his highness' pleasure |

You shall to th' Tower' (1.1.203–4). Tried at Westminster Hall, a 'barge' is prepared for Buckingham (2.1.98); he will trace the journey from the west to the east of Shakespeare's city that we have undertaken in this book, the length of London's streets and river measuring out the degree to which he has fallen.

Buckingham is not the only character condemned to the Tower by Henry during the course of the play. In fact the structure of *Henry VIII* can be described as a series of cycles by which its protagonists repeatedly rise to prominence and then fall in the most dramatic of ways, the Tower recurring as a motif signifying the dizziest heights to which one might aspire but also the most extreme loss of favour an early modern subject can imagine. Buckingham's downfall prefigures both what will happen to Anne and at the same time the fate that befalls former favourite and supporter of the royal divorce Thomas Cranmer, Henry's Archbishop of Canterbury. He is beset by Catholic factions seeking to have him condemned for heresy; 'make your house our Tower,' commands the King (5.1.106). 'Is there no other way of mercy | But I needs must to th' Tower, my lords?' he asks, 'Must I go like a traitor thither?' (5.2.126–27, 130). In fact Cranmer will be spared this fate at this particular moment in time, King Henry restoring the Archbishop to favour by appointing him godfather to the Princess Elizabeth, but this brush with fate reminds the audience that the Tower remains not only a constant presence but also a constant threat, and that just as easily as royal preferment is bestowed so too can it be taken away. Writing under the patronage of the King, at a time when plays and books were frequently censored or even burned, Shakespeare must have been acutely conscious of this fact.

Buckingham's awareness of his own vulnerability is made especially clear when he recognizes a parallel between his (alleged) betrayal, for which he will be sent to the Tower, and his own father's uprising against Richard III, risking the same fate (1.2.193–96). It is certainly not lost upon Buckingham that history can repeat itself, and that the wheel of fortune continues to turn unstoppably:

> My noble father, Henry of Buckingham,
> Who first raised head against usurping Richard,
> Flying for succour to his servant Banister,
> Being distressed, was by that wretch betrayed,
> And, without trial, fell. God's peace be with him.
> Henry the Seventh succeeding, truly pitying
> My father's loss, like a most royal prince,
> Restored me to my honours and out of ruins
> Made my name once more noble. Now his son,
> Henry the Eighth, life, honour, name, and all
> That made me happy at one stroke has taken
> For ever from the world.

(2.1.107–18)

As the royal succession brings gains and losses in favour, so the dangers contingent upon reliance on the monarch's preferment are also passed from father to son.

Succession in *Henry VIII*

We have seen the ways in which the question of succession, symbolized by the Tower of London, is a recurring motif in *Henry VIII*. The play receives its dramatic impetus, after all, from the King's desire for an heir, which motivates – or excuses – his divorce from Katherine and subsequent marriage to Anne, mother of the future Elizabeth I. It is striking that a play Shakespeare co-wrote with Fletcher so late in his own career, at a moment in which the bestowing of his literary reputation onto his successors must have been prominent in his mind, is preoccupied by the issue of succession, constantly looking to the Tower as the place where the process of formalizing each new monarch's status begins (and where some reigns also come to their end, as will Anne's). But there is another reason for this preoccupation with succession, we would suggest, a reason that owes much to the political moment in which the two playwrights wrote. For as recent critics have found, the succession crises with which the Tudor dynasty is so strongly associated (Henry VIII's desire for an heir, Edward VI's premature death without issue and Elizabeth I's refusal to marry, reproduce or specify her intended successor) in fact continued well into the Stuart era. As Lisa Hopkins has written, James I's succession was problematic in both England and Scotland, depending as it did on the effective deposing of his own mother, Mary Queen of Scots. His sole surviving male offspring in 1613, Charles, was seen as a weak and questionable prospect for a future king. Court rumours suggested that he might be a changeling, an imposter placed in a royal crib after the real prince was taken – an unlikely story but one that reflects the degree of anxiety about the prospect of him one day ruling the nation felt by early modern Londoners (Hopkins, 6, 17). As Hopkins says, 'for close on 70 years English Renaissance drama both feeds off the question of the succession and proves itself a notably flexible medium for discussing it' (156). In such a climate it is perhaps not surprising that Shakespeare and Fletcher were drawn to dramatize Henry VIII's concerns about producing a legitimate heir suitable to rule his kingdom upon his death, and to treat the consequences of such concerns so unflinchingly.

A more immediate context for the play's anxieties about the political future of the English nation can be found in the juxtaposition of two contrasting events that had taken place in the royal family in the months leading up to *Henry VIII*'s first performance. On 6 November 1612 King James' firstborn son, Henry, Prince of Wales, died at St James's Palace, after a short and sudden illness (now thought to be typhoid). Already a popular figure, Henry was a patron of the arts and symbol of courtly chivalry around whom a kind of cult of personality had sprung up. The young prince's death was widely mourned, by poets including Thomas Campion, John Donne, George Herbert and Walter Raleigh, amongst others, who had espoused Henry as the ideal future king. The national outpouring of grief that resulted from his death also delayed the planned marriage of his sister, the Princess Elizabeth, to Frederick, elector palatine and future king of Bohemia, who had arrived in England to secure the match on 16 October. Their formal betrothal finally took place on 27 December and their marriage ceremony was celebrated throughout London on Valentine's Day, 14 February 1613. The union was particularly welcomed because of Frederick's status as one of the leading figures of European Protestantism, thus seeming to guarantee England's place amongst the reformed nations and ensuring the peaceful future that was the pacifist King James' most heartfelt ambition.

Henry VIII reflects this extraordinary period of English history as much as it tells the history of the Tudor monarch himself. McMullan has described the play's oscillations in mood and the mixture of positive and negative emotions established in the Prologue's opening speech, which mirrors the juxtaposition of grief with joy felt by the country at large at this moment:

> Think ye see
> The very persons of our noble story
> As they were living; think you see them great,
> And followed with the general throng and sweat
> Of thousand friends; then, in a moment, see
> How soon this mightiness meets misery;
> And if you can be merry then, I'll say
> A man may weep upon his wedding day.
>
> (1.0.25–32)

The 'general throng and sweat | Of thousand friends' seems to place us on a bustling London street, much like the one from which the three Gentlemen will later view Anne's procession from the Tower to the Abbey for her coronation. Through this speech we are made to feel the mixed emotions that foretell the changing fortunes of the play's noble characters and which, we have argued, is symbolized by the presence of the Tower in the drama. The prologue's curious final line, 'A man may weep upon his wedding day' seems not only to inflect the happiness of the present moment with a premonition of the sorrow Henry VIII's marriage to Anne will bring, but also to reflect the current mood of the nation, as celebrations of Princess Elizabeth's marriage were tempered by sadness at the recent loss of her brother, James' eagerly anticipated successor.

Henry VIII is then a play that reflects the current political climate of Jacobean London in its concern for the future security of the nation and sense of precariousness pertaining to the succession of both the monarch and his newly established Protestant church. Critics have noted the drama's emphasis upon historical veracity and the frequent recurrence of the word 'truth' and its associated variants throughout the play (see McMullan, introduction, 3). But as has been also noted, Shakespeare and Fletcher's drama is not straightforwardly a history play, containing elements of romance, tragicomedy and even masque, and in any case this genre is itself notorious for adjusting the past in order to fit the present demands of the stage. At a key moment in the play the dramatists alter the location of the feast celebrating Anne's coronation, for example; her journey from the Tower to Westminster culminates at 'York Place' in *Henry VIII*, a departure from the sources, where it is made clear that the event was marked in Westminster Hall itself (4.1.94). The apparent reason for this change seems to be that it allows Shakespeare and Fletcher to remind their audience of the recent downfall of Cardinal Wolsey; York Place was his former palace in London. As the First Gentleman observes: 'You must no more call it "York Place" – that's past; | For since the Cardinal fell, that title's lost. | 'Tis now the King's, and called "Whitehall" ' (4.1.95–97). 'And therefore the same was called York Place', writes John Stow, 'which name so continued until the year 1529, that King Henry VIII took it from Thomas Wolsey, Cardinal and Archbishop of York, and then gave it to name Whitehall' (367). The playwrights adjust history in order to serve their dramatic ends, neatly juxtaposing Wolsey's fall with Anne's rise in a reminder that she too ultimately is vulnerable, even at the moment in which she might seem all-powerful. This modification of historical truth is designed to evoke a dramatic truth instead, and also perhaps serves as a political comment on James I's reputation for revelry and excess. The King had recently ordered a new banqueting house to be constructed at York Place in 1606 (a building that would famously burn down in 1619 to be replaced by the Inigo Jones-designed structure that still stands today and which is described in our second chapter). *Henry VIII* is thus engaged with different kinds of history and different ideas of what history means within the city where it was created. In much the same way, this book has also been concerned to trace the history of Shakespeare's London through his plays and to place his dramatic works back into the past life of his city.

Conclusion

The relocation of Anne's coronation feast from Westminster Hall to York Place allows Shakespeare and Fletcher to make another important point, too, drawing our attention to the fact that any attempt to be true to history must contend with the fact that the past itself is not stable and static but rather in constant flux. This, while true of history in general, is particularly true of the history of London, which, as we have seen in this study, is always and never the same. Even as the two gentlemen onlookers at Anne's coronation in *Henry VIII* evoke 'York Place', so they are forced to recognize its name has already been altered to 'Whitehall'. In Shakespeare's city of constant change we see the rhythms of *Henry VIII* writ large as forward progress is held in constant tension with a circling back upon the past, revisiting history and registering the changes between that moment and the present as we go.

Henry VIII itself returns to many of the locations we have explored in this book, specifically evoking those particular London settings that held a fundamental importance in Shakespeare's imagination, and which he encountered in his

day-to-day life. The city is perhaps most vividly rendered in the
ribald prose chatter of the Porter and his Man in act five, scene
three, where many of these places are explicitly named and
which we will draw upon here in summing up our arguments.
They evoke the spectacle of early modern executions, whose
'audience' (5.3.58) had a seemingly macabre appetite for the
most gruesome punishments and who seem to have been the
intended market for Shakespeare's *Titus Andronicus*, a play that
attempts to redeem otherwise senseless violence through the
language of martyrdom, as we saw in our first chapter. The
suburb-dwellers, gathered to watch 'the ladies, | When they pass
back from the christening' of the Princess Elizabeth at
Westminster Abbey (5.3.70–71) reflect the concentric circles of
power that converged on Whitehall in Shakespeare's *Richard II*
and in his own day, the subject of our second chapter. The unruly
apprentices whose uprising informs the action of *Romeo and
Juliet* are evoked here as 'the hope o' th' Strand' (5.3.50), the
location of our third chapter and focus for the class struggles
that dominate both that play and *Henry VIII*'s obsession with
the lowly origins of certain key characters (such as Cromwell).
The 'youths that thunder at the playhouse' (5.3.57) here mirror
London's young population of theatre-goers, who included the
students at the Inns of Court whose finely tuned legal wit often
seems to have been the ideal audience imagined by Shakespeare,
and whose moot debates offer an important framework for our
understanding of the pivotal trial scenes found in both this play
and *The Merchant of Venice*, as we argued in our fourth chapter.
The religious reforms that echoed throughout Shakespeare's city
and that take centre stage in *Henry VIII* as well as *Hamlet*, the
subject of chapter five, were focused on the imposing structure
of 'Paul's' and the intellectual maelstrom of its printing industry
(5.3.14). The 'Moorfields' neighbourhood of the Bedlam
Hospital, focal point for our study of medicine in *King Lear* is
alluded to here with a reminder that the field itself was once
used for archery practice (5.3.31); medical discourse is present
throughout *Henry VIII*, particularly in descriptions of
Buckingham's 'choler' at his sentencing (2.1.34) and Katherine's

sickness (4.2.2–4). The play's concern with worldly goods, emblematized in the transferred ownership of York Place and also evoked here in the mention of the 'Fair' at which working-class Londoners spent their hard-earned income (5.3.66), as well as the threat of the 'Marshalsea' debtors' prison (5.3.83), places us back in the world of *Timon of Athens*, a play that is thoroughly immersed in the commercial realities of Shakespeare's London as we saw in Chapter 7. Finally, the distractions available on early modern Bankside with its famous 'Parish [Paris] Garden' (5.3.2) here reflect London's growing entertainment industry that had recently culminated in the opening of the new Blackfriars theatre for which Shakespeare wrote his highly experimental play, *The Tempest*, whose evocation of early modern scientific practices was the subject of our final chapter.

We have thus retraced the steps of our journey through Shakespeare's London. We have also returned to the beginning of the progress through the city that we have shared with the playwright, circling back to the idea of London as a microcosm with which we began; the play's dense and highly specific act five, scene three embodies the city's universality, its ability to contain multitudes and to evoke whole worlds of meaning within the confines of its neighbourhoods and streets. In a technique we have seen repeated throughout the plays examined in this study, details of life in the early modern metropolis are here used to render the events of *Henry VIII* all the more vivid to its first audiences and, at the same time, to transcend the specifics of time and place, reaching beyond the world of the play to a more universal realm of human experience. The plethora of allusions to early modern London in this scene bring Shakespeare's city to life in one of the final moments of his career as a playwright, a career in which the city has been a constant presence in his works even while ostensibly absent. It is fitting that Shakespeare himself is absent at this moment and that Fletcher apparently authored the scene; London's foremost playwright passes the mantle to one of his successors here. We can, perhaps, read the scene as

Fletcher's tribute to his collaborator, a poet who could express all of human life in rich and beautiful words, and a tribute too to their shared city, where all of human life was found.

On the afternoon of 29 June 1613 a fire broke out at the Globe Theatre, 'and fastened upon the thatch of the house and there burned so furiously,' writes Londoner Thomas Lorkins, 'as it consumed the whole house and all in less than two houres (the people having enough to do to save themselves)' (quoted by McMullan, 58). The play being performed there at the time was *Henry VIII*. Shakespeare's theatre was destroyed; the space that had accommodated the entire world of his imagining and in which he had explored every aspect of life in his city was no more. The Globe would be rebuilt; *Henry VIII* was itself revived at the theatre in 1628, sponsored by the then Duke of Buckingham, who seemingly (and misguidedly) sought to secure his own political position by having it performed there. And again it would be rebuilt in 1997, as the modern Shakespeare's Globe, a new home for his plays in today's London. The Globe theatre is in this sense always and never the same. As we have seen through our exploration of Shakespeare's plays in this book, the same is true of early modern London.

WORKS CITED

Adelman, Janet, *Suffocating Mothers: Fantasies of Maternal Origin in Shakespeare's Plays, 'Hamlet' to 'The Tempest'* (London, 1992)

Ahnert, Ruth, *The Rise of Prison Literature in the Sixteenth Century* (Cambridge, 2013)

Archer, Ian W., *The Pursuit of Social Stability: Social Relations in Elizabethan London* (Cambridge, 1991)

Aubrey, John, *Aubrey's Brief Lives*, ed. John Buchanan-Brown (London, 1972)

Bacon, Francis, 'Of Regiment of Health' in *The Major Works*, Oxford World's Classics, ed. Brian Vickers (Oxford, 1996), 403–405

Bailey, Amanda, '*Timon of Athens*, forms of Payback, and the Genre of Debt', *English Literary Renaissance* 41:2 (2011), 375–400

Baker, Christopher, *Religion in the Age of Shakespeare* (London, 2007)

Baker, J.H., 'The third university 1450–1550: law school or finishing school?' in Jayne Elisabeth Archer, Elizabeth Goldring and Sarah Knight, eds, *The Intellectual and Cultural World of the Early Modern Inns of Court* (Manchester, 2011), 8–24

Barton, Anne, 'The London Scene: City and Court' in Margreta De Grazia and Stanley Wells, eds, *The Cambridge Companion to Shakespeare* (Cambridge, 2001), 115–28

Bixby, Suzanne, 'Hamlet', www.talkinbroadway.com/regional/boston/boston7.html

Blayney, Peter W.M., *The Bookshops in Paul's Cross Churchyard* (London, 1990)

Boose, Lynda E., 'The Comic Contract and Portia's Golden Ring,' *Shakespeare Studies* 20 (January, 1988), 241–54

Boulton, Jeremy, *Neighbourhood and Society: A London Suburb in the Seventeenth Century* (Cambridge, 1987)

— 'The Poor Among the Rich: Paupers and the Parish in the West End, 1600–1724', in Paul Griffiths and Mark S.R. Jenner, eds, *Londinopolis: Essays in the Cultural and Social History of Early Modern London*, (Manchester, 2000), 197–225

Bright, Timothy, *A Treatise of Melancholie, &c.* (London, 1586)

Brooke, Arthur, 'The Tragical Historye of Romeus and Juliet' Geoffrey Bullough , ed., in *Narrative and Dramatic Sources of Shakespeare: Volume 1*, (London, 1964)

Buck, George, *A Discourse or Treatise of the third universitie of England. &c.* (London, 1615)

Burton, Robert, *The Anatomy of Melancholy* (1621), eds, Thomas C. Faulkner, Nicholas K. Kiessling and Rhonda L. Blair, 6 vols. (Oxford, 1989)

'Campion, Edmund [St Edmund Campion] (1540–1581),' Michael A.E. Graves, in *The Oxford Dictionary of National Biography* (Oxford, 2004)

'Carey, Henry, first Baron Hunsdon (1526–1596),' Wallace T. MacCaffrey, in *The Oxford Dictionary of National Biography* (Oxford, 2004)

Carroll, William C., ' "The Base Shall Top Th'Legitimate": The Bedlam Beggar and the Role of Edgar in *King Lear*,' *Shakespeare Quarterly* 38.4 (Winter, 1987), 426–41

Chronicle of the Grey Friars of London, ed. John Gough Nichols (London, 1852)

Cormack, Bradin, 'Locating *The Comedy of Errors*: Revels Jurisdiction at the Inns of Court,' in Jayne Elisabeth Archer, Elizabeth Goldring and Sarah Knight, eds, *The Intellectual and Cultural World of the Early Modern Inns of Court* (Manchester, 2011), 264–85

The Book of Common Prayer: The Texts of 1549, 1559, and 1662, (ed.) (Oxford, 2011)

Davies, John, *Microcosmos: The Discovery of the Little World &c.* (Oxford, 1603)

De Grazia, Margreta, 'The Ideology of Superfluous Things: *King Lear* a Period Piece,' in Margreta De Grazia and Peter Stallybrass, eds, *Subject and Object in Renaissance Culture*, (Cambridge, 1996)

Dekker, Thomas, 'A Creditor' and 'A Prisoner', in Thomas Overbury et al., *His Wife with New Additions of Characters* (London, 1622)

— *The Dead Terme &c.* (London, 1608)

— *Dekker His Dreame & c.* (London, 1620)

— *Lantern and Candle-Light & c.* (London, 1609)

Deiter, Kristen, *The Tower of London in English Renaissance Drama: Icon of Opposition* (New York, 2008)

Dillon, Janette, *Theatre, Court and City, 1595–1610* (Cambridge, 2000)

Donne, John, 'Satire 1' in *Selected Poetry*, ed. John Carey (Oxford, 1996), 1–4

'Donne, John (1572–1631),' David Colclough, in *The Oxford Dictionary of National Biography* (Oxford, 2004)

Eagleton, Terry, *Sweet Violence: The Idea of the Tragic* (Oxford, 2003)

Earle, John, *Micro-cosmographie &c.* (London, 1628)

Eisenstein, Elizabeth L., *The Printing Revolution in Early Modern Europe* 2nd edn. (Cambridge, 2005)

'Elizabeth I (1533–1603),' Patrick Collinson, in *The Oxford Dictionary of National Biography* (Oxford, 2004)

Erne, Lukas, *Shakespeare as Literary Dramatist* (Cambridge, 2003)

Foakes, R. A., ed., *Henslowe's Diary*, 2nd edn (Cambridge, 2002)

Foxe, John, *Acts and Monuments &c.* (London, 1563, 1570)

— 'John Foxe's The Acts and Monuments Online' www.johnfoxe.org/index.php (Sheffield, 2011)

Gesta Grayorum, &c. (London, 1688)

Goldberg, Jonathan 'Carnival in *The Merchant of Venice*,' *Postmedieval: A Journal of Medieval and Cultural Studies* 4 (2013), 427–38

Greenblatt, Stephen *Hamlet in Purgatory* (Princeton, 2001)

— 'Introduction' to *The Tempest, The Norton Shakespeare: Essential Plays and the Sonnets*, ed. Stephen Greenblatt et al. (New York and London, 1997)

— *Renaissance Self-Fashioning From More to Shakespeare*, 2nd edn (Chicago, 2005)

Greenes Groats-Worth of Wit &c. (London, 1592)

Groves, Beatrice, *Texts and Traditions. Religion in Shakespeare 1592–1604* (Oxford, 2007)

Hall, John, *Select Observations on English Bodies* (London, 1657)

'Hall, John (1574/5?–1635),' Joan Lane, in *The Oxford Dictionary of National Biography* (Oxford, 2004)

Harkness, Deborah E., *The Jewel House: Elizabethan London and the Scientific Revolution* (New Haven, 2007)

Harman, Thomas, *A Caveat for Common Cursitors, &c.* (London, 1567)

The Harper Collins Study Bible, New Revised Standard Version with the Apocryphal/Deuterocanonical Books, ed. Wayne A. Meeks (London, 1993)

Harsnett, Samuel, *A Declaration of Egregious Popish Impostures, &c.* (London, 1603)

Heylyn, Peter, *Microcosmus, or A little description of the great world &c.* (Oxford, 1621)

'Hoby, Sir Edward (1560–1617),' Louis A. Knapfla, in *The Oxford Dictionary of National Biography* (Oxford, 2004)

Hoeniger, F. David, *Medicine and Shakespeare in the English Renaissance* (Newark, DE, 1992)

Hopkins, Lisa, *Drama and the Succession to the Crown, 1561–1633* (Farnham, 2011)

'Howard, Thomas, fourth duke of Norfolk (1538–1572)', Michael Graves, in *The Oxford Dictionary of National Biography* (Oxford, 2004)

Howard, Jean *Theater of a City: The Places of London Comedy, 1598–1642* (Philadelphia, 2007)

Hutson, Lorna, 'The evidential plot: Shakespeare and Gascoigne at Gray's Inn,' in Jayne Elisabeth Archer, Elizabeth Goldring and Sarah Knight, eds, *The Intellectual and Cultural World of the Early Modern Inns of Court* (Manchester, 2011), 243–63

Jackson, Ken, ' "I know not | Where did I lodge last night?": *King Lear* and the Search for Bethlem (Bedlam) Hospital,' *English Literary Renaissance* 30.2 (Spring, 2000), 213–40

'John [John of Gaunt], duke of Aquitaine and duke of Lancaster, styled king of Castile and Léon (1340–1399),' Simon Walker, in *The Oxford Dictionary of National Biography* (Oxford, 2004)

Johnson, David, *Southwark and the City* (London, 1969)

Jones, Gwilym, *Shakespeare's Storms* (Manchester, 2013)

Jonson, Ben, *Every Man Out of His Humour*, ed. Helen Ostovich, The Revels Plays (Manchester, 2001)

Jorden, Edward, *A Briefe Discourse of a Disease Called the Mother* (London, 1603)

Kantorowicz, Ernst, *The King's Two Bodies: A Study in Mediaeval Political Theology* (Princeton, NJ, 1957)

Kastan, David Scott, *Shakespeare and the Book* (Cambridge, 2001)

Knight, Sarah, 'Literature and drama at the early modern Inns of Court' in Jayne Elisabeth Archer, Elizabeth Goldring and Sarah Knight, eds, *The Intellectual and Cultural World of the Early Modern Inns of Court* (Manchester, 2011), 217–22

Lenton, Francis, *The Young Gallants Whirligig* (London, 1629)

Lesser, Zachary, and Peter Stallybrass, 'The First Literary Hamlet and the Commonplacing of Professional Plays,' *Shakespeare Quarterly* 59 (2008), 371–420

Lewalski, Barbara K., 'Biblical Allusion and Allegory in *The Merchant of Venice*,' *Shakespeare Quarterly* 13.3 (1962), 327–43

'Lopez [Lopes], Roderigo [Ruy, Roger], (c.1517–1594),' Edgar Samuel, in *The Oxford Dictionary of National Biography* (Oxford, 2004)

Lupton, Donald, *London and the Countrey Carbonadoed &c.* (London, 1632)

MacGregor, Neil, *Shakespeare's Restless World* (London, 2012)

Marlowe, Christopher, *The Jew of Malta* (London, 1633)

Mebane, John S., *Renaissance Magic and the Return of the Golden Age* (Lincoln, Nebraska, 1989)

Melnikoff, Kirk, 'Nicholas Ling's Republican *Hamlet* (1603)', in Marta Straznicky, ed., *Shakespeare's Stationers: Studies in Cultural Bibliography* (Philadelphia, 2013), 95–111

Merritt, J.F., *The Social World of Early Modern Westminster: Abbey, Court and Community* (Manchester, 2005)

Minshull, Geffray, *Essays and Characters of a Prison and Prisoners & c.* (London, 1618)

Moffett, Thomas, *Insectorum sive Minimorum Animalium Theatrum & c.* (London, 1634)

Montaigne, Michel de, *The Essayes, or Morall, Politicke and Militarie Discourses*, trans. John Florio (London, 1603)

— 'On the resemblance of children to fathers,' in *The Complete Essays*, trans. M.A. Screech (London, 1987), 858–89

Mukherji, Subha, *Law and Representation in Early Modern Drama* (Cambridge, 2006)

Muldrew, Craig, *The Economy of Obligation: The Culture of Credit and Social Relations in Early Modern England* (New York, 1998)

Mullaney, Steven, *The Place of the Stage: License, Play, and Power in Renaissance England* (Ann Arbor, 1988)

Munro, Ian, *The Figure of the Crowd in Early Modern London: The City and its Double* (New York, 2005)

Nicholl, Charles, *The Lodger: Shakespeare on Silver Street* (London, 2007)

Norden, John, *Speculum Britanniae: The First Parte, a Description of Middlesex (1593)* (New York, 1971)

Ovid, *Metamorphoses*, trans. Arthur Golding (London, 1567)

Palmer, Daryl W., 'Histories of Violence and the Writer's Hand: Foxe's *Actes and Monuments* and Shakespeare's *Titus Andronicus*', in

David M. Bergerson, ed., *Reading and Writing in Shakespeare* (Newark, DE, 1996), 82–115

Pearl, Valerie, *London and the Outbreak of the Puritan Revolution: City, Government and National Politics, 1625–1643* (London, 1961)

Peat, Derek, 'Mad for Shakespeare: a Reconsideration of the Importance of Bedlam,' *Parergon* 21.1 (2004), 113–32

Peterson, Kaara L., *Popular Medicine, Hysterical Disease, and Social Controversy in Shakespeare's England* (Farnham, 2010)

Pettigrew, Todd, *Shakespeare and the Practice of Physic: Medical Narratives on the Early Modern English Stage* (Newark, DE, 2007)

Platter, Thomas, account of his visit to London (1599), in E.K. Chambers, ed., *The Elizabethan Stage*, 4 vols. (Oxford, 1923, repr. 2009), vol. 2, 364–7

Plowden, Edmund, *Les commentaries, ou les reportes de Edmunde Plowden, &c.* (London, 1571)

Prockter, Adrian, and Robert Taylor, eds, *The A to Z of Elizabethan London* (London, 1979)

Ripley, George, *The Compound of Alchemy* (London, 1591)

Salkeld, Duncan, 'Literary Traces in Bridewell and Bethlem, 1602–1604,' *The Review of English Studies*, New Series 56.225 (2005), 379–85

Shakespeare, William, *The Tragical Historie of Hamlet Prince of Denmarke* (London, 1603)

— *Hamlet*, eds, Ann Thompson and Neil Taylor, Arden Third Series (London, 2006)

— *King Henry IV, Part 2*, ed. Ronald Knowles (London, 1999)

— *The Second Part of King Henry IV*, ed. A. R. Humphreys, Arden Second Series (London, 1966)

— *Henry V*, ed. T.W. Craik, Arden Third Series (London, 1995)

— *King Lear*, ed. R.A. Foakes, Arden Third Series (London, 1997)

— *Love's Labour's Lost*, ed. George Hibbard, Oxford Shakespeare (Oxford, 1990)

— *The Merchant of Venice*, ed. John Drakakis, Arden Third Series (London, 2010)

— *Richard II*, ed. Charles R. Forker, Arden Third Series (London, 2002)

— *Romeo and Juliet*, ed. René Weis, Arden Third Series (London, 2012)

— *The Tempest*, eds Alden T. Vaughan and Virginia Mason Vaughan, Arden Third Series (London, 2011)

— *Timon of Athens*, eds Antony B. Dawson and Gretchen E. Minton, Arden Third Series (London, 2008)

— *Twelfth Night*, ed. Keir Elam, Arden Third Series (London, 2008)

— *Titus Andronicus*, ed. Jonathan Bate, Arden Third Series (London, 1995)

— and John Fletcher, *Henry VIII (All is True)*, ed. Gordon McMullan, Arden Third Series (London, 2000)

'Shakespeare, William, 1564–1616,' Peter Holland, in *The Oxford Dictionary of National Biography* (Oxford, 2004)

Sharp, Buchanan, 'Shakespeare's *Coriolanus* and the Crisis of the 1590s', in Buchanan Sharp and Mark Charles Fissel, eds, *Law and Authority in Early Modern England* (Newark, DE, 2007), 27–63

Shirley, James, *The Witty Fair One* (London, 1633)

'Sidney, Sir Philip (1554–1586),' H.R. Woudhuysen, in *The Oxford Dictionary of National Biography* (Oxford, 2004)

Simonds, Peggy Munoz, ' "My Charms Crack Not": The Alchemical Structure of *The Tempest*', *Comparative Drama* 32 (1998), 538–70

Slights, William W.E., *The Heart in the Age of Shakespeare* (Cambridge, 2008)

Southwell, Robert, *The Collected Poems of S. Robert Southwell*, eds Peter Davidson and Anne Sweeney (Manchester, 2007)

Spiller, Elizabeth, 'Shakespeare and the Making of Early Modern Science: Resituating Prospero's Art', *South Central Review* 26 (2009), 24–41

Stallybrass, Peter, Roger Chartier, J. Franklin Mowery and Heather Wolfe, 'Hamlet's Tables and the Technologies of Writing in Renaissance England,' *Shakespeare Quarterly* 55 (2004), 379–419

Stock, Angela, and Anne-Julia Zwierlein, 'Introduction: Our scene is London' in Dieter Mehl, Angela Stock and Anne-Julia Zwierlein, eds., *Plotting Early Modern London: New Essays on Jacobean City Comedy* (Aldershot, Hants., 2004), 1–26

Stow, John, *A Survey of London written in the year 1598*, with an introduction by Antonia Fraser, (Stroud, Gloucs., 2009)

Strachey, William, 'True Reportory of the Wracke, and Redemption of Sir Thomas Gates,' in Samuel Purchas, *Purchas his Pilgrimes* (London, 1625)

Taylor, John, *The Praise and Virtue of a Jail and Jailers & c.* (London, 1623)

Topsell, Edward, *The History of Four-Footed Beasts* (London, 1607)

Vaughan, Alden T., 'Trinculo's Indian: American natives in Shakespeare's England', Peter Hulme and William H. Sherman, eds, *The Tempest and its Travels* (London, 2000), 49–50

Verstegan, Richard, [*Theatre of Cruelty*] *Theatrum Crudelitatum* (Antwerp, 1587)

'Wriothesley, Henry, third earl of Southampton (1573–1624),' Park Honan, in *The Oxford Dictionary of National Biography* (Oxford, 2004)

SUGGESTED FURTHER READING

In addition to the works cited above, the following may be of interest should you wish to learn more about Shakespeare's London. We have broken this list into sections for ease of reference.

Other plays featuring Shakespeare's London

Francis Beaumont, *The Knight of the Burning Pestle* (1607)
Richard Brome, *The New Academy* (1636)
— *The Weeding of Covent Garden* (c.1632)
— *The Sparagus Garden* (1635)
Thomas Dekker, *The Shoemaker's Holiday* (1599)
— & Thomas Middleton, *The Roaring Girl* (c.1607-10)
— & Thomas Middleton, *The Honest Whore* (Parts One and Two) (c.1605-6)
— & John Webster, *Northward Ho* (c.1605-7)
— & John Webster, *Westward Ho* (c.1604)
John Ford, *'Tis Pity She's a Whore* (c.1629-33)
Robert Greene, *A Disputation Between a Hee Conny-Catcher and a Shee Conny Catcher* (1592)
William Haughton, *Englishmen for My Money, or A Woman Have Her Will* (1598)
Thomas Heywood, *The Wise Woman of Hoxton* (c.1605)
— *If You Know Not Me, You Know Nobody, Parts I* and *II* (c.1604-5)
— *The Fair Maid of the Exchange* (1607)
Ben Jonson, *The Alchemist* (1610)
— *Bartholomew Fair* (1614)
— *Every Man out of His Humor* (1599)
— with George Chapman & John Marston, *Eastward Ho!* (1605)

— *Epicoene* (1609)
Thomas Kyd, *The Spanish Tragedy* (c.1587)
John Marston, *The Dutch Courtesan* (c.1604)
Thomas Middleton, *A Trick to Catch the Old One* (c.1607-8)
— *A Chaste Maid in Cheapside* (c.1613)
— *Michaelmas Term* (1604)
— *The Revenger's Tragedy* (1606)
— & Thomas Rowley, *The Changeling* (1622)
John Webster, *The White Devil* (1612)

Mapping the history of London

Jeremy Boulton, 'London 1540–1700' in P. Clark (ed.) *The Cambridge Urban History of Britain 1540–1700*, vol. II (Cambridge, 2000)

Kent Cartwright, 'The Folger 1560 View of London', *Shakespeare Quarterly* 29.1 (Winter, 1978): 67–76

Paul Griffiths, *Lost Londons: Change, Crime and Control in the Capital City 1550–1660* (Cambridge, 2008)

Richard Helgerson, *Forms of Nationhood: The Elizabethan Writing of England* (Chicago, 1992)

J. Howgego, *Printed Maps of London, c.1533–1850*, 2nd edition (Folkstone, 1978)

J.F. Merritt, (ed.) *Imagining the City: Perceptions and Portrayals of Early Modern London from Stow to Strype 1598–1720* (Cambridge, 2001)

Lena Cowen Orlin, (ed.) *Material London, ca. 1600* (Philadelphia, 2000)

— 'Temporary Lives: Lodgings in Early Modern London', *Huntington Library Quarterly* 71.1 (2008): 219–42

Gail Kern Paster, *The Idea of the City in the Age of Shakespeare* (Atlanta, GA, 1985)

M.J. Power, 'The east and west in early-modern London' in E.W. Ives, R.J. Knecht, and J.J. Scarisbrick (eds) *Wealth and Power in Tudor England* (1978), 167–85

Adrian Prockter and Robert Taylor, *The A to Z of Elizabethan London* (London, 1979)

John Schofield (ed.) *The London Surveys of Ralph Treswell* (London, 1987)

Paul S. Seever, *Wallington's World: A Puritan Artisan in Seventeenth-Century London* (Stanford, 1988)

Peter Slack, 'Perceptions of the metropolis in seventeenth-century England' in P. Burke, B. Harrison and P. Slack (eds) *Civil Histories* (Oxford, 2000)

Robert Tittler, *Townspeople and Nation: English Urban Experiences, 1540–1640* (Stanford, 2001)

Peter Whitfield, *London: A Life in Maps* (London, 2006)

City comedy

Brian Gibbons, *Jacobean City Comedy* (1968, rev. edn 1980)

Jean E. Howard, 'Shakespeare and the London of City Comedy', *Shakespeare Studies* (Tokyo, Japan) 39 (2001): 1–21

— 'Stage Masculinities, National History, and the Making of London Theatrical Culture', in Lena Cowen Orlin (ed.), *Center or Margin: Revisions of the English Renaissance in Honor of Leeds Barroll* (Selinsgrove, PA, 2006), pp. 199–214

T.B. Leinwand, *The City Staged: Jacobean Comedy, 1603–1613* (1986)

Dieter Mehl et al (eds), *Plotting Early Modern London: New Essays on Jacobean City Comedy* (Ashgate, 2004)

Shakespeare and his contemporaries in London

Katherine Duncan-Jones, *Ungentle Shakespeare: Scenes from his Life* (London, 2001)

Bart Van Es, *Shakespeare in Company* (Oxford, 2013)

James D. Mardock, *Our Scene is London: Ben Jonson's City and the Space of the Author* (New York, 2008)

Charles Nicholl, *The Lodger: Shakespeare on Silver Street* (London, 2007)

— *The Reckoning: The Murder of Christopher Marlowe* (London, 1995)

Carlo Pagetti, 'Shakespeare's Tales of Two Cities: London and Rome', in Maria Del Sapio Garbero (ed.), *Identity, Otherness and Empire in Shakespeare's Rome* (Surrey, 2009)

James Shapiro, *1599: A Year in the Life of William Shakespeare* (London, 2005)

Robert Shaughnessy (ed.), *The Cambridge Companion to Shakespeare and Popular Culture* (Cambridge, 2007)

J.L. Simmons, 'A Source for Shakespeare's Malvolio: The Elizabethan Controversy with the Puritans', *The Huntington Library Quarterly* 36.3 (May, 1973): 181–201

Stanley Wells, *Shakespeare & Co.* (London, 2006)

Playhouses

Herbert Berry, 'The View of London from the North and the Playhouses in Holywell', *Shakespeare Survey* 53 (2000): 196–212

O.L. Brownstein, 'A Record of London Inn-Playhouses from c.1565–1590', *Shakespeare Quarterly* 22.1 (Winter, 1971): 17–24

Christie Carson and Farah Karim-Cooper (eds.) *Shakespeare's Globe: A Theatrical Experiment* (Cambridge, 2008)

Giles E. Dawson, 'London's Bull-Baiting and Bear-Baiting Arena in 1562', *Shakespeare Quarterly* 15.1 (Winter, 1964): 97–101

Richard Dutton (ed.), *The Oxford Handbook of Early Modern Theatre* (Oxford, 2009)

Andrew Gurr, *Playgoing in Shakespeare's London* (Cambridge, 1987)

— *The Shakespearean Stage: 1574–1642*, 3rd edn (Cambridge, 1992)

— *The Shakespeare Company, 1594–1642* (Cambridge, 2004)

Andrew Gurr and Mariko Ichikawa, *Staging in Shakespeare's Theatres* (Oxford, 2000)

J.T. King, *Casting Shakespeare's Plays: London Actors and their Roles, 1590–1642* (Cambridge, 1992)

James P. Lusardi, 'The Pictured Playhouse: Reading the Utrecht Engraving of Shakespeare's London', *Shakespeare Quarterly* 44.2 (Summer, 1993): 202–27

Tyburn

Thomas P. Anderson, 'Reading Martyred History in *Titus Andronicus*', in *Performing Early Modern Trauma from Shakespeare to Milton* (Ashgate, 2006), 19–56

Anne Dillon, *The Construction of Martyrdom in the English Catholic Community, 1535–1603* (Aldershot, 2002)

John Klause, 'Politics, Heresy and Martyrdom in Shakespeare's Sonnet 124 and *Titus Andronicus*', in James Schiffer (ed.), *Shakespeare's Sonnets: Critical Essays* (New York, 1999), 219–40

Ethan Shagan (ed.) *Catholics and the 'Protestant Nation': Religious Politics and Identity in Early Modern England* (Manchester, 2005)

Anne Sweeney, *Robert Southwell: Snow in Arcadia – Redrawing the English Lyric Landscape 1586–95* (Manchester, 2006)

Alexandra Walsham, *Charitable Hatred: Tolerance and Intolerance in England, 1500–1700* (Manchester, 2006)

The Strand

Ian Archer, 'Popular Politics in the Sixteenth and Early Seventeenth Centuries', in *Londinopolis, c.1500–1750: Essays in the Cultural and Social History of Early Modern London*, eds. Paul Griffiths and Mark S.R. Jenner (Manchester, 2001)

David Kathman, 'Grocers, Goldsmiths, and Drapers: Freemen and Apprentices in the Elizabethan Theater', *Shakespeare Quarterly* 55.1 (Spring, 2004): 1–49

Julie Sanders, *The Cultural Geography of Early Modern Drama, 1620–1650* (Cambridge, 2011)

Whitehall

Anne Barton, 'The London Scene: City and Court', in Margreta De Grazia & Stanley Wells (eds), *The Cambridge Companion to Shakespeare* (Cambridge, 2001), 115–28

David Bevington, David L. Smith and Richard Strier (eds), *The Theatrical City: Culture, Theatre and Politics in London, 1576–1649* (Cambridge, 1995)

Chris Fitter, ' "The Quarrel Is between Our Masters and Us Their Men": *Romeo and Juliet*, Dearth, and the London Riots', *English Literary Renaissance* 30.2 (Spring, 2000): 154–83

Alexander Leggatt, chapter 4, '*Henry IV*', in *Shakespeare's Political Drama: The History Plays and the Roman Plays* (London, 1988), 79–114

Ian Munro, *The Figure of the Crowd in Early Modern London: The City and its Double* (Basingstoke, 2005)

A.D. Nuttall, from *A New Mimesis: Shakespeare and the Representation of Reality* (New Haven, repr. 2007), 143–62

Stephen Orgel, *The Illusion of Power: Political Theater in the English Renaissance* (Berkeley, 1975)

Adam Zucker and Alan B. Farmer, (eds) *Localizing Caroline Drama: Politics and Economics of the Early Modern English Stage, 1625–1642* (Basingstoke, 2006)

The Inns of Court

Christopher Brooks, *Law, Politics and Society in Early Modern England* (Cambridge, 2010)

Constance Jordan and Karen Cunningham, (eds) *The Law in Shakespeare* (Basingstoke, 2010)

Victoria Kahn, *Rhetoric and Law in Early Modern Europe* (New Haven, 2001)

Alan H. Nelson, Chapter 16, 'The Universities and the Inns of Court', in Richard Dutton (ed.), *The Oxford Handbook of Early Modern Theatre* (Oxford, 2009), 280–91

Paul Raffield, *Images and Cultures of Law in Early Modern England: Justice and Political Power, 1558–1660* (Cambridge, 2007)

St Paul's

Peter W.M. Blayney, *The Bookshops in Paul's Cross Churchyard* (London, 1990)

Douglas A. Brooks, *From Playhouse to Printing House: Drama and Authority in Early Modern England* (Cambridge, 2000)

Eamon Duffy, *The Stripping of the Altars, Traditional Religion in England c.1400–1580* (New Haven: 1992)

Lukas Erne, 'Shakespeare and the Publication of His Plays', *Shakespeare Quarterly* 53.1 (Spring, 2002): 1–20

John Freeman, 'This Side of Purgatory: Ghostly Fathers and the Recusant Legacy in *Hamlet*', in Dennis Taylor and David N. Beauregard, eds, *Shakespeare and the Culture of Christianity in Early Modern England* (New York: 2003), 222–60

John Jowett, *Shakespeare and Text* (Oxford, 2007)

David Scott Kastan, *A Will to Believe: Shakespeare and Religion* (Oxford, 2014)

John N. King, Introduction to *Foxe's 'Book of Martyrs' and Early Modern Print Culture* (Cambridge, 2006), 1–20

Zachary Lesser, *Renaissance Drama and the Politics of Publication: Readings in the English Booktrade* (Cambridge, 2004)

Paul's Cross Project http://vpcp.chass.ncsu.edu/

Alison Shell, *Shakespeare and Religion*, The Arden Critical Companions (London, 2010)

James Simpson, *Under the Hammer: Iconoclasm in the Anglo-American Tradition* (Oxford, 2010)

Bethlehem (Bedlam) Hospital

Catherine Arnold, *Bedlam: London and its Mad* (London, 2008)

William C. Carol, 'Songs of Madness: The Lyric Afterlife of Shakespeare's Poor Tom', *Shakespeare Survey* 55 (2008): 82–95

Ken Jackson, *Separate Theaters: Bethlem ('Bedlam') Hospital and the Shakespearean Stage* (Newark, DE., 2005)

Mary Lindemann, *Medicine and Society in Early Modern Europe* (Cambridge, 2010)

Kenneth Muir, 'Madness in *King Lear*', *Shakespeare Survey* 13 (1966): 30–40

Roy Porter, *Madness: A Brief History* (Oxford, 2002)

— *Blood and Guts: A Short History of Medicine* (London, 2002)

Benjamin Reiss, 'Bardoloatry in Bedlam: Shakespeare, Psychiatry and Cultural authority in 19thC America', *English Literary History* 72.4 (2005): 769–97

Southwark

Douglas Bruster, *Drama and the Market in the Age of Shakespeare* (Cambridge, 1992)

Emily Cockayne, *Hubbub: Filth, Noise and Stench in England, 1600–1770* (New Haven, 2007)

Roslyn Lander Knutson, *Playing Companies and Commerce in Shakespeare's Time* (Cambridge, 2001)

Lena Cowen Orlin, *Locating Privacy in Tudor London* (Oxford, 2007)

— 'Women on the Threshold', *Shakespeare Studies* 25 (1997): 16–23

Peter Stallybrass & Allon White, Chapter 1, 'The Fair, the Pig, Authorship', in *The Politics and Poetics of Transgression* (Cambridge, 1986), 1–26

Lime Street

Ian Donaldson, *Jonson's Magic Houses: Essays in Interpretation* (Cambridge, 1997)

Paula Findlen, 'Jokes of Nature and Jokes of Knowledge: The Playfulness of Scientific Discourse in Early Modern Europe', *Renaissance Quarterly* 43.2 (Summer, 1990): 292–331

John Shanahan, 'Ben Jonson's *Alchemist* and Early Modern Laboratory Space', *The Journal for Early Modern Cultural Studies* 8.1 (Spring/Summer, 2008): 35–66

Steven Shapin, 'The House of Experiment in Seventeenth-Century England', *Isis* 79.3 (September, 1988): 373–404

You might also enjoy . . .

Antony Burgess, *Nothing Like the Sun* (London, 1964)

— *Dead Man in Deptford* (London, 1993)

Germaine Greer, *Shakespeare's Wife* (London, 2007)

Neil MacGregor, *Shakespeare's Restless World* (London, 2012)

Sally O'Reilly, *Dark Amelia* (Brighton, 2014)

Liza Picard, *Elizabeth's London: Everyday Life in Elizabethan London* (New York, 2005)

Nicholas Robins, *Walking Shakespeare's London* (London 2004)

S. Schoenbaum, *Shakespeare's Lives* (Oxford, 1991)

Richard Tames, *Shakespeare's London on Five Groats a Day* (London, 2009)

INDEX

Numbers in bold refer to the Figures

The A to Z of Elizabethan London, 37
Adelman, Janet, 161
Agincourt, battle of, 11–12
Alchemy, 206–9
Aldgate, 5
Alighieri, Dante
    The Divine Comedy, 132–3
Alleyn, Giles, 13
Anglican Church (*see* Church of England)
Anhert, Ruth, 181
Anjou, Duke of, 59
Apprentices
    riots, 234
Aquinas, Saint Thomas, 133
Aragon, Katherine of, 221
Archer, Ian, 91
Arden (Forest of), 92
Arundel, Earl of, 5, 36
Askew, Anne, 40
assumpsit, as legal principle, 107
Aubrey, John, 3

Bacon, Francis, 154
Bacon, Roger
    Mirror of Alchemy, 199
Bailey, Amanda, 179
Baker, Christopher, 137, 142
Baker, J.H., 108
Bankside, 48, 104, 234

Barton, Anne, 60–61
Bate, Jonathan, 24
Bear-baiting, 6, 7, 14, 29, 164, 184
Bedlam (Bethlehem Hospital), 17, 147–8, 151, 153, 161–9, 184, 186, 191, 234
Beeston, Christopher, 163
Belott-Mountjoy case, 99–101
    Shakespeare's testimony, **100**
Bible, The
    Genesis, 129
    Exodus, 132
Bishopsgate, 5, 7, 17, 87 147, 163
Blackfriars, 227
    hall, 221
    playhouse, 18, 121, 180, 182, 197, 213–17, 221, 234
    Shakespeare's property, 192, 223
Blount, Edward, 139
Boleyn, Anne, 19
Bonds, 104–7, 177
Book of Common Prayer, 137, 138, 139
Book of Orders, 91
Boose, Lynda, 113
Borough High Street, 186, 189

Boulton, Jeremy, 3, 78
Braun and Hogenberg map of
        London, 3–6, **4**, 7
Bridewell prison, 163–4
Bright, Timothy
        Treatise on Melancholie,
            159
Brooke, Arthur
        *The Tragical History of
            Romeus and Juliet*, 83
Buck, George (Master of the
        Revels), 107
Buckingham, Duke of, 19
Buckingham Palace, 5
Bull-baiting, 6, 7, 14, 29
Bullough, Geoffrey, 83
Burghley, Lord, 55
Burton, Robert
        Anatomy of Melancholy,
            159, 160

Calvin, John, 134, 135
Campion, Edmund, 33–6,
Campion, Thomas, 230
Candlewick Street, 227
Canon Row, 55–6
Carroll, William C., 166
Catholicism (Roman), 123, 130,
            131, 132, 135, 144
        Purgatory, 132–3
        Recusants, 75
        Seven Sacraments, 133–5
Cecil, Sir Robert, 55, 79
Césaire, Aimé, 202
Chancery Lane, 117
Chancery courts, 16, 114–20
Chapman, George, 180
        Eastward Ho! (co-author,
            with Jonson and
            Marston), 181

Charing Cross, 3, 5, 76, 77
Charles I, King, 49, 230
Chartier, Roger, 138
Cheapside, 125
Chettle, Henry, 180
Chiasmus (rhetorical figure),
            53–4, 61–5, 67
*Chronicle of the Grey Friars of
        London*, 131
Church of England (Anglican
        Church), 75
City Fathers, 7, 8, 58, 225
City of London, 5, 107, 114,
            182, 184, 223, 227
Clink prison, 186–7, 189
Coke, Edward, 107
Colclough, David, 109
Cole, James, 196, 197
College of Physicians, 151,
            153
Collinson, Patrick, 70, 72
Common law, 16, 113–20
Conduits (water pumps), 63,
            37, 110
Cope, Sir Walter, 79
Cormack, Bradin, 114
Coronation of English
        monarchs, 19, 55,
            65–72, 223–4
Coryat, Thomas, 203
Covent Garden, 3, 51
Crane, Ralph, 217
Cranmer, Thomas, 41–2
Crosby Place, 87
Cummings, Brian, 137

Daborne, Robert, 180
Danter, John, 28
Davies, John
        Microcosmos, 10

Debt, 173–6, 179–91, 89–92
Dee, John, 206
De Grazia, Margreta, 166
Deiter, Kristen, 224–5
Dekker, Thomas, 165, 180, 190
    The Dead Terme, 28
    'Paules Steeples
        Complaint' 127
    Dekker His Dream, 181
    The Honest Whore (Part
        One) (co-author,
        with Middleton),
        165, 180
    The Honest Whore (Part
        Two) (co-author, with
        Middleton), 180
    Lanthorne and Candlelight,
        184
    Northward Ho! (co-author,
        with Webster), 165
    The Roaring Girl, 181
    The Shoemaker's Holiday,
        180
Dillon, Janette, 75
Dissection, 156
Donne, John, 109–10, 121, 230
    Dean of St Paul's, 109
    'Satire I', 109–10

Earle, John
    Micro-cosmographie, 125
Eastcheap, 89
Edward I, King, 77, 117
Edward VI, King, 69, 123,
        131, 230
Eisenstein, Elizabeth, 137
Eleanor of Castille, Queen, 77
Eleanor Cross 76, 77
Elizabeth I, Queen, 27, 55, 56,
        59, 69–70, 70–1, 74,
        78, 79, 107, 123, 128,
        129, 131, 134, 153,
        206, 226, 230
Elizabeth II, Queen, 68
Elizabeth, Princess (later
        Elizabeth of Bohemia),
        230, 231, 232
    betrothal to Frederick, elector
        palatine, 231
Ely House, 47, 49–51
Equity, as legal principle, 16,
        115
Erne, Lukas, 136
Essex, Robert Devereux, Earl
        of, 27, 78, 153
    uprising and execution, 27
Executions, 14, 21–5, 224,
        225, 234
    of Anne Askew, 40
    of Edmund Campion, 35
    of Thomas Cranmer, 41–2
    of the Earl of Essex, 27
    of Roderigo Lopez, 153

Fenchurch Street, 196
Fleet Hill (see Ludgate Hill)
Fleet River, 121
Fletcher, John, 165
    Henry VIII (co-author, with
        Shakespeare), 18,
        221–36
    The Two Noble Kinsmen
        (co-author, with
        Shakespeare), 221
Foakes, R.A., 152
Forker, Charles R., 63
Fortune Theatre, 180
Foxe, John
    Acts and Monuments (Book
        of Martyrs), 40, 137

Frederick, elector palatine
        (later King of
        Bohemia), 230, 231
    betrothal to Princess
        Elizabeth, 231
Frobisher, Martin, 203

Galen, 150, 151, 153, 154, 155,
        156, 157, 158
George's Inn, 184
Gerard, John
    The Herbal, 199
Gesner, Conrad
    New and Old Physicke, 199
Gilbert, George, 34
Globe Theatre, 6, 7, 8, 11, 13, 18,
        62, 87, 104, 128, 132,
        139, 180, 186, 221
    fire (1613), 236
    first reconstruction, 236
    modern reconstruction,
        44, 142
    relocation from Shoreditch,
        13
    as wooden 'O', 11–12
Glover, Mary, 152–3, 160
Goldberg, Jonathan, 110–11
Great Fire of London (1666), 6,
        124
Greenblatt, Stephen, 95, 128, 133
Greenes Groats-Worth of Wit, 3
Groves, Beatrice, 134
Gunpowder Plot, 136

Hall, John, 149–51
    Select Observations, 149–50,
        158
Hall, Sir Peter, 142
Harington, Sir John, 27
Harkness, Deborah E., 197

Harman, Thomas
    A Caveat, 166, **167**
Harsnett, Samuel
    A Declaration, 161
Harriot, Thomas, 203
Haughton, William, 180
Hathaway, Anne, 1
Hatton Gardens, 49
Heneage, Sir Thomas, 55
Henisch, George
    Princeiples of Geometry, 199
Henry VIII, King, 69, 123, 131,
        147, 165, 223, 230, 232
Henry, Prince of Wales, 230, 232
Henslowe, Philip, 104
    Diaries, 28, 179, 182
Herbert, George, 230
Heylyn, Peter
    Microcosmus, 10
Hibbard, George, 109
Hoby, Sir Edward, 55–6
Hoeniger, F.D., 159–60
Holborn, 49
Holinshed, Raphael
    Chronicles, 64, 136
Holland's Leaguer, 184
Hooke, Robert, 163
Hopkins, Lisa, 230
Howard, Jean, 191
Howard, Thomas, Duke of
        Norfolk, 93
Hunsdon, Henry Cary, Baron
        (Lord Chamberlain),
        58
Hutson, Lorna, 112
hysterica passio, 152, 159–61

Iconoclasm, 123–4, 131–2, 135
Inns of Court, 16, 103, 107–13,
        114, 120, 121, 184, 234

Gray's Inn, 108, 114
    Gesta Grayorum, 108
Inner Temple, 114
Inns of Chancery, 114,
    117–18
Lincoln's Inn, 109, 114
Middle Temple, 103, 108,
    114
moot debates, 111–12
revels, 108, 111
Insectorum Theatrum (Theatre
    of Insects), 137, 195,
    199

Jackson, Elizabeth, 152
Jackson, Ken, 164
James I, King, 7, 49, 56, 72, 77,
    228, 230, 232, 233
Johnson, David, 186
Jones, Gwilym, 204
Jones, Inigo, 233
Jonson, Ben, 180
    The Alchemist, 207
    Batholomew Fair, 113
    Eastward Ho! (co-author,
        with Chapman and
        Marston), 181
    *Every Man Out of His
        Humour*, 125, 126,
        181
Jorden, Edward
    A Briefe Discourse, 152
Jourdain, Sylvester, 201
Judaism, 116–20
    House of Converts, Chancery
        Lane, 117–18

Kantorowicz, Ernst, 69–70
Kastan, David Scott, 136
King's Bench Prison, 189–92

King's Men, 7, 72, 121
King's Two Bodies, 68–72, 110,
    160
Knight, Sarah, 110
Kyd, Thomas, 113
    Spanish Tragedy, 7, 30

Langley, Francis, 104, 180
Leadenhall Street, 196
Leicester, Robert Dudley, Earl
    of, 78, 153
Lenton, Francis
    *The Young Gallants
        Whirligig*, 216
Lesser, Zachary, 140
Lewalski, Barbara, 116
Lime Street, 18, 195–8, 201
    residents of, 196
Ling, Nicholas 139, 140–2, 144
    commonplace markings on
        Hamlet, **141**
L'Obel, Mathias de, 196, 198
    Plantarum, 199
London
    Anglo-Saxon, 61
        Thorney Island
            (Westminster), 61
    early modern
        beehive, depiction as, 9, 10
        challenging environment,
            58
        diversity, 7–8, 10, 49
        microcosm, figuration as,
            9–13, 235
        names thereof, 10
        population, 3, 9
        riots, 27
        theatre audiences, 13,
            24, 28, 29, 36, 45,
            222, 234

theatre, imagined as, 10
theatre industry, economics
    thereof, 179–84
medieval, 8, 47,
    floods, 61
London Bridge, 6, 184
London walls, 5, 7, 18
Long Ditch, 61
Lopez, Roderigo, 153–4
Lord Chamberlain's Men, 7, 27,
    58, 104–5, 163
Lorkins, Thomas, 236
Ludgate Hill (Fleet Hill), 121,
    125
Lupton, Donald
    *London and the Country
        Carbonadoed*, 9
Luther, Martin, 134, 142
Lyly, John, 180

MacGregor, Neil, 87
Mainy, Richard, 161
Manningham, John, 103
Mannoni, Octave, 202
Marlowe, Christopher, 113
    Doctor Faustus, 7
    The Jew of Malta, 7, 154
    Tamburlaine the Great, 7
Marshalsea prison, 235
Marston, John, 180
    Eastward Ho! (co-author,
        with Chapman and
        Jonson), 181
Martyrdom, 14–15, 21–5,
    31–42, 234
    of Catholic priests, 14, 31–6
    of Protestants, 40–2
Mary I, Queen, 40, 123, 226
Mary, Queen of Scots, 230
Masques, 85, 182, 218

Massinger, Phillip, 180
Mebane, John, 207
Merritt, J. F., 78, 79
Meteren, Emmanuel van, 196
McMullan, Gordon, 221, 231,
    232, 236
Microcosm, 9–13, 235
Middleton, Thomas, 165,
    171–93, 180–1
    The Changeling (co-author,
        with Rowley), 29
    *The Honest Whore (Part
        One)* (co-author, with
        Dekker), 165
    Michaelmas Term, 181
    The Revenger's Tragedy, 29,
        181
    The Roaring Girl, 181
    *A Trick to Catch the Old
        One*, 181
    Timon of Athens (co-author,
        with Shakespeare), 18
    A Yorkshire Tragedy, 181
Millington, Thomas, 29
Minshull, Geffray, 171, 190
Moffet, Thomas, 195, 196
Montaigne
    'Of Caniballes', 205
Moorfields, 234
Moorgate, 5, 163
Morley, Henry, 107
Mukherji, Subha, 113
Muldrew, Craig, 174
Mullaney, Steven, 185, 198
Munro, Ian, 87

National Theatre
    production of *Timon of
        Athens* (2012), 193
Nelson, Horatio, Lord, 77

New World, or the 'Americas',
     200–5
Nicholl, Charles, 100–1
Norden, John
     Speculum Britanniae, cover
          image, 6, 49, 50, 62–3,
          79, 83, 84

Old Bailey, 121
Ovid (Publius Ovidius Naso)
     Metamorphoses, 26, 37, 39,
          40, 136

Palmer, Daryl, 35
Paracelsus, 150, 151, 160
Paris Garden, 234
Peacham, Henry, 26
Pearl, Valerie, 186
Peat, Derek, 166
Penny, Thomas, 195, 196
Persons, Robert, 34, 35
Peterson, Kaara, 152, 158, 161
Plague, 27–28, 48, 58, 151
Platter, Thomas, 10, 11, 184,
     198
Pliny, 158
Plowden, Edmund, 69
Protestantism (English), 123,
     130, 132, 134–5, 137,
     142, 144
     Auto-Didacticism, 138
     Confession, 129
Puritans
     hanged in early modern
          London, 22–3
     opposition to theatre, 58,
          168

Raleigh, Sir Walter, 78, 230
Red Bull Theatre, 180

Reformation (Protestant,
          English), 14, 34, 43–4,
          58, 78, 123, 130, 131,
          133, 134, 137, 142,
          144, 147, 234
     of mourning rituals, 43
     of the Sacraments, 44, 133–5
Revenge Tragedy, 29–31
Rich, Richard, 199
Richard II, King, 66, 70, 93, 225
Ripley, George, 207
Rome, 8, 25, 33
Rose Theatre, 7, 27, 28, 29, 179
Rowley, William
     The Changeling (co-author,
          with Thomas
          Middleton), 29
Royal Shakespeare Company
     (RSC), 142
     production of Richard II
          (2008), 70, 71

Salkeld, Duncan, 163–4
Sam Wanamaker Playhouse,
     213–14, 214
Sartre, Jean-Paul, 113
Savoy, 5,
     John of Gaunt's palace, 49–51
Shakespeare, John, 78, 93, 132,
     193
Shakespeare, William
     arrival in London, 1–6
     children (Susanna, Hamnet
          and Judith), 1, 149
     'First Folio' (Mr. William
          Shakespeare's
          Comedies, Histories,
          and Tragedies), 139,
          217, 219
     interest in publication, 136

'lost years', 3, 34
marriage to Anne Hathaway, 1
obtains Coat of Arms, 92–3
plays
    Antony and Cleopatra, 25
    As You Like It, 11, 86,
       186
    The Comedy of Errors,
       108
    Cymbeline, 186
    Hamlet, 17, 29, 43, 120,
       121–45, 148, 159, 166,
       234
    Henry IV part 1, 7, 48, 89
    Henry IV part 2, 48, 89,
       114, 125
    Henry V, 8, 11–13, 14, 48,
       81
    Henry VI, Part One, 128
    Henry VIII (co-author,
       with Fletcher), 18, 53,
       59, 75, 221–36
    Julius Caesar, 25
    King Lear, 17, 61–2, 145,
       147–69, 186, 188, 192,
       211, 234
    Love's Labour's Lost, 109
    Macbeth, 148, 166
    Measure for Measure, 101
    The Merchant of Venice,
       16, 99–120, 154,
       189–90, 191, 222, 234
    A Midsummer Night's
       Dream, 86, 89, 186
    Othello, 148
    Richard II, 15, 47–72, 75,
       136, 234
    Richard III, 225
    Romeo and Juliet, 15–16,
       73–97, 234

    The Tempest, 18, 137,
       195–219, 222, 223, 234
    Timon of Athens, 18, 105,
       234, 171–93
    Titus Andronicus, 7, 15,
       21–45, 63, 137, 139,
       234
    Twelfth Night, 103
    The Two Noble Kinsmen
       (co-author, with
       Fletcher), 221
    The Winter's Tale, 159,
       186
poems
    The Rape of Lucrece, 58
    Venus and Adonis, 58
religious leanings, 130
Sharp, Buchanan, 91
Shirley, James
    The Witty Fair One, 125
Shoreditch, 7, 13, 104
Sidney, Sir Philip, 59
    Astrophil and Stella, 128
    The Defense of Poesy, 128
    The Old Arcadia, 59
Silver Street, 99, 102
Simonds, Peggy Munoz, 207
Slade, John, 107
    Slade's Case, 107
Slights, W.E., 156
Slinger, Jonathan, 70, **71**
Smith, John, 201
Smithfield, 34
Somerset, Edward Seymour,
    Duke of, 5, 131
Somerset House, 78, 131
Southampton, Henry
    Wriothesley, Earl of,
    58, 108, 182
Southwark, 6, 17–18, 27, 184–9

Southwell, Robert, 35–6
    'I Dye without Desert', 36
Spanish Armada, 128, 129
Spanish Inquisition, 129
Spencer, Sir John, 87
Spiller, Elizabeth, 210
Spitalfields, 3
Stationers' Register, 28
Stallybrass, Peter, 138, 140
St Dunstan's in the West, church
    of, 121
St Laurence Pountney, church
    of, 227
St Paul's, 121–45, 184, 186,
    198, 204
    cathedral (Old St Paul's,
        pre-1666), 5, 17, 49,
        120, 124, 127, 131,
        147, 234
    churchyard (Cross Yard), 122,
        135, 136, 138, 139
    early modern book-trade, 17,
        28, 158, 234
    Paul's Cross, 136
    Paul's Walk, 124–7, 135
    Paul's Walkers, 125
    spire destroyed, 6
    Wren, Christopher, as later
        architect of, 6, 121,
        122, 123, 124
St James's Palace, 230
Stock, Angela, 10
Stow, John,
    Survey of London, 5, 6, 51,
        61, 66, 99, 196, 197,
        232
Strachay, William
    'True Reportory,' 201
Strand, 5, 15–16, 73–97, 136,
    184, 186, 234

Stratford Upon Avon, 1, 2, 14,
    21, 78, 92, 96, 132,
    149, 192, 223
    Guildhall Chapel, 132
Succession, 26–7, 224, 229–33,
    235
Suffolk, Lord, 5
Sumptuary Laws, 74
Swan Theatre, 104–5, 180
Sweeney, Anne, 33

Talbot, John (Earl of
    Shrewsbury), 128
Taylor, John, 189
Taylor, Neil, 142
Temple Bar, 77
Thames, River, 6, 51, 61, 76, 80,
    184
The Theatre, 7, 104
Thompson, Ann, 142
Topsell, Edward, 203
Tourner, Cyril, 180
Tower of London, 18–19, 34, 59,
    72, 222–9, 231, 232
    Tower Hill, 224
    White Tower, 225
Trafalgar Square, 77
Tyburn, 14–15, 21–45, 184
Tynan, Kenneth, 113

Vaughan, Alden T., 204
Venice, 105
    Venetian Carnival, 111
Verona, 73, 74, 76, 86, 87, 92,
    93, 97
Verstegan, Richard
    Theatre of Cruelty, 31–3, **32**

Walsingham, Sir Francis, 128
Warner, David, 142

Webster, John, 113, 165
  The Duchess of Malfi, 29
  Northward Ho! (co-author,
    with Dekker), 165
Weis, René, 82, 91
West End, 3
Westminster, 3, 5, 15, 48–72,
    77, 91, 107, 184, 223,
    225, 227, 232
  Abbey, 66, 224, 227, 231
  Bedchamber, 60
  Court of Requests, 99
  Great Chamber, 60
  Presence Chamber, 60
  Privy Chamber, 60
  Star Chamber, 56
  Westminster Hall, 35, 56, 60,
    61, 62, 65–72, 99, 227,
    232, 233

White, Edward, 29
White, John, 200
White, Margaret, 163
Whitehall, 49–72, 166,
    223, 232, 233,
    234
  Whitehall Palace, 49, 60,
    61, 76
    banqueting hall, 49,
      233
Williams, Tad, 202
Windsor, 56, 93
Wolsey, Thomas, Cardinal,
    232

Yates, Edward, 34
York Place, 232, 233, 234

Zwierlein, Anne-Julia, 10